BOOK OF
JESUS CHRIST
A STORY OF CHRIST THE MESSIAH

WAYNE SHERMAN

authorHOUSE

AuthorHouse™
1663 Liberty Drive
Bloomington, IN 47403
www.authorhouse.com
Phone: 833-262-8899

Published by AuthorHouse 10/18/2024

ISBN: 979-8-8230-3455-5 (sc)
ISBN: 979-8-8230-3456-2 (e)

Library of Congress Control Number: 2024920741

Dedications

I am dedicating this book to:

My friend and sceptic, Reg Howard,
who encouraged me to start this book

My wife, Marlene,
who encouraged me to complete it

My Lord and Saviour,
Jesus, the Christ and Messiah

Contents

Introduction and Part I

A three part document

Acknowledgment

I have a friend who is by nature a sceptic and is constantly pushing me to do a better job of expressing my Christian faith. He was one of several close friends who encouraged me to publish my first book, "A Synopsis of the Bible". Now he has been again encouraging me to investigate and publish a book specifically about the life, messages, and divinity of Jesus Christ. He has also recommended that this effort should be based on the first four books of the New Testament (Matthew, Mark, Luke, and John) only, to assure the earliest and most first-hand knowledge of Jesus. He has stated that he looks for proof through multiple backup documentation to verify that something is true. My friend's urging has given me quite a challenge, but I intend, through this document, to try to meet such a challenge. However, I felt that in order to put the story of Christ in perspective, I needed to book-end the accounts of Jesus in the four gospels with two other volumes, one about what the Old Testament said about a coming Messiah, and also the story of what happened following Jesus' crucifixion, that turned the record of his life, his teachings, and his sacrificial death into a worldwide religion.

Document Foreword

This effort has taken me into a whole new realm of study and research, to establish what Jesus did and said that so impressed a whole generation of the Hebrew people to not only believe in Him as the son of the most high God, but to also indicate why his story was so powerful that it caused it to be spread throughout the known world and through 2000 years of human history. This growth of Christianity from one man and a few of his followers to a whole world religion is, as I see it, a truly remarkable (even miraculous) occurrence, and to me, not really explainable without divine control.

Document Introduction

I am not a Bible scholar, and I do not hold any theological degrees. I also have no background in the languages in which the Bible and the story of Christ were originally written. I am thus depending on current Bible research and translations in this effort. I am now retired. However, during my career, I was a master troubleshooter, able to solve some very complex technical problems in very large scale computers and communications networks for the US Department of Defense. As I performed my job, I saw, unfortunately, how people often accepted and acknowledged the fixes, corrections, and improvements without recognizing the necessary effort and expertise that went into them (one of my bosses said "the system just matured"). Thus, I can, with this background and experience, see first hand how people can look at God's creations, but not recognize his hand in them. With this understanding, I believe that my particular reference points are complimentary to the validation of the truths of the data within this document.

I performed computer and communications problem solving work through logical processes, by thinking both globally and in detail at the same time, and I was quite successful at it. Thus, I have approached the subject of this book in the same manner. And hopefully, the readers will see the logic and the truth in this writing, rather than thinking in terms of serendipity, happenstance, or coincidence. My overall objective in this book is to present the Jesus of the New Testament of the Bible in a way that will allow even the most ardent sceptics among us to more fully comprehend and possibly understand that there is and intelligent creator of the universe, and that he has a plan, mission, and objective for the human race as presented through the Jewish prophets, and then last of all and most prominently, through Jesus as the promised "Christ". And, hopefully, I offer this information in such a way that even those sceptics will not only recognize this plan, mission, and objective but also to completely accept and believe in Jesus as their personal life guide and objective of awe and worship.

I know I have taken on a huge effort, considering that an uncountable number of more educated, dedicated, committed, and brighter than me, have worked on this before. But I believe that, with my skills and background, I can measurably help those who are still on the fence to accept and believe

References

For this writing, my primary reference is the English Standard Version (ESV) translation of the Judeo/Christian Bible. I have also used secondary references, where appropriate and available, such as other English language Bible translations, Wikipedia (the on-line encyclopedia), numerous Bible Concordances, and Harper's Bible dictionary. I have also interjected other supporting items, such as corroborating historical data from other sources and words and suggestions from trusted Christian friends, and also my own musings.

A Definition of terms

The term "Christ" is used a number of times in the Bible to indicate a king above all kings, a Saviour of the people, and an eternal being.

The term "Messiah" is also sometimes used in the Bible and has basically the same definition as the "Christ"

The name "Emanuel" that appears in the prophesies of Isaiah is also synonymous with "Messiah" and "Christ" in its meaning.

The name "Jesus" was a fairly common name used for male children in New Testament times (and even today among Hispanic people). It is also very similar to or synonymous with the name "Joshua", the name of an Old Testament leader. It means "God with us" or "Saviour".

I have sometimes used the words "an evil presence" to indicate a power for wrong, otherwise personalized as Satan, the Devil, Beelzebul, etc.

I have also used the words "God", "Lord", "most high God", or "the Creator God" to indicate the all powerful, all knowing, creator of the time, space, eternity, the heavens, the earth, and life on earth. *I, as well, note that the Bible also indicates that this all knowing, all powerful entity is a continuing, all-present observer and controller of his creations. I have also noted that the Bible also indicates, one of the creations, the human race, has been given three elements that distinguish them from other living beings. One is a higher intellect than other the living creatures to be able to ponder and reflect on God and his creations. The second is the knowledge of the absolutes of good and evil, (which must inherently involve rules and laws to live by). And the third element is unfortunately the free will to or not to obey or even believe in those rules and laws, or in the existence of the creator himself.*

Tools for support and emphasis

You, the reader, will also note that I have used italics to set apart my observations and thoughts, parentheses to provide some clarification, and bold print for Bible quotes and for points I consider important.

Story Organization

I have divided this document into three parts. The first part is a compendium of Old Testament prophesies fore-telling Christ, his life, and his mission. The title of this part is **"The forecasts of Christ"**. The second part is based on the four gospels; Matthew, Mark, Luke, and John, which tell of the life, actions, messages, sacrificial death, return to life, and divinity of the Christ while on earth. The title of this volume is **"The Life of Christ"**. The third part is about how and why the life and teachings of Christ became a world-wide religion. The tile of this part is **"The Impact of Christ"**.

I, long ago, came to believe in Jesus as my lord and savior and as a guide on how to live my life. If the writing of this book will encourage others to believe as well, especially those with a logical or scientific bent in their personalities (such as my friend and I), it will have accomplished its purpose.

<u>SO LET US BEGIN</u>

Part I - THE FORECASTS OF CHRIST

Introduction

As I indicated above, the primary source for this Part is the Old Testament of the Judeo/Christian Bible, as it appears in English Standard Version (ESV) translation. I have also used as secondary resources: Bible commentaries, Harper's Bible Dictionary, Wikipedia, Bible concordances, and comments by trusted friends. This part is a synthesis of the prophesies about the coming Messiah in the Old Testament, along with some of my interpretations and some interesting old and New Testament comparisons.

As a logical person, I like to look at things chronologically in order of their occurrence in time. Therefore, I have started this document by describing the historical settings for, and looking at various predictions of the Christ as documented in the historical settings in the Old Testament of the Bible. Thus, I have begun at the very beginning with the first few words of the Old Testament "In the Beginning" (See Genesis 1:1). I, in no way, consider myself a prophet, trying to predict meanings for the future. However, I have, on occasion, given my own interpretations to words and events to tell what I think they meant in the global scheme of things.

Part I Section 1 - Moses and the Torah

Authorship of the first five books of the Bible, called the Torah, are attributed to the man, Moses, an early very important person in the Old Testament. These five books are especially remarkable in that they represent very early, if not the first known written narratives in the world history of languages. It appears that all the stories of history prior to Moses were passed on only by word of mouth. It also appears that before Moses, the only things written down were records of business transactions.

The Hebrews, at the time of Moses birth, were slaves of the Egyptian king (Pharaoh). Moses is described in the Bible as a son of a Hebrew mother, who, in an attempt to avoid an edict by the Pharaoh that all male Hebrew newborns in his kingdom should be killed, placed him in a reed basket and launched it into the Nile river, where he was discovered by the Pharaoh's daughter, and apparently raised to adulthood in the Pharaoh's court (See Exodus 2:1-10 in the Old Testament).

Note that a similar royal kill-order for male children also is described in the New Testament to have occurred shortly after the birth of Jesus in Bethlehem, when the king of Judea, Herod the Great, proclaimed that all the male children under the age of two, in and around Bethlehem (where Jesus was born), should be killed (See Matthew 2:16 in the New Testament). Interesting parallel!

At about forty years old, Moses rejected his Egyptian upbringing and turned back to his Hebrew heritage. After a life crisis (he killed an Egyptian slave-master and was found out) (see Exodus 2:11-14), he fled from Egypt and established a new life elsewhere among a tribe of nomads, the Midianites. He was later called by God, to go back to Egypt to try to obtain freedom from slavery of his Hebrew people.

Moses, as an adopted son of the Pharaoh's daughter, apparently was trained as a ruler of people, and as such he knew he needed not only to obtain freedom for his people, but also to establish them as a nation, separate and away from Egypt (where they had lived for previous four hundred years, the last number of years as slaves to the native Egyptians). Thus, apparently he knew that he had to give his people a history and heritage (*Genesis*), to convince them to leave their homes and existing culture, and to lead them out of Egypt (*Exodus*), to give them a new set of laws and, a new culture, and a new way of life (*Leviticus*), to establish a sense of belonging to a unified movement, even though they still identified themselves as belonging to several separate tribes based on their ancestors, the twelve sons of Jacob (*Numbers*), to give them the courage to endure all the setbacks they might encounter in the process (*Deuteronomy*), and to look forward to resettling in a new territory to be known as the "promised land".

After the Hebrews escaped from Egypt, they became nomads, moving from place to place in the Sinai peninsula. They set up their camps in an area together, but separated by their various tribes based on their descendancies. One of the important things that Moses did after he lead the Hebrews out of Egypt, was to design and set up a special tent to be the center of the tribal camps for worship of the Creator God, who was his guide in saving the Hebrew people from slavery and molding them into a new nation. It was called a "tabernacle". He also specified the ways in which it was configured, how it would be set up and taken down each time it was moved, and even down to the design of the dress of the priests and servants who tended it. (One of the items in the tabernacle was a curtain (veil) between its "Holy" and "Most Holy" sections. It appears that Moses intended that only a very select few of the believers would be allowed to pass through the veil. *(This curtain will be important in the second part of this document.)* Another of the items to be created was the "Ark of God", a seat for God, to be placed in the Most Holy area of the tabernacle. The Hebrew people moved a number of times before they entered the promised land. And each time the people moved, the tabernacle was set up in the middle of the camp, until it was finally set up permanently in the land promised to them by God.

There is no specific record of the existence of the Moses of the Old Testament except in the Judeo/Christian Bible. However, the name Moses was sometimes used in the ancient Egyptian culture, including a pharaoh named Tut-moses.

In doing all these things, whether or not he fully understood God's plan, Moses set the course of a separate people group, chosen by the creator God, who through many trials and culling processes, became the progenitors of the person who is now recognized by a significant portion of the world's population to be the son of the creator God and eternal ruler of all mankind.

Old Testament history before Moses (Genesis)

Now let's start with the first of the Mosaic books, Genesis. In doing so I hope to point out how there was a continuous plan to reach the culmination of the establishment of the lordship of Jesus as the Christ, the promised one.

In the first few words of Genesis, the first book of the Judeo/Christian Bible are the words **"In the beginning God <u>said</u>......."** (See Genesis 1:1 in the Old Testament). In other words, God used his voice (his word) to speak into being all space, time, energy, and matter. *In the book of John in the New Testament, the apostle John opened his gospel with the statement **"In the beginning was the <u>Word</u>, and the <u>word</u> was with God, and the <u>word</u> was God. He (referring to Jesus) was in the beginning with God"** and is being identified by John as the voice of creation. In this brief, bold, statement John ties Jesus (an assumed mere human) into the creation of the universe. And thus, by this verbiage, John also said that Jesus was not a mere human but the "word" of the God of all creation, and the instrument by which God created (see John 1:1-3 in the New Testament) . Wow. What an assertion.*

Then in Genesis, after the establishment of light, the cosmos, the earth, and life on the earth, God created humans, in the person of Adam and Eve. God placed them in an earthly paradise where they had all the essentials of life. However, God planted a tree in that paradise, who's fruit Adam and Eve were told not to eat . This was the tree of the knowledge of good and evil (See Genesis 2:16-17). Unfortunately, due to the encouragement of an evil presence in the form of a serpent, they ate the fruit of that tree, and discovered the difference between right and wrong (See Genesis 3:1-6). And as a result, they also realized that their lives involved wrongs, and as well, that their lives were not eternal but were going to end. This was an awful burden they brought on themselves and the whole human race. *However, in the fullness of time, the <u>word</u> came to humanity in the form of Jesus of Nazareth, who offered to restore eternal life, through the process that required belief that Jesus was the promised Christ, the prophesied son of the creator God. **(If this idea seems a leap at first glance, I hope, though this document, to prove that this assertion is actually the truth.)***

Further in Genesis, it is documented that Adam and Eve had two sons, Cain and Abel (See Genesis 4:1). And an interesting and traumatic event took place with these two sons. Both believed in God, and felt the need to bring sacrifices to him. But Cain's grain sacrifice was rejected in favor of a blood sacrifice brought by Abel (See Genesis 4:3-5). *This, to my understanding, represented the first inkling of the requirement for a death of a living being to be a worthy sacrifice. And, thus, in the New Testament, Jesus died as that worthy sacrifice for humanity (See numerous New Testament references to that sacrificial death, which I will specify in the second part of this document).*

And of course, the same evil presence, was there to oppose a worthy sacrifice, as were the Jewish leaders in the New Testament, each of whom in turn caused the death of Jesus.

Genesis, in Chapter 8, also displayed the first significant culling of humanity in the "great flood", where only a few people, chosen by God, survived (the family of Noah). *This also established the idea that purity came through the washing of water, foretelling the baptism of Jesus before he entered his ministry.* And then it documented the selection several generations later, of a single family and a single son of that family "Abraham" to be the progenitor of the people group who would, under the later guidance of Moses, become the Hebrew nation. It also identified the strip of land between the Jordan River and the east end of the Mediterranean Sea to be the "promised land" where Abraham should settle. And in addition, it specifies that this area would be the eternal inheritance of the descendants of Abraham. Then, Genesis proceeded to tell the story of Isaac, Abraham's son, and also of his grandson Jacob. It interestingly told that Jacob was a flawed (blemished) man. He stole his brother's birthright (See Genesis 25:29-34). He then stole his father's blessing (See Genesis 27). And when he traveled back to the land of his father's relatives to find a wife, he tricked his future father-in-law into giving him two of his daughters as wives instead of one, and he also stole a large part of his father-in-law's domestic flocks (Genesis 29-31). However, it turns out that Jacob's trickery was part of God's plan to create his chosen people. But, there were consequences. On his way back to his home with his two wives and his new-found riches, he somehow got into a fight with an angel, which resulted in a dislocated hip, so that he became crippled for the rest of his life. The angel he fought with told him that from then on he would be known as **"Israel"** (a striver with God) (See Genesis 32:22-28). So from then on, his descendants would be called the "Children of Israel". Then Genesis told of the process by which that people group, the family of Jacob, (Abraham's grandson) moved to Egypt, four hundred plus years before Moses was born.

The creation of the nation of Israel (Exodus, Leviticus, Numbers, and Deuteronomy)

The descendants of Jacob lived in Egypt for about 400 years. They had initially been welcomed into Egypt by the Pharaoh. Over that 400 years, their numbers grew from a small clan of about 100 people, to a population of several million. But some years after their arrival, due to changes in Egyptian leadership, they became slaves of the Egyptians, and were forced into slave labor to build Egyptian cities. During this period, they began to be called Hebrews. Then, Moses arrived on the scene as described above, and lead them out of Egypt across an arm of the Red Sea into the Sinai peninsula. But this Exodus came with a price. In order to convince the Pharaoh to let the Hebrews leave, God imposed a series of plagues on Egypt that destroyed crops, polluted the water, made people ill, and eventually a plague that killed the firstborn of the Egyptians. With this plague the Pharaoh finally relented and gave the Hebrews permission to leave the country. But Moses did more that lead a rebellion. As indicated above, he gave them a heritage, laws to live by, and a reason band together to form a nation

Three very important events that set the course of history for the Children of Israel

Besides the historic information and the laws and rules for living in the book of Exodus, there are three very important events that influenced the direction of the people of Israel toward the birth, mission, and the "blood" sacrifice of Jesus.

The first event, The Passover

The first of these three events was the establishment of the Passover feast. Moses had gone to the Pharaoh before each of the first nine of the ten plagues that fell on Egypt as documented in Exodus, and either predicted or initiated them. However, for the tenth and last plague (deaths of the first born of every Egyptian family), Moses did something else. He directed the Hebrew people to protect themselves from death by telling them that each household must slaughter a lamb, eat the flesh of the lamb, and paint the doorposts of their houses with its blood. This protected the Hebrew people from death of their firstborn in the tenth plague (See Exodus 12:1-8). This action not only involved a blood sacrifice but added an earthly purpose for it, in that it was to save human lives. This set the precedent for the other, numerous, ritual sacrifices recorded in the rest of the Torah, and guided worship for the Hebrew people throughout the remainder of the Old Testament. This event, in finality, set up the course and significance of the "Lord's Supper, and the venue for the death of Jesus as the final and ultimate Passover Lamb.

The "Last Supper" of Jesus, as recorded in the New Testament, was a celebration of the Passover (See Matthew 26:17). As Jesus and his disciples were eating the Passover meal, Jesus took some bread and told the disciples it was his flesh and to eat it. Then he took a cup of red wine and told his disciples to drink it, stating that it was his blood, and thus establishing that he was himself the Passover lamb (See Matthew 26:26-28). (The account of this action also appears in Mark 14:22-24, and Luke 22:14-17.)

The second event, The Ten Commandments

The second of these events was the creation of the Ten Commandments, given to the Hebrews after they left Egypt. These ten basic laws were given to Moses by God on two stone tablets. And they became the foundation for all the other laws and rules for living, contained in the rest of the Torah. The first four of these commandments were the directions and admonitions about the worship of God. The fifth was about love and respect for family and heritage. And the final five were rules for dealing with fellow human contemporaries. Incidentally, these last five have since been the bases for civil law of almost all civilized nations in the world. (A relief of Moses, holding the tablets containing the Ten Commandments, is the central sculpture at the top of the portico of the U.S. Supreme Court building in Washington DC.) The Ten Commandments appear in both Exodus 20:2-17 and in Deuteronomy 5:6-21. *Jesus, in his ministry, condensed these Ten Commandments and changed their tenor from laws to be obeyed into two statements of faith, to be emblazoned, not on stone tablets, but in believers' hearts, when he said **"Love the Lord with all your heart, soul,***

and mind, and love your neighbor as yourself" *(See Matthew 22:37-40 in the New Testament).* Actually, the first part of this statement was a quote of Moses in Deuteronomy 6:5-6.

The third event, The establishment of encampment order and the tabernacle

After the Hebrews escaped from Egypt, under God's direction, a very important order of encampment was established that gave the descendants of each of the twelve tribes who were the decedents of Jacob/Israel a specific area in which to set up their tents. And in the center of this encampment was a special, sacred tent and courtyard containing the earthly seat of God. It was called the Tabernacle, where God was to be continually worshiped. .

Prophesies about Christ in the Torah

The recognition of the idea of an eternal king

Besides the history lessons and laws in the Torah, there began to be a set of prophesies in those books that told of an eternal ruler for Hebrew people, but not a king in the sense of the Egyptian Pharaoh or later earthly Hebrew kings like Saul or David. The first such was the story of Abraham's contact with Melchizedek, the king of the city of Salem. Abraham recognized him as not just an earthly ruler but also **"a priest of the most high God"** to whom Abraham brought sacrifices of the spoils of a war he had just won (See Genesis 14:17-20). *In the New Testament book of Hebrews, it was pointed out that there is no corresponding reference in the Old Testament to Melchizedek's birth or death, nor either to the beginning or the ending of his rule. The author of the New Testament Book of Hebrews, identified Jesus as the Christ* **"in the order of Melchizedek"** *(See Hebrews 7:1-3), a living entity, preceding Moses, with no beginning and no end.*

A substitute sacrifice for a human life and that an offspring of Abraham would be a blessing to all humanity

In Genesis 22, God tested Abraham by telling him to sacrifice his son Isaac. Abraham demonstrated that he was willing to do this, even though Isaac was the heir that God had promised him. In demonstrating his willingness, at God's direction, to offer as a "blood sacrifice" his only legitimate son, God gave him, as a substitute, a Ram (Male sheep) caught in some nearby bushes, and promised him that **"...in your offspring shall all the nations of the earth be blessed."** (See Genesis 22:18). *I believe that this prophesy was both a short term one about Isaac and also a long term one about the Christ as the lamb of God.*

A salvation image on a pole

In Numbers 21:5-9 is the story about a time when the Children of Israel spoke against God and Moses, and were assailed with "fiery serpents" that when bitten by one caused them to die. So God told Moses to make an image of such a serpent and place it atop a pole for all to see. And those who looked at the serpent on the pole were healed. In the New Testament, Jesus was nailed to the cross (a pole) for all to see as a symbol of life, not death. Even the Roman Centurion in charge of Jesus' execution said **"Truly this man was the Son of God"** (See Mark 15:39)..

The preparation of the chosen people and the chosen one

Jesus was born in Bethlehem of the territory of Judah, about ten miles south of Jerusalem, not too far from where Abraham had lived. However, Jesus earthly parents were from Nazareth (having moved to Bethlehem due to an order from the Roman government for the purpose of leveeing a tax). But after a couple of years they were forced to move to Egypt, to avoid an order from the king of Judea (Herod the Great) to kill all male babies in and around Bethlehem. After the death of Herod, Jesus' family moved back to Nazareth, where he grew up. Nazareth was located in an area that once was the part of the Northern Kingdom of Israel, about seventy five miles north of Jerusalem. Why a "Northern Kingdom" will be explained below. About 700 years before Jesus was born, the kingdom of Assyria had decimated the northern kingdom of Israel and carried away all the leaders and a significant part of the population, and resettled them in an area that is now in the northern part of Iraq. This was most likely in the area near the modern city of Mosul. Subsequently, the Assyrians relocated a group of undesirables into the land vacated by the Hebrew captives. However, the remaining Hebrew people in the area of the northern kingdom, in an area called Galilee, apparently were not deported, and held onto their faith in God. In the Chapter 6 of the book of Numbers, there was created the "Nazarite" vow. This vow required a period of a time of intense study and worship of God the Creator, of fasting and avoidance of anything having to do with wine or grapes, and to not shave. *I have often wondered if the New Testament city of Nazareth in Galoilee might have been the ancient center of those who had taken the Nazarite vow. In any case, after Jesus had come from Nazareth of Galilee and had been baptized in the Jordan River by John the Baptist, he was driven into the wilderness for "40 days" (a period of time) to be tempted by Satan (the evil presence) (See Mark 1:9-13 in the New Testament). Was Jesus, in truth, an epitome of the ancient Nazarite? I believe so, and I believe that the Nazarite vow was created for, and as a prophesy, of Jesus.*

The promise of another future great leader

Then in Deuteronomy, Moses predicted that a prophet like Moses would arise to speak to the people. Moses quoted God, who said to him **"The Lord your God will raise up for you a prophet like me from among you, from your brothers—. It is to him you shall listen"** (See Deuteronomy 18:15). **And again God said "I will raise up for them a prophet like you from among their brothers. And I will put my words in his mouth, and he shall speak to them all that I have commanded him."** (See Deuteronomy 18:18). This appears to be a prophecy of Jesus. However, Jesus was not quite like Moses, in that Moses, despite his great accomplishments, was a sinner, because he had killed an Egyptian (See above) and had demonstrated unnecessary unrighteous anger while producing a water source for his Hebrew followers in the wilderness **"at a place called Massah"** (See Exodus 17:2-7). As a result, even though he had lead the Hebrews for forty years through the wilderness, he died and was buried there. So he was not allowed by God to enter the land of promise (See Deuteronomy 34:4) .

Part I Section 2 - Old Testament history from the Torah to King David

A number of the Old Testament books told of the history of the Hebrew people after they entered the "Land of Promise" and lived their lives there over a period of about one thousand five hundred years. These books were Joshua, Judges, First and Second Samuel, First and Second Kings, First and Second Chronicles, Ezra, and Nehemiah. (Then there was a historical gap between Second Chronicles and Ezra, which was partially filled by the prophetic books of Jeremiah and Ezekiel. And there was another gap in Bible records after Nehemiah until the the time of the New Testament.)

The first leader of the Hebrews after Moses was Joshua

After Moses died, leadership of the Hebrews fell first to Moses' chosen successor, Joshua. Through a series of wars and conquests, he lead the Hebrew people to conquer the land that had been promised to them by God, and to its establishment under its new name, Israel, as the homeland for the Hebrews. Incidentally, the name "Joshua" appears to be an archaic pronunciation or spelling of the name "Jesus". During this conquest, and area of the conquered land was specifically set aside and assigned to be the the home of each of the Hebrew tribes. At the end of the conquest of this **"Promised Land"**, the tabernacle was set up at Shiloh in the area of Israel assigned to the tribe of Ephraim as the center of worship of God. But again, like Moses, Joshua proved imperfect, not always following God's guidance, in that he allowed a number of the previous city-states in the new land to continue to exist, along with their corrupt forms of worship. Thus, once the land was settled by the Hebrew people, they unfortunately started turning away from the God that had empowered Moses, and began to add in worship practices of the false gods of the archaic city-states, some involving sex worship (Baal) and ritual prostitution. Others supported the killing of babies and young children (Molech), and others tried to give animal gender to God by worshiping the "Queen of Heaven". All this was done as a practice of adoration to these false gods.

The time of the Judges

Also, because they turned away from God, the creator of the universe, as their leader, they became basically leaderless in the land that they had conquered, and became prey for raiding parties and invading armies of surrounding nations. They did have wise men among them who were called on to adjudge legal disputes among the people, but there was no longer a power structure that would protect them from outside attack, or even disputes between the Hebrew tribes..

From among the Hebrews from time to time, there arose natural leaders and heros of the people, who are identified in the book of Judges. Notable among them were Gideon and Samson. They temporarily rescued their people for the invaders and raiders. But their victories were only short lived, and these two heros also proved to be flawed (blemished) human beings. (See Judges 6:11 through 8:35 and Judges 13:2 through 16:31).

Israel's First King (Saul)

Throughout this period, the Israelites longed for a king to lead them as a warrior and hero, who would demonstrate human strength and leadership in earthly combat and conquest, and who would pass his throne to his son and grandson. They offered the position to Gideon but he turned it down (See Judges 8:22-23). Later a judge named Eli passed his judicial authority to Samuel his foster son, who was so prevailed upon by the people for an earthly king that he gave in, and let them go ahead and find a person who could be crowned king. But Samuel, in doing so, warned the people about the problems that would be associated with an earthly king (See 1 Samuel 8:10-18). Moses had earlier predicted that the Israelites would establish an earthly king over them, and had also previously warned against excesses that would tempt such a king (See Deuteronomy 17:14-20). The leading people nevertheless decided to determine who the king would be by "casting lots", instead of asking God first. But God did allow them to do this, maybe just to prove a point (See 1 Samuel chapters 9 through 14.) They chose a strong, good looking, super-hero type named Saul, who stood physically head and shoulders above everyone else. Unfortunately, he demonstrated excessive ego, in that he defied Samuel in offering Mosaic sacrifices. However, he was successful in wars against neighboring countries who had been suppressing and taxing the Israelites. He also expanded to territory of Israel and established its borders. But, besides, being egotistical, he also turned out to have somewhat of a paranoid and schizophrenic personality, demonstrating unreasonable fits of anger, and pursuing and attacking individuals who he thought threatened him.

I feel that this is an appropriate place to discuss the casting of lots, in order to make important decisions. Apparently, the casting of lots was considered in Biblical times to be a fair, unbiased way to make choices, and God did allow this. This method was used at least three times in the Bible to make such decisions, but each time there were consequences. This first time was when the Hebrew tribes were given their own unique territories in the new promised land of Israel. Joshua and his subordinates carried out this action. The long range consequence was that a number of generations later the nation of Israel was split in two, along tribal lines. The second time was when a group of dedicated men cast lots to choose a king for Israel. The choice was Saul, who turned out to be a disappointment, resulting in God making his own choice, David, to replace him. The third time was in the New Testament when, after the betrayal of Judas, the eleven remaining disciples cast lots to determine Judas' successor. They chose another follower of Jesus, named Matthias. Apparently, this choice did not satisfy God, because, he selected Paul of Tarsus instead. Thus, it appears that even with the best intentions, and even when those attempts are considered fair and unbiased by Godly people, men's choices often come short of God's plan.

Israel's Second King (David)

God recognized Saul's shortcomings early on, and rejected Saul as king (See 1 Samuel 15). So God sent Samuel to find a worthy replacement for him. Samuel was directed by God to the vicinity of Bethlehem in the area that had been settled by Judah, one of Jacob's sons. And he was drawn to the family of Jesse. (Just to tie things together, Jesse was the grandson of Boaz and Ruth. The story of Ruth was documented in the Old Testament book of Ruth. She was a woman of the nation of Moab, who's people had once been enemies of Israel. However, she migrated to Bethlehem and met and married Boaz, and became the grandmother of Jesse.) *To me, this is a prime example of God's plan to, when appropriate, introduce desirable traits via inter-racial marriage into the Hebrew gene pool, a conclusion that might be drawn from our mixed society today.*

Jesse had eight sons. Samuel met the older seven of them and decided that none would be God's choice to replace Saul. So he asked to see the eighth son who was in the field tending Jesse's flocks. The eighth son was named David. When Samuel met him, he immediately recognized that David was God's chosen one, and he ceremonially poured oil over David's head and pronounced him to be the next king of Israel (See 1 Samuel 16:1-13).

However, this selection was apparently not publicized because of two succeeding events that indicated that Saul did not initially know of this selection of David to be his successor. The first event was precipitated because David was apparently an excellent and recognized musician. Thus, he was selected to play and sing for Saul, to help calm him down during his fits of rage and paranoia. This didn't always work because one time Saul threw a spear at David during one of the music sessions. Fortunately he missed.

The second was when Saul was leading an army against a neighboring country, Philistia. That country had a hero, a huge warrior named Goliath. Afraid to engage in outright conflict, the two armies were camped on either side of a valley, apparently waiting for a provocation to engage. Every day, Goliath would appear in the valley to challenge anyone from Saul's army in a winner-take-all individual combat. No one in the Israeli camp was willing to take the challenge. It happened that David's older brothers were in Saul's army. David was apparently either too young for combat and was needed to tend his father's farm, but he happened to be visiting his brothers in Saul's camp when Goliath was making his challenge. He offered to take on Goliath, and his offer was surprisingly accepted by Saul. Apparently he must have been known to be proficient with the slingshot as a weapon. David went into the valley, and as Goliath approached, David hit him on the forehead with a stone from his slingshot with such force that it possibly fractured Goliath's skull and knocked him out cold. David proceeded then to take Goliath's sword and cut off his head. This threw the Philistine army into a panic and they ran from the field. Then the Israeli army pursued and killed many of them.

This was a turning point in the relationship between Saul and David, because when they returned to Saul's capital, the crowds that greeted them shouted that Saul had **"killed thousands"**, but David had **"killed tens of thousands"**. This added to Saul's paranoia, and resulted in him beginning to hate and fear David. On top of that, Sauls first son, Jonathan, developed a strong friendship with David, and on occasion protected him from his father's wrath. For most of the rest of Saul's reign, David became a hunted man, trying to avoid being assassinated by Saul. Sometime later, both Saul and three of his sons, including Jonathan, were killed in combat, and after a short, unpopular reign by a surviving son of Saul, David was officially crowned king of Israel.

To confirm the fleeting nature of an earthly leader, unfortunately, there appears, so far, no evidence of king Saul's existence except for Biblical accounts in 1 Samuel 8-31 and briefly in 1 Chronicles. This does not mean that he did not exist. *(The only reasons we know so much more about the Egyptians is that they happened to build many of their structures out of hard, enduring stone instead of brick and wood. Even in Egypt, many structures built of less permanent brick and wood have not survived and are, in modern times, only being discovered because of interest in the more permanent ones in that country.)*

Ever since David was king of Israel, he has been considered a model hero of the people of Israel. He had been venerated as the founder of the Davidic dynasty of kings. He was a strong believer and worshiper of God, and was blessed by God in many ways. His kingdom was secure throughout his reign. He was victorious in battle, and extended the borders of Israel, and he died, not in battle, but of old age. David is credited with many of the songs of praise, worship, and prophesy that are documented in the book of Psalms in the Old Testament. And the "Star of David" has become a crowning symbol of the Jewish faith for thousands of years.

But David also turned out to be a flawed man, blemished in many ways. He eventually did all the bad things that both Moses and Samuel warned the people that a king would do. Before he became king, he raided and desecrated the tabernacle where God had been worshiped for centuries. After he became king, he heavily taxed the people, built an army, and married many wives, some for political gain. He was also responsible for the deaths of two of the husbands of women he took as his wives. During his reign, one of his sons, "Absalom", tried to kill him or force him into exile. However, Absalom was killed by Joab, David's military leader. Also, David conquered the town of Salem, (remember Melchizedek), renamed it Jerusalem, and set it up as his capital city. There he set about to build for himself an opulent palace, and determined to also build a temple there as a replacement for the tabernacle then located in the town of Shiloh (but God prevented him from doing that because of his many sins).

However, despite David's accomplishments, again there appears, so far, very little evidence of king David's existence except for Biblical accounts in 1 Samuel 16-31, all of 2 Samuel, 1 Kings 1:1-4, and also extensively in 1 Chronicles 11-29.

Prophesies about Christ, Joshua to King David

The books of the history of the nation of Israel demonstrate a microcosm of all humanity, where without consistent un-flawed guidance, temporal failure is inevitable. However, buried in the history of the rise and fall of the nation of Israel, there are sparks of hope in the prophesies of those who could see beyond the immediate and mundane.

Life after death (Job)

Probably the most ancient of these books of history appears as the **Book of Job**. In the Judeo/ Christian Bible, the book of Job is placed after the end of the history books of Israel. However, the setting for this book seems far earlier, in an area of the world and a time when human populations were small and were clustered around tribal centers. Job believed in God, but was afflicted with all sorts of problems. His children were all killed in a natural disaster, and his riches were stolen from him. He became ill from a serious, painful skin disease, and his wife told him to "Curse God and die". But he continued to believe in God, even though he seriously questioned why God had allowed these things to happen to him. And he was tormented by so-called friends who insisted he had done wrong and was being punished for it. However, during all of this, he made this remarkable confession of faith **"For I know that my redeemer lives and at the last he will stand upon the earth. And after my skin has been thus destroyed, yet in my flesh I shall see God, whom I shall see for myself, and my eyes shall behold, and not another"** (Job 19 25-27). This statement, to me, not only expressed his belief in his life after death, but also a prophesy of God in human form (Christ), that Job will be made whole in his after-life, and that he will be with God.

Life after death (King David)

Even though King David was a warrior and used his powers and later his authority to wage wars and to kill, he was also a poet, a musician, and a very deep lover and respecter of God. In some ways he was also a prophet, with apparently a deep understanding God and his plans for Israel and all of humanity. As proof, a significant number of the songs in the book of Psalms were accredited to his authorship. Some were prayers to God. Some were praises of God, and thanksgiving for his love, power, and majesty, and thanks for his protection. Some were confessions of his sins and pleading for forgiveness. Some were sermons and instruction. Others were or included prophesy. The seventeenth psalm ends with a hint of afterlife, when David wrote **"as for me, I shall behold your face in righteousness; when I awake, I shall be satisfied with your likeness"**. Contained in the most well known of his poems, the twenty third psalm, which begins **"The Lord is my shepherd....."** but its ending that caused me to point out the prophesy in it, is a pretty clear prediction of life after death **".... and I shall dwell in the house of the Lord forever."** David also ended the thirtieth psalm with the words **"Oh Lord my God, I will give thanks to you forever."** Also, David ended psalm fifty six with the words **"For you have delivered my soul from death, yes my feet from falling, that I might walk before God in the light of Life."** And psalm one hundred thirty three ends with the phrase **"For there the Lord has commanded the blessing, life evermore."** Also, Psalm one hundred thirty nine ends with the phrase **"....and lead me in the way everlasting"**, and Psalm one hundred forty ends with the words **"the upright shall dwell in your presence"**.

A premonition of the Crucifixion, death, and resurrection (King David)

A thousand years before Jesus was born, king David penned Psalm twenty two with words, which forecast what would happen to Jesus as he was being executed on the cross in verses 16-18, which says **"they have pierced my hands and feet, I can count all my bones, they stare and gloat over me, they divide my garments among them, and for my clothing they cast lots."**. (For conformation see John 19:22-24). (Note that nailing someone to a cross was not a know method of execution in the time of king David.) Also, the first words of this Psalm in verse 1 were significantly the very same as some of the last words spoken by Jesus as he was dying on the cross, **"My God, my God, why have you forsaken me?"** (See Matthew 27: 46 and Mark 15:34). Then in Psalm 23 David predicts Jesus' death **"even though I walk through the shadow of death"**. Then following in Psalm 24, David proclaimed Jesus resurrection and ascension into heaven **"Lift up your heads, O gates! And be lifted up, O ancient doors, that the king of glory may come in. Who is the king of glory? The Lord, strong and mighty."**

A prediction of the Eternal Christ (King David)

Among the psalms of David, Psalm one hundred ten is a very interesting and remarkable prophesy of the Christ. In verses 1-4 it reads **"The Lord said to my Lord, sit at my right hand until I make your enemies your footstool. The Lord sends forth from Zion your mighty scepter. Rule in the midst of your enemies. Your people will offer themselves freely on the day of your power in holy garments. From the womb of the morning, the dew of your youth will be yours. The Lord has sworn and will not change his mind. You are a priest forever after the order of Melchizedek."** David was not talking about himself because he referred to "My Lord", (one greater than himself). See also Mark 12:35-37 in the New Testament where Mark quoted Jesus as he referenced David's Psalm. This was of course based on the original account in Genesis where Abraham met and gave alms to Melchizedek. And also note a similar reference to Melchizedek in the New Testament book of Hebrews Chapter 7. And it said **"a priest forever".** It should be noted that David wrote Psalm 110 about a thousand years after Abraham, about four hundred years after Moses, and nearly a thousand years before Jesus was born. This, to me, is certain proof of consistency of God's divine plan in the Old Testament.

A prediction that the Christ would be on God's right hand and would be called the "Son of Man" (Asaph)

Asaph was not mentioned in any books of the Bible except Psalms. However, in Psalms he is recognized as its second most prolific author. In Psalm 80, Asaph, as a representative of the people of Israel, pleaded with God to restore Israel's fortunes, after numerous calamities. In verses 14-19 he wrote **"Turn again, O God of hosts! Look down from heaven, and see; have regard for this vine, the stock that your right hand planted, and for the son you made strong for yourself. They have burned it with fire and cut it down; may they perish at the rebuke of your face! But let your hand be on the man of your right hand, the <u>son of man</u> who you have made for yourself! Then we shall not turn back from you; give us life, and we will call upon your name! Restore us, oh Lord God of hosts! Let your face shine that we may be saved."**

Part I Section 3 - Old Testament history King Solomon and beyond

Israel's Third King (Solomon)

As David neared the end of his life, there was a brief attempt by another of David's sons, Adonija, to take over the kingship of Israel, but David declared the second son of Bathsheba, Solomon, as his heir. Solomon took over David's plans to build a temple to replace the tabernacle, and thus, built the first temple in Jerusalem, and moved in all the priests, tabernacle workers "Levites", and the worship artifacts there (including the Arc of the Covenant). He also continued military conquests, expanding Israel's territory to the north as far as present day Turkey, including control of most of Syria. He was considered a very wise man and is identified as the author of three books of the Old Testament; Proverbs (except for the last two chapters), Song of Solomon, and Ecclesiastes. His reputation expanded to territories and kingdoms well beyond his own, as attested by a visit by the queen of Sheba. (Sheba has been identified as a kingdom that included the areas of modern Oman, Aden, Yemen, Eritrea, and Ethiopia, countries surrounding the Horn of Africa at the south end of the Red Sea). He built a number fortifications and military bases, and acquired more wives than even his father David. Unfortunately, in later life he turned away from the God of David and Moses. As apparently noted in his last writing, Ecclesiastes, it seems to reflect Solomon's change in thinking in that he said that "all is vanity", so it is most important to just enjoy life as it comes, and forget about the greater values. However, Solomon did end his book of Ecclesiastes with the following: **"The end of the matter; all has been heard. Fear God and keep his commandments, for this is the whole duty of man."** See information on Solomon's reign in 1 Kings 1-11 and 1 Chronicles 29:22 through 2 Chronicles 9:31. Interestingly, in Chapter 30 of Proverbs (actually attributed to Agur, son of Jakeh the Oracle) there is an excellent prediction of the coming Christ and his powers, as follows: **"Who has ascended to heaven and come down? Who has gathered the wind in his fists? Who has wrapped up the waters in a garment? Who has established all the end of the earth? What is his name, <u>and what is his son's name</u>? Surely you know!"**

Again, little is historically known about Solomon outside the Bible except, interestingly enough, in the history and legends of Aden, Yemen, and Ethiopia, the part of the world that once was the kingdom (or "queendom") of Sheba.

The split

Apparently, since the settlement of the Hebrews in Israel, there had continually been some dissension among the children of Israel between the descendants of the tribe of Judah and the tribe of Ephraim. I suspect that a reason might have been because the center of worship (in the tabernacle) which was originally set up by Joshua at Shiloh in the territory of the tribe of Ephraim, was moved to the new temple in Jerusalem by Solomon in the territory of the tribe of Judah. Thus the Ephraimites may have felt that it had been stolen from them. In any case, after Solomon died, the nation of Israel split into two separate countries, the southern kingdom headed by king Rehoboam, Solomon's son, and the northern kingdom headed by king Jeroboam, an Ephraimite who had been an official of Solomon's court. The northern kingdom retained the name Israel, and the southern kingdom became known as Judah. The capital of Israel (the northern kingdom) was established in the city of Samaria, near Shiloh where the tabernacle had originally been located. This northern kingdom had the most population and the most riches, and with their riches, they built opulent palaces in Samaria. But the southern kingdom had the temple, the center of worship of God. This fact was apparently a continuing sore spot between the two kingdoms, because, like in the Muslim world today where believers make religious pilgrimages to Mecca, there were regular pilgrimages by believers in the northern kingdom to the temple in Jerusalem for holy day events. *Jesus is recorded in the New Testament as making these trips several times.*

The end of the Northern Kingdom

After the split, the Northern kingdom became racked with discontent and rebellion. There were no successful efforts for the northern kingdom kings to pass their reign to their heirs. Kings were often forcibly deposed and sometimes assassinated. Neighboring countries often conducted raids into Israel. And Israel lost control of Syria, which after reestablishing its sovereignty, raided and plundered both Samaria and Jerusalem. Some of the northern kings tried to kill the believers and set up worship of Baal as a substitute for worship of God, but this effort was thwarted on several occasions, once most notably by the prophet Elijah in a proof-of-divinity contest (See 1 Kings 18). But the bulk of the people turned their backs on God. Then, Shalmaneser, the king of Assyria (who's capital was the city of Nineveh in the Tigris/Euphrates river valley in what is now northern Iraq), decided to conquer and subjugate Israel, which he did. He and his successor, Sargon II, also took captive most of the population of the city of Samaria and the surrounding areas and deported them. Then they brought in undesirables from Assyria to take their place. *The descendants of these undesirables intermarried with some of the remaining Israelites and were later called Samaritans in the New Testament.* The city of Samaria, with its opulent palaces, was razed to the ground, and the site was abandoned. The northern kingdom lost its identity as a nation, and the people as a kingdom were lost to history. *To me this was another culling by God to purify the race of people who would later produce Jesus, the promised Christ.* The Assyrians later, under their new king, Sennacharib, son of Sargon II, also tried to conquer Judah but were thwarted by God. (Sennacharib's entire army died of a mysterious cause, in their camp in one night outside the walls of Jerusalem.)

The end of the Southern Kingdom

The southern kingdom (Judah) existed for several hundred years under the leadership of descendants of David, including a number of years after the Assyrian destruction of the northern kingdom. Several of these kings were good, restoring rites of the Passover and the sacred holidays, resurrecting the Mosaic laws and rituals, and restoring and repairing the temple. However, some of them were awful. Furthermore, every one of even the best of these kings had flaws in their personal lives and decisions. Even though Judah survived the attack by the Assyrians, raids by neighboring nations (like Egypt) continued to occur, especially as the leadership started to weaken. Toward the end of the Davidic dynasty, a Judaic king naively showed the riches of the temple to emissaries of Babylon, (the next kingdom to arise in the Tigris/Euphrates valley after the decline of Nineveh). So Nebuchadnezzar, the king of Babylon, decided to invade Judah and plunder those riches. He did so, successfully conquering Judah, and, just as Shalmaneser did earlier to Israel, and took captive a large number of the citizens of Judah and resettled them in the area of the deltas of the Tigris and Euphrates rivers in what is now southern Iraq. (Among those deported by Nebuchadnezzar were Ezekiel and Daniel (see the books of Ezekiel and Daniel in the Old Testament). And Nebuchadnezzar not only expropriated the temple riches but also destroyed the temple itself, razing it and burning it to the ground.

Thus, with these deportations and for many years after these events, there was effectively no-longer a nation of descendants of Jacob. A new nation would eventually arise from the return of some (another culling) of those who were deported by Nebuchadnezzar, plus some of those who were left behind during the deportations and exile. However, this new nation would be called Judea, not either Judah nor Israel.

*To me, this whole process tended to prove several things. First, despite being very early confronted with a knowledge of good and evil, the process of learning the real nuances of this knowledge is often very difficult to grasp and quite frequently becomes buried in temporal thinking. Second, people generally yearn for direction and leadership. The wiser of the temporal leaders in the Old Testament tried unsuccessfully to point them to God instead of civic, earthly leaders such as kings, but people didn't listen, just the same as today. The earthly individuals, chosen by people for guidance and leadership, without exception, proved to be wanting in some characteristics of their lives. Third, competition, prejudice, bigotry, greed, sexual urgencies, envy, pride, anger, the desire for self preservation, the desire for power and material things, and the establishment of false comfort zones, are all powerful influences on human thinking. These can, as even today, seriously cloud objective judgement. Fourth, aging is inevitable and nothing earthly is permanent and must come to an end. Fifth, "**Nothing is new under the sun**" (See Ecclesiastes 1:9), and the same mistakes will be made over and over again, as can be seen in the Old Testament of the Bible and all of human history.*

There are some significant corroborating reports in recently discovered records of the time of the kings and nations of both Israel and Judah, in archives of Egypt, Assyria, and Babylon.

The Return of the remnant and the rest of Hebrew history before Jesus

About 70 years after the last deportation from Judah of the descendants of Israel, only about seventy thousand of them returned to Jerusalem. *(This to me was another culling of the people to purify them for the coming of Christ.)* However, these few, under the Hebrew priest Ezra, set about to rebuild the temple in Jerusalem. But by that time, there were those living in the areas of the former kingdoms of Judah and Israel who strongly objected to this reestablishment, and forced a hold on the work. So a few years later Nehemiah, a Hebrew and official in the Persian court, came with another group of Hebrew people to Jerusalem from their exile in the valley of

Babylon, who rebuilt the Jerusalem city walls. They brought with them a descendant of David, named Zerubbabel, who they thought would become king of the reestablished kingdom of Israel. However, apparently he didn't work out because the reestablished Israel fell into a period of darkness and became subject first to Alexander-the-Great and then his minions, the Seleucids. Then it came under the authority of a group of rebels called the Maccabees. Then it came under the control of the Roman Empire, who set up its rule under a non-Hebrew puppet king, Herod the Great. Herod the Great ruled the reestablished nation of Israel, (which by then was called Judea), until shortly after the birth of Jesus. And during his reign Herod rebuilt the temple again and also built several pyramids and palaces. *And I think may have thought of himself as the promised saviour (Messiah) of the Hebrews.*

Part I Section 4 - Post-Split Old Testament prophets who foretold Christ, and their prophesies

Besides the portents in Genesis and Exodus and the prophecies of Moses, Job, and King David, after the split between northern and southern Kingdoms, there were several Old Testament prophets that had specific things to say about the coming Christ. All of the prophets below appeared during this period. They and their prophesies appear in the Old Testament, as follows:

Isaiah, the prophet

David's son, Solomon, was considered a very successful king. He also had some very good thoughts in his writings about wise and moral living. However, his writings appear to be about more earthly thought and wisdom rather than about consideration of God the Creator. After him, and for almost four hundred fifty years, the Kings of the separate nations of Judah and Israel seemed more interested in maintaining their kingdoms than thoughts of God.

But, about the time of the invasion of Israel (the northern Kingdom) by Shalmaneser, the king of Assyria, and the destruction of that nation by him, there came the prophet Isaiah in the southern kingdom. Isaiah lived to see Israel destroyed, and also through the ups and downs of Judah during the reigns of succeeding alternatively good and bad rulers of that country, until it became obvious that Judah was doomed as well. He tried, with varying success, to influence the thinking and actions of those kings. But in the end, he just had to watch the inevitable. In addition to the documentation of what was happening to Judah in its last days, Isaiah made some extensive prophecies about the coming Messiah. *Some scholars consider that what is written in Isaiah is a result of two or three different authors, writing over a period of about two hundred years. However, they discount the possibility that Isaiah was able to prophesy about things that happened after the last deportation and the return of the seventy thousand. In rebuttal, I believe that if Isaiah could predict the coming of Christ seven or eight hundred years later, he could also have certainly predicted the return of the Hebrews from the last captivity. Therefore, I prefer to believe that Isaiah was one long lived person, as was Daniel (see below).* Isaiah was considered a major prophet of the Old Testament, prolifically producing predictions about the fates of Judah,

Israel, and also about other surrounding middle eastern nations and peoples. Also, he has been considered the primary source of predictions about the coming Christ. In reading the book of Isaiah, his prophesies seem sometimes disjointed, more like those of an oracle than other Old Testament prophets. Also, sometimes he speaks in the past tense as though some of his predictions had already occurred, even though they were still in the future. And he often uses the name Israel when he is referring primarily to the nation of Judah. *(I suspect that this was a concession to the idea that all were descendants of Jacob/Israel, even though Judah is the only surviving national entity.)* However, he was quite specific in many areas dealing with the Christ's future birth, actions, and treatment by his contemporaries. A number of these prophesies were used in the libretto of the Handel's Messiah and also are often used in numerous writings and sermons. Examples of his predictions about the Christ are as indicated below.

Isaiah's Prophesies about the Christ

Here are just some of the more obvious of Isaiah's prophesies concerning the coming of the Christ.

Isaiah 4:2 (*Christ to be honored by some*) **"In that day the branch of the Lord shall be beautiful and glorious, and the fruit of the land shall be the pride and honor of the survivors of Israel."**

Isaiah 7:14 (*Christ's birth*) **"Therefore the Lord himself will give you a sign. Behold, the virgin shall conceive and bear a son, and shall call his name Emanuel (God with us)".**

Isaiah 9:1b *(Christ will come from Galilee)* **"...but in the latter time he has made glorious the way of the sea, the land beyond Jordan, Galilee of the nations."**

Isaiah 9:2 (*Christ, the light of the world*) **"The people who walked in darkness have seen a great light; those who dwelt in the land of deep darkness on them the light has shined."**

Isaiah 9:6-7 (*Christ's power, identity, and promise of eternal life*) **"For to us a child is born, to us a son is given; and the government shall be upon his shoulders, and his name shall be called Wonderful, Counselor, Mighty God, Everlasting Father, Prince of Peace. Of the increase of his government and of peace, there will be no end, on the throne of David and over his kingdom to establish it and to uphold it with justice and with righteousness from this time forth and forevermore."**

Isaiah 11:1-5 (*Christ's heritage, purpose, justice, and omnipotence*) **"There shall come forth a shoot from the stump of Jesse and a branch from his roots shall bear fruit. And the Spirit of the Lord shall rest upon him, and the Spirit of wisdom and understanding, and the Spirit of counsel and might, the Spirit of knowledge and the fear of the Lord. And his delight shall be in the fear of the Lord. He shall not judge by what his eyes see, or decide disputes by what his ears hear, but with righteousness he shall judge the poor and shall decide with equity for the meek of the earth; and he shall strike the earth with the rod of his mouth, and with the breath of his lips he shall kill the wicked. Righteousness shall be the belt of his waist, and faithfulness the belt of his loins."**

Isaiah 11:10 (*Christ, the beacon for all humanity*) "**In that day the root of Jesse, who shall stand as a signal for the people, of him shall the nations inquire, and his resting place shall be glorious**".

Isaiah 25:8-9 (*Christ's gifts of salvation and eternal life to his people*) "**He will swallow up death forever; and the Lord God will wipe away tears from all faces, and the reproach of his people he will take away from all the earth, for the Lord has spoken. It will be said in that day, behold, this is your God; we have waited for him, that he might save us. This is the Lord; we have waited for him; let us be glad in his salvation.**"

Isaiah 35:4-6 (*Christ's charter and his miracles*) "**Behold, your God will come with vengeance, with the recompense of God. He will come and save you. Then the eyes of the blind shall be opened, and the ears of the deaf unstopped; then shall the lame man leap like a deer, and the tongue of the mute sing for joy.**"

Isaiah 40:3 (*A prediction of John the Baptist who introduced Christ to the world*) "**A voice cries in the wilderness, prepare the way of the Lord; make straight in the desert a highway for our God.**"

Isaiah 40:10-11 (*Christ's love and caring as a good shepherd*) "**Behold, the Lord God comes with might and his arm rules for him; behold, his reward is with him. He will tend his flock like a shepherd; he will gather the lambs in his arm; he will carry them in his bosom.**"

Isaiah 42:1-4 (*God's certification of Christ and his commission*) "**Behold my servant, whom I uphold, my chosen, in whom my soul delights; I have put my spirit upon him; he will bring forth justice to the nations. He will not cry out aloud or lift up his voice, or make it heard in the street; a bruised reed he will not break, and a faintly burning wick he will not quench; he will faithfully bring forth justice. He will not grow faint or be discouraged till he has established justice in the earth, and all nations wait for his law.**"

This scripture is quoted in Matthew 12:18-21 in the New Testament, but in Matthew there is an interesting change in the wording where the word "gentiles" is substituted for "nations". This change appears to make Christ's witness a personal witness to individuals rather than political entities. This will be very important to the nature of the salvation offered by Jesus.

Isaiah 49:6 (*The Christ will be the saviour to not only Israel but all the peoples of the earth*) "**It is to light a thing that you should be my servant to raise up (only) the tribes of Jacob and to bring back (only) the preserved of Israel; I will make you as a light for (all) the nations, that my salvation may reach to the ends of the earth**".

Isaiah 52:13-15 and 53:1-12 (*A story of the person, the power, the life, the fate, and the purpose of the Christ, in a nutshell*) "**Behold my servant shall act wisely; he shall be high and lifted up and shall be exalted. As many were astounded at you, his appearance was so marred, beyond human semblance, and his form beyond that of the children of mankind. So shall**

41

he sprinkle many nations, kings shall shut their mouths because of him; for that which has not been told them they see, and that which they have not heard they understand. Who has believed what he has heard from us? For he grew up before him as a young plant, and like root out of dry ground; he had no form or majesty that we should look at him, and no beauty that we should desire him. He was despised and rejected by men; a man of sorrows, and acquainted with grief, and as one from whom men hide their faces. He was despised and we esteemed him not. Surely he has borne our griefs and carried our sorrows; yet we esteemed him stricken, smitten by God, and afflicted. But he was wounded for our transgressions; he was crushed for our iniquities; upon him was the chastisement that brought us peace, and with his stripes we are healed. All we like sheep have gone astray; we turned, every one, to his own way; and the Lord has laid on him the iniquity of us all. He was oppressed, and he was afflicted, yet he opened not his mouth, like a lamb that is led to the slaughter, and like a sheep that before his shearers is silent, so he opened not his mouth. By oppression and judgement he was taken away; and as for his generation, who considered that he was cut off from the land of the living, stricken for the transgression of my people? And they made his grave with the wicked and with a rich man in his death, although he had done no violence, and there was no deceit in his mouth. Yet it was the will of the Lord to crush him; he has put him to grief, when his soul makes an offering for guilt. He shall see his offspring; shall prolong his days; the will of the Lord shall prosper in his hand. Out of the anguish of his soul he shall see and be satisfied; by his knowledge shall the righteous one, my servant, make many to be accounted as righteous, and he shall bear their iniquities. Therefore I will divide him a portion with the many, and he shall divide the spoil with the strong, because he poured out his soul to death and was numbered with the transgressors; yet he bore the sin of many, and makes intercession for the transgressors." (*There are so many parallels and prophecies of Jesus, the Christ the Messiah in the above words that it is impossible to cite them all here, but they definitely show up in the New Testament.*

Isaiah 59:20 (A direct prophesy of the coming of Christ as a saviour for the Hebrews) **"And a redeemer will come to Zion to those in Jacob who turn from transgression declares the Lord."**

Isaiah 61:1-2 (Quoted by Jesus in his hometown (Nazareth) synagogue when he first introduced himself as Christ, the redeemer) **"The spirit of the lord is upon me, because the Lord has anointed me to bring good news to the poor; he has sent me to bind up the broken hearted, to proclaim liberty to the captives, and opening of the prison to those who are bound, to proclaim the year of the Lord's favor."**

Even though sometimes written in the past tense and in poetic form, all of these prophesies of Isaiah, put together, lay out a nearly complete picture for what those of about 700 BC would expect in a future Christ/Messiah.

Jeremiah the prophet

Jeremiah appeared on the scene in Judah after Isaiah as a second major prophet, very near the end of the Davidic dynasty. And his life story tells of the fall of Jerusalem, the destruction of the temple, and the deportation of many of the citizens. It also tells of failed attempts by the survivors to reestablish order in the chaos and the eventual travel of Jeremiah and others to Egypt, where tradition says that Jeremiah died. Much of the book of Jeremiah is a record of his attempts to warn the people of what was coming (death and destruction). He was opposed by a number of other so-called prophets and temple priests, who kept telling the people that God would protect them and not to be concerned. At one point his opponents beat him and put him in stocks, and he was threatened with death several times. Most of Jeremiah's prophesies are about the coming destruction and disasters, seventy years of exile and eventual return of the people to rebuild the temple and the city. But he also had some things to say about the coming Christ.

<u>Jeremiah's prophesies about Christ</u>

One particular prophesy of Jeremiah was about the coming Christ in Chapter 23:5-6, as follows: **"Behold the days are coming declares the Lord, when I will raise up for David a righteous branch, and he shall reign as king and deal wisely, and shall execute justice and righteousness in the land. In his days Judah will be saved, and Israel will dwell securely. And this is the name by which he will be called: The Lord is our righteousness."** (Jeremiah also repeats this in Jeremiah 33:15-16.)

A second of Jeremiah's prophesies in chapter 31:15 is cited in the second chapter of Matthew in the New Testament as a forecast of the murdering of the male children in Bethlehem by King Herod in an attempt to kill the Messiah: **"Thus says the Lord; A voice is heard in Ramah, lamentation and bitter weeping. Rachel is weeping for her children; she refuses to be comforted for her children, because they are no more."**

Another of his prophesies was about a "New Covenant" as follows in Jeremiah 31:31-34: **"Behold the days are coming, declares the Lord, when I will make a new covenant with the house of Israel and the house of Judah, not like the covenant I made on the day when I took them out of the land of Egypt, my covenant which they broke, though I was their husband, declares the Lord. But this is the new covenant I will make with the house of Israel after those days declares the Lord; I will put my law within them, and I will write it on their hearts. And I will be their God, and they shall be my people. And no longer shall each one teach his neighbor and teach his brother, saying 'Know the Lord', for they shall all know me, from the least of them to the greatest, declares the Lord. For I will forgive their iniquity, and I will remember their sin no more."** *To me and many others, that new covenant is Jesus, his sacrifice, and his offer of salvation, and the demonstration through him of God's unconditional love for mankind.*

Another of Jeremiah's prophesies was about security for Israel, Judah and Jerusalem as follows in Jeremiah 33:14-16. It promises a righteous branch from David **"shall execute justice and**

righteousness in the land". *However, I am not sure about the meaning of this particular promise. Maybe it will be revealed in the future.*

Ezekiel the prophet

Ezekiel appeared on the scene as a third major prophet and one of the early captives of Nebuchadnezzar, who was resettled in what is now southern Iraq. Most of his prophesies were about bad things that would happen to Babylon and other middle eastern countries, and particularly concerning Jerusalem and the temple there, who's destruction was eminent. He also, through a lot of dreams and visions, tried to encourage the resettled people to hold fast their belief in God. He predicted the rebuilding of the temple in Jerusalem and described its design and the rituals to be performed there in very great detail. He, interestingly, spoke of himself as the "Son of Man", a term Jesus often used to identify himself during his ministry. Ezekiel also prophesied about Christ. And, in addition, he prophesied about the Holy Spirit, which was foretold by Jesus as an entity (or spirit) who would follow him. (See Luke 24:49 and John 20:22-23 in the New Testament)

Ezekiel's prophesies concerning the Christ

In Ezekiel 34:23-24 he quoted God as saying **"And I will set up over them one shepherd, my servant David, and he shall feed them: he shall feed them and be their shepherd. And I the Lord will be their God, and my servant David shall be prince among them."**

And in Ezekiel 36:26-27 he also quoted God as saying **"And I will give you a new heart, and a new spirit I will put within you. And I will remove the heart of stone and give you a heart of (***living***) flesh. And I will put my spirit within you, and cause you to walk in my statutes and be careful to obey my rules."** *To me, this is a pretty clear prediction that the Christ will bring a new set of rules for living, driven by the heart and not by the law.*

Daniel the prophet

Nebuchadnezzar was king over a very powerful middle eastern country about 600 BC. The capitol of this kingdom was the city of Babylon on the Tigris River. He fought against and conquered a number of neighboring countries, including Judah. In order to prevent subsequent rebellions by those countries, he captured a significant portion of the populations of those countries and resettled them elsewhere. Daniel was one of the people of Judah who were deported from Judah to Babylon about the same time as Ezekiel. But Daniel was one of a young elite sub-group who were considered the best and brightest among those deported. He was assigned to be part of King Nebuchadnezzar's court. He gained favor with Nebuchadnezzar by accurately interpreting a dream, and was promoted to a high position among the king's advisors. And, in the process of interpreting the dream, Daniel witnessed to him about God. But Nebuchadnezzar was an egotistical man and tried to aggrandize himself by building a huge statue of himself and ordering his subjects to worship it. Three of Daniel's compatriots refused to do so and were throne into a furnace. However, they came out unburned, and Nebuchadnezzar praised God for the miracle. Daniel was blessed with a long life, surviving as a court advisor to Nebuchadnezzar's son and grandson, and even to the Darius, the king of the Medes and Persians who invaded and conquered Babylon. Daniel was able also to witness to Darius and was able to convince Darius to believe in God after Daniel survived from being thrown into a den of Lions. Daniel made a number of prophesies about future events. Among them, one was about God, who he called **"The Ancient of Days"** and three were about the coming Messiah. The ones about the Messiah are as follows.

Daniel's prophesies about the Christ and his kingdom

Daniel chapter 2 tells about the dream of Nebuchadnezzar had had that he did not understand. Daniel described the dream thus: The king dreamed of a magnificent statue of a man with a head of gold, an upper body of silver, a lower body of bronze, and legs of iron, but with feet of clay. Daniel described the gold head as the kingdom of Babylon, but that there would be three succeeding earthly kingdoms, followed by a kingdom that would be set up by God that would exist forever. The dream came true. Nebuchadnezzar's kingdom was followed first by the Persians (silver), then by the Macedonians (In the person of Alexander The Great) (bronze), and then the Romans (iron). And then the weakness and destruction of Judea, but the survival of God's eternal kingdom, with the advent of Christ.

In Daniel 7:13-14 *This one appears to be about a first coming of Christ* **"I saw in the night, visions, and behold, with the clouds of heaven there came one (Christ) like the 'Son of Man', and he came to the 'Ancient of Days' (*God*) and was presented before him. And to him was given dominion and glory and a kingdom, that all peoples, nations, and languages should serve him; his dominion is an everlasting dominion, which shall not pass away, and his kingdom, one that shall not be destroyed."**

And in Daniel 12:1-3 *This one appears to be about a second coming of Christ* **"At that time shall arise Michael *(the Christ?)*, the great prince who has charge of your people. And there shall be a time of trouble, such as never has been since there was a nation till that time. But at that time your people shall be delivered, everyone whose name shall be found written in the book. And many of those who sleep in the dust of the earth shall awake, some to everlasting life, and some to shame and everlasting contempt."** Interesting, this scripture also is apparently the first to identify that there are two states of the after-life. One to "everlasting life" (heaven) and one to "shame and everlasting contempt" (hell).

The Prophet Hosea

After the book of Daniel in the Old Testament are a number of books written by or about a series of what are called "minor prophets". A majority prophesied about immediate or impending events that would effect Israel and Judah, but four of them would have some specific and interesting words about the coming Christ. Hosea was the last prophet of the northern kingdom before it fell to the Assyrians. He was a witness to the moral decay of that nation at its end. And this decay apparently resulted in a personal tragedy for him. Hosea tells how God directed him to marry a prostitute. She bore him children, but then she left him and returned to prostitution. The book of Hosea is the story of his efforts to win her back. He compares his love for her and his successful efforts to redeem her, to that of God's efforts to win back the children of Israel after they had prostituted themselves to other Gods. But there is one of his prophesies that is specifically cited in the New Testament about Jesus, as per below.

Hosea's prophesy about the Christ

Hosea 11:1 is quoted in Matthew chapter two in reference to Jesus return from Egypt after he and his family fled there to avoid Jesus being killed by King Herod. **"When Israel was child, I loved him and out of Egypt I called my son."** And in Hosea 6:2 he predicted of Christ **that "After two days he will revive us, on the third day he will raise us up, that we may live before him."** *This is a prediction of the resurrection of Christ on the third day, and the gift of eternal life for his followers.*

The Prophet Joel

In Joel 3:12, Joel acknowledges that God is ruler and judge of all nations (not just Israel), and also what Jehoshaphat did (one of the kings of Judah after the split (See 2nd Chronicles 20:6). More on this in Volume II about Jesus' second coming.

The Prophet Jonah

Jonah was a particularly interesting person in that he was more of a preacher than a prophet because he had the power of persuasion to lead people to belief in the Lord God of Israel. But he was a rebel and refused to follow God's direction to witness to Israel's enemy, Assyria. As a result, he was thrown into a stormy sea by a boat crew and was swallowed by a large fish, especially prepared for that purpose by God. Thus, he was effectively dead for three days, then was vomited up alive on the shore by the fish on the third day. **His three days in a symbolic tomb was mentioned in the New Testament as a prediction of Jesus' death and resurrection after three days in the tomb.** *Interestingly enough, the large God-prepared fish, was a symbol of both the tomb and the salvation of the Christ, because it saved Jonah from drowning, after he was "baptized" in the sea (See Jonah 2:5-6).*

But there is another remarkable and almost eerie precursor and predictor of Christ's mission on earth, in that before Jonah was swallowed by the fish, Jonah was on a boat that was about to sink in a stormy sea. It was determined by the ship's crew that Jonah was the cause of their predicament. So Jonah offered himself as a sacrifice to save the ship and it's crew, **and the crew became believers in God because of Jonah's sacrifice** (See Jonah 1:12-16).

The prophet Micah

Another of those minor prophets was Micah. He was a contemporary of the prophet Isaiah, and just as Isaiah, was a witness to the gradual decay of Judah before it was conquered by Nebuchadnezzar.

<u>Micah's prophesies about the Christ</u>

In Micah 4:2b-3a *Is a forecast of Christ's judgement* **"For out of Zion shall go forth the law, and the <u>word</u> of the Lord from Jerusalem. He shall judge between many peoples, and shall decide for strong nations far away."** *To me, this is not only a prophecy of the coming of Christ, but also that he would be sovereign over not only Israel, but also the whole world.*

In Micah 5:2 *Is a forecast of Christ's birthplace* **"But you, O Bethlehem Ephrathah, who are too little to be among the clans of Judah, from you shall come forth for me one who is to be ruler in Israel, whose coming forth is from old, 'ancient of days'".***(The same name for God that appeared in Daniel)* *This sounds like Micah was predicting David. However, he obviously was not talking about David, because Micah lived several hundred years after David. So he was pretty obviously predicting not David, but his descendent Jesus.*

The prophet Zechariah

Zechariah was one of the minor prophets. He prophesied late in the Old Testament period during the time of Ezra and Nehemiah, after the return of the exiles to Jerusalem after the Medes and Persians had conquered Babylon. He had several visions about the coming Christ as follows.

<u>Zechariah's prophesies about the Christ</u>

In Zechariah 9:9 *A forecast of Jesus' triumphal entry into Jerusalem as commemorated on Palm Sunday.* **"Rejoice greatly, O daughter of Zion! Shout aloud, O daughter of Jerusalem! Behold your king is coming to you; righteous is he, humble and mounted on a donkey, on a colt, the foal of a donkey."** *A prophesy specifically about Jesus' triumphal entry into Jerusalem.*

In Zechariah 12:10 *A forecast of the spirit of Christ, of his side being pierced (on the cross), and his death as the son of God.* **"And I will pour out on the house of David and the inhabitants of Jerusalem a spirit of grace and pleas for mercy, so that, when they look on him whom they have pierced, they shall mourn for him, as one mourns for an only child, and weep bitterly over him, as one weeps over a firstborn."**

In Zechariah 13:1 *A forecast of the sin-cleansing power of Christ.* **"On that day there shall be a fountain opened for the house of David and the inhabitants of Jerusalem, to cleanse them from sin and uncleanliness."**

In Zechariah 14:6-9 *A forecast of the new day of Christ.* **"On that day there shall be no light, cold, or frost. And there shall be a unique day, which is known to the Lord, neither day or night, but at evening time there shall be light. On that day living waters shall flow out from Jerusalem, half of them to the eastern sea and half of them to the western sea. It shall continue in summer as in winter. And the Lord will be king over all the earth. On that day the Lord will be one and his name one."** *This is to me again, a prediction that Christ will be sovereign of not just the Hebrews, but of all the peoples of the earth.*

In Zechariah 14:21b *An interesting possible forecast of Christ driving the money changers from the temple.* **"And there shall no longer be a trader in the house of the Lord of hosts on that day."**

Another prophesy by Zechariah starts with the **thirteenth verse of chapter 2 and continues through the whole of chapter 3**. You, the reader of this document need to read it. *To me, it is one of the most intriguing and mysterious passages in the Bible, and, I think, might stand almost equal to Isaiah chapter 53 in describing the Messiah. I will not quote it here but rather hold off until the second volume, as it, I believe, will have much more meaning in light of the words and events of the gospel passages in the New Testament. It does identify an individual called "Joshua (the Old Testament pronunciation of Jesus) the high priest", and describes certain events about him. This may also be the seminal prophesy that identifies the name "Jesus" with the "Christ." As you read this you will also note that it talks about a "branch", as, I assume, a reference to Jesus as a descendent of David. Some have inferred that they are referring to two different people, Joshua and the branch, but I think they are one, not two, both to me are the same person, Jesus of the New Testament. Let us assume that Jesus (Joshua) was the ultimate warrior of the Old Testament (See also Psalm 24), preceding David, and the "Branch" (but who came after David) was the Jesus of the New Testament, the ultimate saviour.*

However, Zechariah also prophesied that Zerubbabel, a descendent of David who returned from the Babylonian exile, would be a great king. He apparently facilitated the rebuilding of the Temple, but his legacy disappeared from history until he was later named in the New Testament as an earthly ancestor of Jesus. Some historians indicated that he was accompanied by a priest named Joshua, even though Ezra appears most likely to have been the accompanying priest. And interestingly enough, Nehemiah, who came to Jerusalem a generation or two later to rebuild the Jerusalem wall, makes no mention of Zerubbabel in his book. Also, Zechariah spoke of Joshua in such a way that indicated that he would be someone in the future. Again, this supports the concept that Joshua was the archaic pronunciation of Jesus, and that Zechariah was speaking of the future Messiah.

The Prophet Malachi

Shortly after the rebuilding of the temple and the wall of Jerusalem under the leadership of Nehemiah, apparently the enthusiasm for the reestablishment of the kingdom of Israel waned, especially after the less than expected performance of Zerubbabel as the new king. So Malachi arose as a new prophet to scold the people into honoring God. But he did something else as well. He prophesied the coming of both John the Baptist and Jesus, as below. (This prophesy was penned 500 years before Jesus was born.)

<u>Malachi's prophesies about John the Baptist and the Christ</u>

Malachi 3:1-4 **"Behold, I send my messenger, and he will prepare the way before me. And the Lord you seek will suddenly come to his temple; and the messenger of the covenant in whom you delight, behold, he is coming, says the Lord of hosts. But who can endure the day** of his coming, and who can stand when he appears? For he is like a refiner's fire and like a fuller's soap. He will sit as a refiner and purifier of silver, and he will purify the sons of Levi *(the temple caretakers)* and refine them like gold and silver, and they will bring offerings of righteousness to the Lord. Then the offerings of Judah and Jerusalem will be pleasing to the Lord as in the days of old and as in former years."

Part I Section 5 - A summary of Old Testament Prophesies about Christ

Thus, there are numerous predictions of and about a Christ/Messiah. Here are some of them.

- **that God "spoke" to create light and John said that in the beginning Christ was thespoken word of God   Genesis 1:1-3   John 1:1-3**

- **that God preferred Abel's blood sacrifice   Genesis 4: 3-5**

- **that God baptized and cleansed the earth (the great flood)   Genesis 6:11-7:24**

- **that God provided a blood sacrifice substitute (for Isaac)   Genesis 22:1-13**

- **that God offered life for many with the sacrifice of a lamb (for Israel) (the passover)   Exodus 12:1-13**

- **that Christ, the saviour, would exist   Deuteronomy 18:15   Isaiah 11:1-5   Jeremiah 33:15-16   Daniel 7:13-14   Zechariah 3:1-8   Malachi 3:1-4**

- **that there would be a being who would be Christ   Proverbs 30:4**

- **that he would be a blessing to the whole earth   Genesis 22:15-18   Isaiah 49:1   and 6   Daniel 7:14   Hosea 2:23   Zechariah 2:11**

- **what would he be like   Psalm 24:7-10 Isaiah 11;1-5, 42:1-6, and 52:13   Jeremiah 33:15-16   Daniel 7:13 and 10:4-6**

- **that he would be in human form   Isaiah 52:14-53:3 Daniel 10:4-6**

- **that a voice from the wilderness will forecast him   Isaiah   40:3-5 Malachi 3:1   and 4:5-6**

- **that he would be born to a virgin   Isaiah 7:4**

- **that he would be born in Bethlehem   Micah 5:2**

- **that he would be a descendant of King David   Isaiah 9:7   Jeremiah 23:5-6 Zechariah 13:1 and several other places**

- **but that he would precede and be worshiped by David. Psalm 110:1**

- **that he would be named Jesus (Joshua)   Zechariah 3:1-10**

- **that his early life would be threatened   Jeremiah 31:15**

- **that he would spend time in Egypt   Hosea 11:1**

- **that he would begin his ministry in Galilee   Isaiah 9:1**

- **what his appearance would be like on earth   Isaiah 4:2, 52: and 53:2   Daniel 7:13 and 10:4-6**

- **that he would be badly thought of and treated   Isaiah   53:3, 5, 7-8**

- **that he would be a king   Psalm 24:7-10   Isaiah 9:6   Jeremiah 23:5   Zechariah 3:6**

- **that he would be a servant of God   Isaiah 42:1**

- **that he would be chosen and blessed by God   Isaiah 1-4**

- **that he would be a teacher   Malachi 3:1-3**

- **what he would teach   Deuteronomy 3:18   Jeremiah 31:31-34 Micah 6:8**

- **that he would be a shepherd for his people   Psalm 23:1   Isaiah 40:10   Ezekiel 34:23-24**

- **that he would be a prophet   Deuteronomy 18:15 and 18**

- **that he would be a priest   Zechariah 3:8**

- **that his preisthood would be after the order of Melchizedek   Psalm 110:4**

- **that he would be called "Son of Man"   Psalm 80:17   Daniel 7:14**

- **that he would also be called the "Son of God"   Psalm 2:7**

- **that he would perform miracles   Isaiah 35:4-6**

- **that he would teach in parables   Psalm 78:2-4**

- <u>that that he would make a triumphal entry on a donkey</u>   <u>Zechariah 9:9</u>

- <u>that he would drive money changers from the Temple</u>   <u>Zechariah 14:21</u>

- <u>that he would be rejected by his own people</u>   <u>Psalm 22:16-17</u>   <u>Isaiah 53:3</u>

- <u>that his hands and feet would be pierced</u>   <u>Psalm 22:16</u>

- <u>that his side would be pierced</u>   <u>Zechariah 12:10</u>

- <u>that he would offer salvation to the Hebrews</u>   <u>Isaiah 59:20</u>

- <u>that he would be a blessing to all humanity</u>   <u>Genesis 22:18</u>

- <u>that he would die as a sacrifice for our sins</u>   <u>Isaiah 53:5-6, 8 and 11-12</u>

- <u>that he would be hung on a tree (wooden cross) to die</u>   <u>Deuteronomy 21:22</u>

- <u>that people would cast lots for his clothes</u>   <u>Psalm 22:18</u>

- <u>that he would die with criminals and be buried in a rich man's tomb</u>   <u>Isaiah 53:9</u>

- <u>that his time in the tomb was predicted</u>   <u>Hosea 6:2</u>   <u>Jonah 2:5-6</u>

- <u>that his resurrection was predicted</u>   <u>Psalm 30:5</u>

- <u>that he will be a new covenant for humanity</u>   <u>Isaiah 42:6</u>   <u>Jeremiah 31:31-34</u>   <u>Ezekiel 36:26-29</u>

- <u>that there will be life after death for believers</u>   <u>Job 19:25-26</u>   <u>Psalm 23:6 and 73:24</u>   <u>Ecclesiastes 12:7</u>   <u>Isaiah 25:8 and 26:19</u>   <u>Daniel 12:1-2</u>

- <u>that his second coming to earth was predicted</u>   <u>Psalm 24:7-9</u>   <u>ah 35:4 and 66:15-16</u>   <u>Daniel 12:1-2</u>   <u>Zechariah 14:1-7</u>

- <u>that there will a terror with his return</u>   <u>Isaiah 2:12-19</u>

- <u>that his throne would be eternal</u>   <u>Ecclesiastes 3:14</u>   <u>Isaiah 9:7</u>   <u>Daniel 7:14</u>

- <u>that he will be judge of humanity</u>   <u>First Cronicles 16:33</u>   <u>Psalm 1:5 and 75:7</u>   <u>Isaiah 24:1-12, 42:1 and 66:16</u>

- <u>and that the Holy Spirit is real</u>   <u>Isaiah 61:1</u>   <u>Ezekiel 36:26-28 and 37:13</u>

Therefore, Jesus of Nazareth cannot be dismissed as an aberration or just another rebel. And therefore, I believe that it would be very, very hard to not believe that the Jesus of the New Testament is the predicted Christ/Messiah, the Son of God.

Part I Section 6 - The dark period

During the period of time between the book of Malachi and the time of the New Testament (about 400 years), there was a lot of turmoil in the promised land. These were the conquest by Alexander-the-Great, the government by the Seleucids, the government by the Maccabees, the conquest by Rome, and the ascension of Herod the Great. During this period the name of the nation was changed from Judah to Judea, and the people became known as Jews instead of Hebrews or Children of Israel. Also, during this period there was quite a bit of persecution of the believers and worshipers of God. The temple was desecrated and left in disrepair. Priests and temple caretakers (the Levites) were executed, especially during Seleucid period. But when Herod the Great came into power, he built a large pyramid east of Jerusalem and placed a palace on top. He consolidated the territory that once was the area originally assigned to the tribes of the Hebrew people under Joshua. He built a new port city called Caesarea. He also fortified the mesa near the shore of the Dead Sea, called Masada.. He also rebuilt, and expanded the temple in Jerusalem. *I think he may have seen himself as the promised Messiah.* However, the orthodox Jews hated and mistrusted him because he was an Edomite, not a Hebrew in the line of David.

So, some of the Jewish people withdrew to hermitages, one such was the community of Essenes who tried to preserve the Old Testament writings by copying them and storing them in caves in a desolate area of Qumran near the Dead Sea. Others set about to bring together the Old Testament writings into a document called the Septuagint, which was one of the sources for the collection of writings of both the old and new testaments into one Bible under the later direction of Roman Emperor Constantine. Another group began working on an expansion of the old laws of Moses, called the Talmud, which specified in detail such things as ritual bathing and hand washing, and how far a person could travel on the Sabbath before breaking the law. *Such restrictions as codified in the Talmud were already in place in the Jewish law in the time of Jesus, and were often used in judgements against him.*

Augustus Caesar established himself as Emperor of the Roman Empire, garrisoning Roman soldiers in locations around the empire, and assigning civil representatives to protect Roman interests in the territories. Augustus declared a time of Roman peace (Pax Romana) in the empire and directed that a census be taken to determine who were the people he was governing.

Part I Section 7 - The scene is set

Thus, the scene was set for the advent of Jesus and the New Testament. The territory of the Jewish state had been established. The government under Rome was reasonably stable, and Roman civil law was in place. The Hebrew heritage and the prophesies about the coming Messiah had been documented. And it was the right time for something momentous to happen. So, on to Part II of this document.

Part I Section 8 - The Holy Spirit

Although this document is about the Christ, the promised one. I felt I should mention that the Holy Spirit was not a new entity introduced by Jesus, who gave the disciples the power to believe in and understand Jesus as the Christ, and who gave them, at Pentecost, the talent to speak in languages not their own. In fact, the Old Testament is rife with references to the "Spirit of God" (or the Holy Spirit) and the things that the Holy Spirit did for the people of God. As in the following examples:

The Holy Spirit was there in the Cosmos at the Creation, Genesis 1:2

The Holy Spirit gave creative talents to the men who created the worship fixtures for the tabernacle during the Exodus from Egypt, Exodus 31:3 and 35:31

The Holy Spirit gave Joshua and David, respectively, the power to lead Israel, Numbers 27:18 and Second Samuel 23:2

The Holy Spirit was recognized as a guide for Othniel, the first judge of Isreal, Judges 3:10

The Holy Spirit gave Samson the strength to break his bonds when captured, Judges 15:14

Part I - CODA

I have written this "Part I" partly to establish the legitimacy of a Christ/Messiah (who I havell documented in Part II), and partly to satisfy my friend that the Torah and Isaiah were not the only Old Testament documents to tell of a coming Christ. I hope I have achieved both purposes. I also hope that the readers will see that the Old Testament was not just the end of a history of a nation/state but was part of the story of humanity, and also part of a story of God's plan for all of us who are willing to believe (including the sceptics among us), that not only that there exists a super-intelligence who created all we know and beyond, and is now watching over us. And, also that God had a plan to give a right way of living and an eternal life for those who believe in both him and his son and messenger, the Christ, the Messiah.

Part II - THE LIFE OF JESUS, THE CHRIST, THE MESSIAH

Foreword

As indicated in the first part of this document, I am a believer in Jesus Christ and his redemptive power, his majesty, and his caring for humanity. And I feel that I can contribute to the knowledge and beliefs of others by expressing my beliefs, and the justifications for those beliefs. Thus, I have written this three part document to that end. This is the second part of three about Christ the Redeemer. In the first part I provided, to the best of my knowledge and research, the data for the predictions of, and prophesies about Christ, the Messiah, in the Old Testament of the Judeo/Christian Bible. In this second part, I will continue the story of Christ by delving into his life while on earth during the first century AD. In it, I will try be objective as reasonable to show Jesus, a Jewish boy, as the real earthly son of the Most High God as predicted in the Old Testament, and that he was set on earth to provide a design for loving and righteous living, and also a path to the eternal life that was denied to the human race because of their nature as flawed human beings. I start this out by presenting Jesus' birth and early human years, and the sometimes otherwise unexplainable events during that period of his maturation as a human being. Then I continue the story of his introduction to the world as the earthly son of God, his teachings, the miracles he performed, the controversies he stirred up, his death, and his resurrection from the dead. In this process, it is my hope that the readers of this document might accept the evidence in such a way as to consider belief in and acceptance of him as savior. If you are a sceptic, as many of us are, please read on and see if you might be otherwise convinced.

My view of Jesus is that he was a duel persona, both wholly temporal and also wholly eternal. First, as to the eternal, the apostle John started off his gospel with the words **"In the beginning was the Word, and the Word was with God, and the Word was God. He was in the beginning with God. And all things were made through Him, and without Him was not anything made that was made."** In other words, John, the apostle and author of the fourth gospel, said that Jesus, as the word of God, was eternal, and that his voice was the voice of God that spoke into existence, all that was, is, and will be. Second, as to the temporal, he came to earth as a human baby, to a teenage, unmarried woman, in a little town in a minor province of the Roman Empire. And John also continued **"In him was life, and the life was the light of men."** So to me, these words say that he was very much a temporal human person as well. Also, unlike many people who seem to think of Jesus in terms of "meek and mild" I see him as described in Psalm 24:8 **"Who is the king of glory? The lord strong and mighty, the lord mighty in battle!"**. Also many of his acts are not those of meek or mild person, as exemplified by his strong statements as to right and wrong, his frequent condemnation the Israel's rulers, and his dealing with the money changers in the temple (For details of this encounter see later in this document).

References

For this writing, I continue to use as my primary reference, the English Standard Version (ESV) translation of the Judeo/Christian Bible. I have also used secondary references, where appropriate and available, such as other English language Bible translations, Wikipedia (the on-line encyclopedia), and Harper's Bible dictionary for backup and confirmation. I have also continue to interject other supporting items such as Bible concordances, words and suggestions by trusted Christian friends, and my own musings.

A Definition of terms (some as before, others new)

The term "Christ" is used a number of times in the Bible to indicate a king above all kings, a savior of the people, an eternal being, the word of God, the son of God.

The term "Messiah" is also used often in the Bible and has basically the same definition as the "Christ"

The name "Jesus" was a fairly common name used for male children in New Testament times (and even today among Hispanic people). It is also very similar to or synonymous with the name "Joshua", the name of an Old Testament leader. It actually means "God with us" or **"Savior"**.

The name "Emanuel" that appears in the prophesies of Isaiah is synonymous with "Jesus", "Messiah", and "Christ" in its meaning.

The term "wilderness" is often used in the Bible. Many people equate this with desert. But it could be forested or prairie as well. Thus, it meant any fallow or unimproved land that did not normally have human habitation.

The word "disciple" is used frequently in the New Testament. It simply means student of a rabbi or master teacher. Jesus had a following of students (disciples) during his ministry and is sometimes called rabbi by them.

I have sometimes used the words "an evil presence" to indicate a power for wrong, otherwise called Satan, the Devil, Beelzebul, etc.

I have used the words "God", "Lord", "most high God", or "the Creator God" to indicate the all powerful, all knowing, creator of time, space, eternity, the heavens, the earth, and life on earth. (*I as well, note that the Bible also indicates that this all knowing, all powerful entity is a continuing, all-present observer and controller of his creations. And that, as the Bible also indicates, one of those creations, the human race, has been given three elements that distinguish them from other living beings. One is a higher intellect than other the living creatures. The second, is the knowledge of good and evil, (which must inherently involve rules and laws to live by). And third, a free will to obey or not to obey those rules and laws, **including the capability to believe in or, unfortunately, not to believe in God.**)*

Tools for support and emphasis

You, the reader, will also note that I have continued, as in the first volume of this book, to use italics to set apart my observations and thoughts, parentheses to provide some clarification, and sometimes bold print for Bible quotes and for points I consider important and information that I wish to otherwise stress. I have also, to make this document more acceptable in today's culture, have used some more contemporary words and phrases (e.g. "Pregnant" vs. "With Child")

Story Organization

As I said before, this document is divided into three parts. The first part is a compendium of the Old Testament prophesies fore-telling Christ, his life, and his mission. The title of the first part is **"The forecasts of Christ"**. This writing, the second part, is based on the four gospels; Matthew, Mark, Luke, and John, which tell of the life, actions, messages, and divinity of the Christ while on earth, in other words **"The Life of Christ"**. The third part is about how and why the life and teachings of Christ became a world-wide religion. The title of this part is **"The Impact of Christ"**.

As I stated in the first part, I, long ago, came to believe in Jesus as my lord and savior and as a guide on how to live my life. If with the writing of this book I hope that I will be successful in encouraging others to believe as well, especially those with a logical or scientific bent in their personalities (such as my friend and I). If I do then it will have accomplished its purpose.

Part II Introduction

Jesus, the subject of the whole New Testament, lived his whole fairly short life in the Roman province of Judea about two thousand years ago. But he is probably the most written and spoken about person in all of human history. The first four books of the New Testament; Matthew, Mark, Luke, and John, are the most basic writings about the life, purpose, and divinity of Jesus as the promised Messiah, and are together identified as the "Gospels". Most scholars support the idea that they were all penned within about fifty years after Jesus' crucifixion.

The first one to be written was most likely Mark, who is attributed to have been the scribe for Peter the Apostle, who was a close follower and student of Jesus. The tenor of this book appears to be from a point of view of the actions of Jesus, as would fit with the apparent action-oriented personality of Peter.

The second gospel written was most likely Matthew. This book is attributed to the apostle Matthew who was also a close associate and student of Jesus (one of the 12 inner circle disciples). Its tenor is more of that of an orderly administrative mind, because it tells the stories of Jesus in categories (i.e birth, sermons, parables, miracles, arrest and trial, crucifixion, and resurrection). *This would fit the style of writing that could be attributed to an accounting oriented personality, that would match that of a tax collector, which Matthew was identified as such. For some reason, Matthew is called Levi in other parts of the gospels. This might be attributed to the possibility that his ancestors were of the Old Testament tribe of Levi.*

The third book was written by Luke. Luke was the only one of the authors who was not Jewish. Rather, he was a Greek, a convert and follower of the apostle Paul. Luke is normally identified as a clinically trained doctor, who accompanied Paul on several of his mission trips. He, of the four gospel writers, was apparently the only one who did not have a first hand acquaintance with Jesus. But with his logical, scientific mind, and with Paul as his mentor, and benefitting from Paul's in-depth knowledge of the Old Testament laws and prophesies, and also interviews with others who had first hand knowledge of Jesus, he thus was able to put together an excellent study about Jesus, his ministry, his purpose on earth, and his divinity. And as with a scientific approach, he basically ordered his writing on a time-line rather than by subject matter.

The book of John was, most likely, the last written gospel, probably about eighty AD. In his book, John called himself the "Beloved Disciple", *apparently because he felt the closest emotionally to Jesus of all the disciples.* However, when he and his brother, the disciple James, were younger they were called "Sons of Thunder" *probably indicating that they became easily angry.* But since the book of John was written later in his life, it appears that he had mellowed.

The first three gospels are often referred to as "Synoptic Gospels", most likely because they appeared to present a general summary of Jesus life. While the tenor of the gospel of John was more spiritual, presenting a more emotional and intellectual point of view of Jesus. John particularly emphasized the eternal nature of Jesus as the Christ. John also presented the most detail of the ordeal that Jesus went through during the last few days leading up to his crucifixion.

As a precaution, the avid Bible scholar will see some duplications and overlapping of some of the accounts, and one may also find some seeming inconsistencies and discrepancies between accounts of the same events in the different gospels. However, it must be noted that first, the gospels are most likely somewhat biased by the personalities and emotional leanings of the authors, and second, that they were documented thirty to fifty years after the described events occurred, and thus might have been affected by imperfect memories or personal experiences after Jesus' death. Third, the authors may have had different awareness of certain events and statements as they happened because of their individual closeness to the particular events. And fourth, there may have been some variations in meanings of some words and phrases through multiple translations over the past two thousand years. However, I believe that these concerns in no way diminish the basic premises and concepts of the **"Greatest Story Ever Told"**.

As I indicated above, this part is based entirely on the four gospels (the first four books of the New Testament), except that I point out in various places how Jesus did fit and fulfill the prophesies about the Christ/Messiah of the Old Testament.

Part II Section 1 - The Environment Into Which Jesus Was Born

At the time of the birth of Jesus, much of the civilized world, at least in Europe, North Africa, and the Middle East, was at relative peace under the edict of the "Pax Romana" by the Roman emperor Augustus Caesar. Also the currency of business and trade was Roman. The country of Judea was by then a province of the Roman Empire, with Roman soldiers garrisoned at strategic points around the province, and a Roman political leader had been placed in charge of the more important decisions relative to the peaceful governance of the area. At the time of Jesus' birth, a man named Quirinias was such a leader, and he had charge of the area of both Syria and Judea. The Roman Empire did however, allow the customs, religions, and laws of the local areas to remain under the control of local ethnic authorities, as long as they didn't compromise the Roman overall rule, taxation authority, and political order. Thus, they allowed a local king, known as Herod the Great, to rule over Judea. And just previous to the time of Jesus' birth, through some local wars and skirmishes, Herod had been able establish his rule over approximately much of the area that was initially allocated to the "Children of Israel" when it was originally conquered under their leader, Joshua, about fourteen hundred years before. This included te province of Galilee, west and north of the Sea of Galilee, which was populated primarily by Hebrew people who were descended from at least two of the Hebrew tribes who occupied this area under the leadership of Joshua. In fact, most of the people in Herod's kingdom were Jews, and descendants of the original settlers, except for an area about in the middle of the territory that was settled later by emigrants from what is now northern Iraq. They were called Samaritans, and were looked down on as an inferior race by the Jews.

The earthly royal authority of the time

As I indicated in Part I, Herod the Great, within Roman overarching control, had raised the nation of Judea from a low point under the destructive rule of the Selucids (descendants of the leaders of the army of Alexander the Great) and the questionable rule of the Maccabees (a Jewish rebel group). The country had become relatively prosperous and also at peace except for a new rebel group called the Zealots, who didn't like Herod because of his non-Jewish ancestry, (apparently Herod had both Hebrew and Edomite ancestors). (The Edomites were historically sometimes enemies of the Hebrews during Old Testament times.) The Zealots particularly didn't like the Romans, wanting to get rid of them, and that Judea should be reestablished as a sovereign nation. There were apparently occasional small-scale riots and uprisings in Judea at this time mostly due to the Zealots, but nothing of consequence. For the most part, travel was safe and relatively easy do to because of the Roman-built roads, so that believing pilgrims from other parts of Judea and even from places as far away as Greece and Ethiopia could travel to the temple in the capitol, Jerusalem, for worship and to celebrate holy days. Herod had added to regional military fortifications, strengthened the walls of Jerusalem, built a large pyramid southeast of Jerusalem with a palace on top, and had begun a major rebuilding and expansion of the temple itself. *I suspect that he might have been thinking of himself as the promised messiah.*

The earthly civil authority at the time

The laws of the land were under the authority of a semi-religious legislative/judicial group called the Sanhedrin. There were two major political parties who held seats in the Sanhedrin, the Pharisees and the Sadducees. Their governance was strongly religious, (the parties differing only with some disagreement about certain religious beliefs (The Saducees did not believe in life after death.), but both claiming solidarity with the laws of Moses). Their rule and decisions were based on rigorous enforcement of those laws, (as strengthened, updated, and re-invigorated by more recent Jewish scholars ((i.e the Talmud)). *(In other words, no separation of Church and State.)* However, their powers were somewhat limited by overarching Roman law. One of those limitations was that only the Roman governor could order an execution of criminals, as will be seen to be very important later in this volume.

The synagogue culture

Also, during the period prior to Jesus' birth, local groups of the faith started establishing Synagogues. These were local churches where believers could go to hear the word of the Old Testament and listen to teaching of the elders (rabbis). Normally, these services were held on the Sabbath day, the seventh day of the week, the day the Old Testament said that God rested after the creation. Thus, the synagogues were to supplement worship between pilgrimages to the Jerusalem temple. Each synagogue had a trove of scrolls, (or books of the Old Testament on rolled pappus or animal skins that had been copied for them by hand). In addition to houses of worship, the synagogues were the local seats of government and judicial authority, and also apparently the schools for education of Jewish youth.

Travel freedoms and controls

Thus, when Jesus was born, people were free to move from one part of the Roman Empire to another without government restrictions. But also the Roman government could initiate relocation of people in its empire any time it so desired.

Part II Section 2 - Jesus' Missions On Earth

Thus, Jesus came into being in human form at a very fortuitous time when for the first time in human history, a society and culture existed that permitted the introduction and spread of a religious belief well beyond the bound of a local community, a country, or even a region of the world. Was this a time and timing planned by God? I believe it was. And he came to carry out certain missions. They were: (1) to teach a right way of living, thinking, believing and acting, (2) to prove his divinity via miracles, (3) to die as a sacrifice for human sins, (4) to rise from the dead to prove that there was eternal life and to offer it to believers, (5) to promise a later return to gather up his followers at the end of time. So let us further explore those missions.

To Prove His Authority As The Son Of God - The Christ

He needed to do this in order to differentiate himself for other teachers of God's laws and purposes for humanity. He did this in several ways. One was to demonstrate his ability to perform miracles of healing of human diseases and his power over nature. Another was to be recognized as such by John the Baptist and God himself at his baptism. Another was to be pronounced as such by his disciples, the people he spoke to, and even the governing authorities at his trials and execution. Another was his own pronouncement as such in the Synagogue at Nazareth at the beginning of his active ministry. But this mission was not an end in itself. It instead was to validate himself as the official "Word of God", so that the hearers of his teaching and observers of his death and resurrection would fully accept his words and believe in him.

To Teach What To Believe And How To Think, Live, and Act

Another of his missions was his teaching mission, that was to tell the people what to believe and how to live and act. He did this in four primary ways. This teaching process included both explaining the right ways to live, but also telling the ways that would condemn people not only for their actions but even for their thoughts. As tools to accomplish this, he used things such as direct pronouncements and sermons, parables, actions by himself and his disciples, and forecasts of the future (prophesies). In doing this he also validated the basic laws of the Old Testament, the objective definitions of right and wrong.

To Carry Out The Sacrificial Will Of God As The Passover Lamb

This second purpose was to let the people know that he was on the earth to carry out the will of his father (God), to act as a blood sacrifice (remember in Genesis, Abel's sacrefice and the ram as a substitute for Isaac) for forgiveness of the crimes of the people (sins against God, humanity, individuals, wrong thinking and bad philosophies). In doing so he would be the innocent lamb of God to die for the Passover, as originally established in the Old Testament. And via this process he let people know that there was life after death.

To Prove That There Was Life After Death

This was carried out by his personal appearance to many of his disciples after he had died on the cross as proof of life after death.

To forecast His Return To Earth At The End Of Time, To Judge Humanity

He promised at his return, to gather his followers (both those who have previously died and who were still living) from the four corners of the earth and to escort them to heaven.

__And coincident with the carrying out of all five of these missions, many people who came in contact with him became strong believers in him and accepted him not only as a great teacher, but also as the promised Christ/Messiah__ the son of the most high God.

Part II Section 3 - Jesus' Birth And Maturation

Jesus' birth

The gospels relate that there was a teenage girl, a Jewess named Mary, who lived in a little town named Nazareth in northern Israel in the province of Galilee, who was picked out by the God, the creator of the universe, to have a glorious problem. The problem was that, even though she was engaged to be married to an older man, Joseph, and even though she had not yet had sexual intercourse with him or any other man, she became pregnant. The Bible tells us that she was visited by an angel who told her that even though she was still a virgin, she would bear a son, who would be the Son of God. A lot of people consider that somebody lied, and this could not have happened. However, such a virgin birth was predicted by the prophet Isaiah seven hundred years before (See Isaiah 7:14 in the Old Testament). Also, for the most comprehensive account of this event see Luke 1:26-38.

And I have a personal story that suggests that an atypical pregnancy could be possible. Once in Oklahoma City where I grew up, I was visiting my sister at Mercy Hospital as she was recuperating from a gall bladder operation. There, I met a man who had just had surgery on his abdomen. He said that he had been doing fine for most of his life, but had suddenly developed a high temperature and a severe stomach pain. They took an x-ray and found a tumor which they removed. But it wasn't an ordinary tumor. It was a completely formed fetus, that had developed inside of his body but that had died and had started to decay. This really did happen. The hospital people said that this was a remarkable situation and had no explanation. I am in no way saying that this was how Mary's pregnancy happened, but that there are things we still don't know about medical science that could go against the normal assumptions. So I ask the sceptics to have an open mind on this, and believe that a divine power can cause such things that we supposedly enlightened people can't explain.

As I indicated above, Nazareth was a small town. In such a town the normal situation is that practically everybody knows everybody else there, and usually knows what is going on in each other's lives. Mary's pregnancy would have been a serious item of gossip, could have been a very critical concern of and about Mary's family, could have been raised damaging concerns about Mary's morality, and possibly could have resulted in legal charges being brought against her that could have even caused her to be stoned to death. Mary, when she first became pregnant, decided to leave town for a while and visit her cousin Elizabeth who lived just outside Jerusalem. Elizabeth was an older woman, old enough to be past child bearing age. However, she too was unexpectedly pregnant. Mary stayed there for several months before returning to Nazareth. There is a very beautiful and poignant story of Mary's visit to Elizabeth in Luke 1:39-56.

When Joseph found that the woman he was engaged to, was pregnant, he was in a quandary. What should he do? He thought about breaking the engagement quietly to minimize scandal, but he had a dream in which he was informed that he should not break the engagement but go ahead with the marriage. Joseph was also told to name the baby "Jesus". As indicated before this name is a version of Joshua and has the same meaning as Immanuel. These names all mean "God With Us" in the Hebrew language. This story about Joseph is the subject of Matthew 1:18-24.

Then, about that time, Caesar Augustus, issued a decree that there should be a census to determine who lived in his Empire so they could be taxed. Part of the order was for those who could be subject to this Roman tax to move back to the place of their ancestral family to be counted. Joseph was from Bethlehem and a descendant of King David, (as was Mary). Bethlehem was about eighty five miles south of Nazareth, about ten miles south of Jerusalem. So Joseph decided to pick up his carpentry practice and move back to Bethlehem, and he took Mary with him. Apparently, there were a lot of displaced people in Bethlehem, and the only hotel was full. However, the hotel owners made provision for Joseph and Mary to live temporarily in the stable where the horses and livestock were housed. *This actually was not such an awful situation, since at that time a lot of people lived in houses where they lived right along side their livestock.* During the time they were living there Mary gave birth, and used a livestock feed trough (manger) as the baby's crib. As you, the reader, will have noted in Volume I of this document, that both the town and the situation of Jesus' birth were predicted as much as eight hundred years before he was born (See Isaiah 7:14 and Micah 5:2). Again, if the sceptics continue to think of this sequence of events just as coincidence, maybe it is time to start reconsidering.

And if the above is not enough to indicate a divine plan, it happened that **"in the same region there were shepherds out in the field keeping watch over their flocks by night. And an angel of the Lord appeared to them, and the glory of the Lord shone around them, and they were filled with fear. And the angel said to them 'fear not for behold, I bring you good news of great joy that will be for all the people. For to you is born this day in the city of David**

(Bethlehem) a savior, who is <u>Christ</u> the Lord. And this will be a sign for you: you will find a baby wrapped in swaddling cloths lying in a manger (livestock feed trough)' " (See Luke 2:8-12). Wow. The shepherds went immediately to the hotel stable in Bethlehem, met Joseph and Mary and saw the baby lying in the feed trough just as described by the angel. *And the reader will note that the angel also told the shepherds that this baby was* **the Christ (the promised future eternal king, as predicted repeatedly in the Old Testament)**. *Another Wow.*

Baby Jesus in the temple

As was the custom at the time, Joseph and Mary, a week later, traveled the ten miles from Bethlehem to Jerusalem to present the baby Jesus at the temple and have him circumcised. But when they arrived at the temple they were met by a devout old man named Simeon who had been told by God that before he died, he would see **"the Lord's Christ"**. He took Jesus in his arms and said **"Now you are letting our servant depart in peace, according to your word; for my eyes have seen your salvation that you have prepared in the presence of all peoples, a light for revelation to the gentiles, and for glory to your people Israel"** (See Luke 2:20-32). Then shortly after this, an old widow also came up to Joseph and Mary and offered a thanksgiving prayer to God, for the redemption of Israel (See Luke 2:36-38). .

Jesus' young childhood and famiy moves

The Magi

The gospels of Luke and John seem to indicate at this time Joseph and Mary returned to Nazareth with Jesus. However, Luke apparently skipped over a series of events during this period that were important in the life of Jesus. This doesn't mean there is a discrepancy in the gospel of Luke. Please remember that one of the definitions of the word gospel is summary. None of the four gospels cover the whole story of Christ, by definition. In the last chapter of the gospel of John, in the last verse, John states the following; **"Now there are also many other things that Jesus did. Were every one of them to be written, I suppose that the world itself could not contain the books that would be written."**

The first story that was not included in either the Gospel of Luke or John was that there was a group of three astro-scientists (Wise Men) who lived in a country east of Judea, I suspect most likely in the Tigris/Euphrates valley area, who saw a sign in the sky that, to them, indicated the birth of the promised Messiah. *To my thinking, they could have been descendants of Hebrew people who had not returned from captivity with Ezra and Nehemiah, or at least they were worshipers of the Hebrew God, because apparently they were familiar with the Old Testament prophecies.* They decided to travel to Judea to find and worship this Messiah. Of course, they went to Jerusalem, the capitol and worship center of the Jewish faith. They did not find Jesus there, but they gained an audience with Herod the Great and told him of their quest. He told them to search diligently for the baby and after they found him to return to Herod and let him know <u>so he could go and worship him as well (liar-liar)</u>. When the wise men left Jerusalem, the sign in the sky reappeared and led them to Bethlehem to the residence of Joseph and Mary. It seems that by this time, Joseph and Mary were no longer living in the stable (despite numerous manger scene depictions) and had moved into a house. And also Jesus, by this time, may have been at least one year old. They met Jesus and gave him the gifts they had brought for him; gold, frankincense, and myrrh.

*Most people know the names of these gifts, but I suspect very few know of their extreme importance as prophesies of Jesus' life. Gold is an indicator of wealth, power and royalty, kingship. Frankincense is a sweet smelling aromatic sap of the terebinth tree that was used to sweeten the oil used to anoint a priest to certify him for priesthood. Myrrh, is a strong smelling aromatic sap of a bush that grows in the Arabian Desert, that was used in Biblical times as part of the embalming process before burial if a dead body. **Thus, in these gifts, the Wise Men were forecasting the kingship, the priesthood, and the death of Jesus Christ.***

The wise men intended to return through Jerusalem and tell Herod what they had found, but were told in a dream to go back another way. The story of the Wise Men is contained in the gospel of Matthew 2:1-12.

Herod's order to kill, and family moves

But Herod must have consulted his advisors to find out where and when the Christ was to be born. They must have told him that Christ's birth had occurred one to two years before in Bethlehem. So Herod decided to order execution of all male babies under two years old in and around Bethlehem. However, Joseph was warned in a dream that this was going to happen, and he packed up his family and moved to Egypt. And they remained there until Herod the Great died. This story is contained in the gospel of Matthew 2:13-17. The slaughter of the Bethlehem babies was prophesied in the Old Testament book of Jeremiah (See Jeremiah 31:15). It is also interesting similar to the Old Testament edict by the Egyptian pharaoh at time of Moses' birth, where he directed that all male Hebrew babies should be killed (See Exodus 1:22).

Shortly after the Bethlehem killings, Herod the Great died, and his kingdom was spit up under the rule of four of his sons. At that time, apparently Joseph decided to move his family back to Judea. This move from Egypt was prophesied in the Old Testament book of Hosea (See Hosea 11:1). However, rather than going back to Bethlehem, instead he decided to go to Nazareth, bypassing the area now ruled by a son of Herod the Great, named Herod Archelaus, because Joseph was afraid that Archelaus might still want to carry out his father's wishes and try to kill Jesus (See Matthew 2:19-23).

Jesus' education

There is no reference in the New Testament about Jesus growth and education after the return from Egypt until he was about twelve years old. However, I think we can assume that he received the normal education of such male children provided by the elder (rabbi) of the local Nazareth Synagogue. This would have included learning to read and write, and heavy instruction in the history of the Jews from Genesis onwards. Since two languages, Hebrew and Aramaic, were both commonly used in Judea at this time, they were both most likely taught as well, and possibly also a little Greek and Latin to allow understanding of the governing Romans. Just as today, there were several age levels in this process. The first few years involved teaching of the basics to permit basic contributions to society, with a heavy influence of Mosaic law. Those who excelled, moved on to more rigorous schooling. Then the top students we assigned as disciples to a master teacher, who led them in the finer points of their faith and heritage. These latter students were the ones who would later become scribes, pharisees, and leaders in the faith and government.

As I indicated in Part I, the name of the town where Jesus lived, Nazareth, is suspiciously similar to "Nazirite" the name of the old order of super dedicated believers. And I have an inkling that Nazareth might have been a historic seat of the Nazirite culture. And as such, the teaching there could have been extra rigorous. I assume Jesus was subject to this education process, and apparently was a star of the Synagogue, because later in his life, events occurred there that would define his path, and also what happened in the Jerusalem temple when he was about twelve years old.

Jesus in the Temple at twelve years old

When Jesus was twelve years old, Joseph, Mary, and Jesus traveled with a group from the area of Nazareth in Galilee to the Jerusalem temple to worship for the Passover celebration. Such a trek would normally take four or five days each way, because they were traveling on foot. They most likely did this every year. But this time it was different. During the visit Jesus became separated from his parents. When Joseph and Mary started back to Galilee, they assumed that Jesus was among those in their traveling party. After a day's journey, they discovered he was not in the group. After searching for him they returned to Jerusalem and after three more days, they found Jesus in the temple, having a dialog with the teachers there. **"And all who heard him were amazed at his understanding and his answers"** (See Luke 2:47). *This of course indicated that his biblical knowledge was remarkable, well beyond what would be even expected from even a well educated twelve year old.* When Joseph and Mary found him, they were obviously upset, and he didn't seem to realize why, because he said **"Why were you looking for me? Did you not know that I must be in my father's house"** (See Luke 2:47). *This answer was particularly profound in that it said many things about Jesus and his mission on earth. First, it said that he knew Joseph was not his biologic father, but rather God. Second, he knew that the temple in Jerusalem was the earthly house of God. And third, that he belonged in the presence of God, his real father. But it also said something else. That was that his human persona was that he was still a teenager, full of his mission but not yet earthly wise enough to know that he was still in need of his parents' care. Psychologists today recognize that the human brain is not completely formed until the person is at least in his or her early twenties. And many teenagers don't seem to recognize that they have a responsibility to and dependence on their parents until not only their education is complete but that their brains are fully formed. So despite his phenomenal knowledge, his actions indicated that he was not yet ready to begin fulfilling his earthly purposes.* For the whole story of Jesus as a twelve year old, see Luke 2:41-52.

Part II Section 4 - Jesus' Early Ministry

Changes in the political situation between the time of Jesus' birth and the beginning of his mnistry

Herod the Great died not long after he ordered the deaths of the young boys in and around Bethlehem. After Herod's death, his kingdom was divided into several parts. Two of the separate parts, Judea and Galilee, came under the kingship of two of Herod's sons. However, due to unrest in Judea, the Romans had taken a more direct control of the area by establishing a Roman governor in Jerusalem. At the time of Jesus's adult ministry, the Roman governor was Pontius Pilate, a political appointee of the Emperor on Rome.

Introduction of John-the-Baptist

Please remember what I said before, that when Mary became pregnant, she went to visit her older cousin, Elizabeth, who was also pregnant at the time. And this is the story of the birth of John the Baptist. Elizabeth was the wife of a priest, Zechariah, who was serving in the temple in Jerusalem. His job was to keep the incense burning in the section of the temple called the Holy of Holies. The angel Gabriel appeared suddenly beside the incense alter and frightened him. But the angel told him not to be afraid and also told him that he would have a very special son who would restore belief in God to many people. He also told him to name him "John". However, Zechariah argued that both he and Elizabeth were too old to have children, so the angel stuck Zechariah dumb, and he was not able to speak until the baby was born. Thus, unable to compete his service, Zechariah went home to his wife, and Elizabeth became pregnant. A healthy boy was born to her. **"And the child grew and became strong in spirit, and he was in the wilderness until the day of his public appearance to Israel"** (See Luke 1:80). *I have a theory. John's boyhood home was in a small town between Jerusalem and the dead sea. This is near the area in which the Essenes had a community "in the wilderness". The Essenes had strong convictions about practicing and preserving the Old Testament laws, (they were the group that hid Old Testament scrolls in the caves at Qumran). The Essenes believed in the simple life, with a serious expectation of the eminent coming of the Christ. They dressed and ate simply and lived monastic lives. One of their important tenants was bathing as a purification ritual. In the gospel of Mark it says* **"John appeared, baptizing in the wilderness a baptism (ritual bathing) of repentance for forgiveness of sins"** *(See Mark 1:4). Most scholars seem to believe that the place where John was baptizing was in the lower Jordan River near where it enters the Dead Sea. This was near the ancient city of Jericho and also not far from the Essene community.*

Thus, I believe John was involved with or influenced by the Essene culture, or maybe himself a member of the Essenes. His message appeared very much that of the Essenes. And he said something else that I think was quite telling, in that the Essenes mantra was to protect the word of God for the descendants of Israel. But, he also said something different that would foretell the spread God's salvation beyond just those people, but to all the people of the world. He said to the Jewish leaders **"And do not presume to say to yourselves 'We have Abraham for our**

father' for I tell you, God is able from these stones to raise up children for Abraham." *(See Matthew 3:9)*

As the son of an eloquent temple priest (See an example of his father Zechariah's sermons in Luke 1:67-79), John must have been a strong and mesmerizing preacher of the word of God, because people from all over Judea came to hear him and to be baptized in the Jordan River. And in doing so, they were confessing their sins. But one of his important messages was that **"After me comes he who is mightier than I, the strap of who's sandals I am not worthy to untie. I have baptized you with water, but he will baptize you with the holy spirit"** (See Mark 1:7-9). Thus John the Baptist is a remarkable fit with the prophesy in Isaiah chapter 40:3 **"A voice cries in the wilderness, prepare the way of the lord"**. And John knew what his role was, and acknowledged it to the temple priests and Levites who were sent to question him (See John 1:19-23).

John-the-Baptist baptized Jesus and testified to his lordship

One day, while John was preaching and baptizing, Jesus came down from Nazareth to be baptized. Apparently, John knew of him, and apparently immediately recognized who he was, because he gave this remarkable testimony about Jesus in a comment to him, **"I need to be baptized by you, and** *(why)* **do you come to me** *(for me to baptize you)***?"**. (See Matthew 3:14). But Jesus said to John **"Let it be so now, for thus it is fitting for us to fulfill all righteousness"** (See Matthew 3:15). In fact John the Baptist knew quite well who Jesus was, as he said in John 1:29 **"The next day he saw Jesus coming toward him, and said 'behold, the Lamb of God, who takes away the sin of the world!'"** And also said in John 1:34 **"And I have seen and borne witness that this is the Son of God."** So John went ahead with the rite of baptism, and immediately after Jesus came up from the water, all those present saw the heavens open up and **"a voice from heaven said 'this is my beloved son, with whom I am well pleased'"** (See Matthew 3:17). And John began telling all in earshot that Jesus was the "Son of God" (See John 1:29-34). Wow, what an acknowledgment.

Jesus was tested by Satan

After Jesus was baptized, he went into the wilderness to be tested by the Devil to insure that he was ready to be the Christ and not fall into temptations of the world. The first test was that the Devil offered him bread (and more broadly, the pleasures of the world such as food, drink, sex, riches, etc.). He turned that down in favor of God's word. Then the Devil suggested he be a sceptic, testing and questioning God's power, to question his belief in God, to question if God was really with him. Jesus told the Devil that this was not right, and he wouldn't do it. Then the Devil offered him unlimited earthly power, to be earthly sovereign of all the earth. And he turned that down as well, and basically said "That's enough testing Satan, go away!" **"For it is written 'You shall worship the Lord your God and him only shall you serve'"**. (See Matthew 4:1-10). *And that is good enough for me to believe in him both as life guide and savior.*

Jesus' first miracle

Only a few days after Jesus returned to Galilee from being baptized, he and his mother were invited to a wedding in Cana, another small town near Nazareth, in the region of Galilee. And some of Jesus' early followers went with them. Apparently, the wedding reception was a big party because the host ran out of wine for the guests. Also, apparently by this time, Mary had become aware that her son had some extraordinary, and unexplainable powers. She turned to him and asked him to do something about it. He said to her, **"Woman, what does this have to do with me? <u>My hour has not yet come</u>."** (See John 2:4). *This last statement seems to indicate that by this time in his life he considered that he had come to understand that he might as a human not yet be ready to start his mission on earth as the Christ or to demonstrate his exceptional powers.* However, Mary ignored his protestations, and told the wedding officials to **"Do whatever he tells you"**. So Jesus told the servants to take six nearby water jars and fill them with water. When they did, he told them to dip some liquid out of one of the jars and take it to the wedding host. When the host tasted it, not knowing it came from a water jar, its taste to him was that of fine wine, and he gladly served it to the wedding guests (See John 2:1-10). **But most importantly, with this act, suddenly his early followers saw Jesus in a new light, not just a significant teacher, and even as John the Baptist told them, the "Son of God", but much more, giving them their first glimpse of his real out-of-this-world powers.** (See John 2:11).

Jesus began his ministry (in Nazareth and his rejection there)

After leaving the wilderness, Jesus began to teach his message. His early ministry was in and around Nazareth. He gained almost immediate notoriety by saying **"Repent for the kingdom of heaven is at hand"**. (See Matthew 4:17) One of the first places he spoke was in his home town (Nazareth) synagogue. Nazareth, of course, was where Jesus grew up. He was schooled in the synagogue there. Everyone there knew him and his family. One day he was attending a Sabbath service and stood up to read from an Old Testament scroll. It turned out to be part of the book of Isaiah. He started reading **"The spirit of the Lord is upon me, because he has anointed me to proclaim good news to the poor: He has sent me to proclaim liberty to the captives and recovering sight to the blind, to set at liberty those who are oppressed, to proclaim the year of the Lord's favor."** (See Isaiah 61:1-2) Then he handed the scroll to the rabbi and sat down. There apparently was a stunned moment of silence, and then he said **"Today this prophesy has been fulfilled in your hearing."** Unfortunately, the townspeople were not convinced, and they became angry at what he was saying, especially after he made some additional statements. Thus, their ire proved the truth that "familiarity breeds contempt", and they drove him out of town and threatened to kill him. (See Luke 4:16-30)

Jesus moved to Capernaum

Having been rejected in Nazareth, Jesus moved to Capernaum, another, larger town in Galilee on the north west coast of the Sea of Galilee. The Sea of Galilee is actually a fresh water lake in the upper part of a fairly deep rift valley that runs from the highlands of Syria to the East branch of the Red Sea. It is fed by the Jordan river from the north. It still contains a plentiful fish population, which in Biblical times, made fishing there a lucrative business. This was the area where Simon, Andrew, James, and John had their fishing businesses. However, the rift valley in which it lies has a tendency to channel winds and otherwise fairly violent weather across the water (see further in this document as a setting for at least two of Jesus' miracles). The Jordan River also flows out of the south end of the Sea of Galilee down the rift valley to its lowest point, occupied by the Dead Sea.

To the east of this lower part of the valley is now the Muslim Kingdom of Jordan and on the west side of the lower Jordan River is now another Muslim occupied area called the West Bank. However, in Jesus' time, both banks of the river were parts of Judea.

The area in and around Capernaum was where Jesus did much of his teaching, and performed several of his miracles. But he also traveled up and down the Jordan west bank on several occasions as part of his mission and to attend holy days in Jerusalem. However, on one of his such travels he went through the Samaritan territory, which was located about half way between the Jordan Valley and the Mediterranean Sea. This trip will be shown later to be a milestone in Jesus's ministry.

Jesus selected his disciples

About this same time, he also started selecting certain of his followers to be his designated inner circle of disciples (students). The first two were disciples of John the Baptist, who pointed out Jesus to them. One was John, the author of the Gospel of John, and the other was Andrew, the brother of a man named Simon. Andrew told Simon, "We have found the Messiah". Later, Andrew introduced Simon to Jesus, who said he should no longer be called Simon but would henceforth be called Peter, the Rock (See John 1:35-42). Matthew and Mark tell the story of Jesus selection of his first four disciples in a little different way. Matthew and Mark both say that Simon, Andrew, John and James (John's brother), were doing maintenance on their fishing boats on the shore of the Sea of Galilee (and Luke said they were out fishing) when Jesus asked them to follow him. This recruitment was a well known Bible quote "Follow me and I will make you fishers of men". (See Matthew 4:18-22 and Mark 1:16-17). And thus, Simon (Peter), Andrew, James, and John became Jesus's first four disciples. The next day Jesus met Philip, who introduced him to Nathanael, who was immediately very impressed and amazed by Jesus's perceptive powers. (See John 1:43-51) So, Philip and Nathanael became Jesus' fifth and sixth disciples. (Unfortunately, not too long after John the Baptist had pointed out Jesus to his disciples, he was arrested for preaching against King Herod's immorality, and would eventually be put to death.) Jesus would go on to call six more young men to join him as disciples. Among them were Matthew, the tax collector and author of the Book of Matthew, and two members of the Zealot movement. They were a second Simon and Judas Iscariot.

A little personal opinion: I feel it necessary to extemporize here and talk about the whys and wherefores of the acceptance of Jesus as the true son of God by his contemporaries. I believe that John and Andrew, and maybe also Philip accepted the Christ-hood of Jesus because they discovered him as a God chosen adult, and he was validated as such by John the Baptist, someone who's words they already respected. And Nathanael accepted him because he recognized Jesus' uncanny observation and insight. However, the local Nazareth townspeople were too familiar with him in the role of a local boy just growing up with other children there. So they had too much assumed prior knowledge of him as he appeared to them as no different from the rest of the children when he was young, even though he might been extraordinarily bright and perceptive. His new declaration of his adult mission just didn't fit with their prior perceptions, and they couldn't handle it. So they reacted in rebellion instead of acceptance. I think this is often a natural, but very negative attitude, that some people have when confronted with new and radically different information. And I think that a lot of us can think of numerous examples of this type of reaction occurring even in today's society.

Part II Section 5 - Jesus as a teacher

JESUS TAUGHT WITH STATEMENTS, SERMONS, AND LECTURES

Jesus spoke with authority

Jesus then began his ministry in earnest. And there apparently was a noticeable difference between the way in which Jesus spoke and the way in which the Jewish believers at the time were used to hearing God's message. And comments to this fact were made comparing Jesus' words to the words of other Rabbis, scribes (religious lawyers), and teachers of the word. This is specifically noted at the end of Jesus' "Sermon on the Mount", Matthew states **"And when Jesus finished these sayings, the crowds were astonished at his teaching. <u>For he was teaching them as one who had authority and not as their scribes</u>"** (See Matthew 7:38). *This, to me, indicates that the teachers and scribes taught by reading from the scrolls and saying that this is what Moses, Isaiah, etc. have said, rather than teaching from their own experience, beliefs, or understanding. Instead Jesus spoke on his own authority,* **presenting himself to be the original source of knowledge, wisdom, and the word; not Moses or the prophets.** Here are some examples of his words when he demonstrated this originality:

"<u>I am</u> the bread of life, he who comes to me shall never hunger, and he who believes in me shall never thirst." (See John 6:35)

"<u>I am</u> the light of the world. Whoever follows me will not walk in darkness, but will have the light of life" (See John 8:12)

"<u>I am</u> the door. If anyone enters by me, he will be saved." (See John 10:9)

"**I am** the good shepherd. The good shepherd lays down his life for the sheep.**"** (See John10:11)

"**I am** the resurrection *(from death)* and the life. Whoever believes in me, though he die, yet shall he live, and everyone who believes in me shall never die.**"** (See John 11:26)

"**I am** the way, and the truth, and the life.**"** (See John 14:6)

"**I am** the true vine.**"** (See John 15:1)

Then in Mark 14 verse 62 there is the most definitive statement of all before his inquisitors in a Jewish leadership council meeting, when they were trying to find a reason to have him punished, They asked him "**Are you the Christ, the son of the blessed?**" *Jesus responded by saying* "**I am, and you will see the Son of Man seated on the right hand of Power, and coming with the clouds of heaven".**

There are quite a lot of additional messages and meanings in the broader contexts of the these statements that I will be exploring further along in this document. But to me, each one of these statements is clear evidence that Jesus was speaking from his own authority, and not on the authority of Moses or of the Old Testament prophets. And almost surprisingly, these statements, and his inherent authority in making them, were clearly accepted without question by many of those who heard them. But there is another quite surprising parallel for these statements, that give them even more authority. This may become clear in the book of Exodus 3:13-14 as follows: **"Then Moses said to God, 'If I come to the people of Israel and say to them. The God of your fathers has sent me to you, and they ask me, "What is his name?" what shall I tell them?' God said to Moses, "I am who I am." And he said 'Say this to the people of Israel, I AM has sent me to you.'"** Another Wow.

The Sermon on the Mount according to Matthew

Mark, Luke, and John start describing Jesus ministries with miracles, but Matthew starts with his Sermon on the Mount. *Remember that I mentioned earlier that I believe that Jesus' healings of physical and mental ailments were not for altruistic purposes, but rather to support belief in him as the Messiah, the Christ, and to gain credence for his words. Also, I think we need to preface his teaching ministry a little by noting that Jesus apparently found places where he could speak to, and be heard by, on one occasion 4000 men plus women and children and on another occasion at least 5000 men plus probably and equal number of women and children at one time (See Matthew 15:38,Mark 6:44, Mark 8:9, and Luke 9:14). This ability to speak to and be heard by that many at one time without the aid of modern microphones, amplifiers, and speakers is in itself a miracle, even if possibly partly explained by the unusual acoustics of his speaking location. The Mormon tabernacle in Salt Lake City, Utah is constructed in such away as to provide exceptional acoustics so that people throughout the auditorium can hear well without amplification, but that is an especially built indoor venue, and it cannot hold nearly 5000+ people. And I have a personal experience that relates to this situation. A few years ago I was flying in a Boeing 747 from California to New Zealand. It was loaded with between 300 and 400 passengers. There was a male steward aboard who had a particularly penetrating voice so that he could be heard throughout the main cabin, without shouting, over the roar of the air and engines and passenger conversations. But again that was in an enclosed space and a lot less people. Also, a friend of mine who has visited the Holy Land said that their guide took their group to a mountainside that led down to the Sea of Galilee that had unusually good voice carrying properties. But even so, Jesus' voice apparently, along with his other exceptional traits, must have had an extraordinary sound-carrying quality that made him heard by thousands at once.*

Jesus Told of God's Support, Compassion, and Expectations
"The Beatitudes"

And Jesus had not only a remarkably projectable voice, but also a landmark message for these crowds. The first part of his message is commonly known as the Beatitudes. *(At this point I am going to do some paraphrasing here to try to make these statements more meaningful to current cultures.)* He started off by telling those suffering depression, or who were in mourning for a personal loss, or who worried or were fearful (chronically depressed), that God's support and comfort were available to them. He told the seekers after higher purpose and calling, that a belief in the most high God could satisfy their hunger. He also said that those who had no anger in their hearts and who cared about others, or were trying make peace between men, were blessed by God. Then he became personal and talked directly to true believers in God, telling them that, even though they might be hated and persecuted by others on earth, that they had a special place in heaven. **But then he also told them that they were the flavor and light of the world, and so they had a responsibility while on earth, to give that flavor and show that light to the world (to be a witness) for the glory of God** (See Matthew 5:3-16).

Jesus Announced His Deity

Jesus then openly stated that he, himself, was the one prophesied as the Messiah/Christ in the Old Testament when he said "I have come..." (See specifically Matthew 5:17). **But he also said emphatically that his arrival did not change anything about the Old Testament laws *(that "good" was still "good" and "evil" was still "evil")* and that even those who believed in him as the Messiah were still responsible to obey the laws of right and wrong, and also anyone who teaches anyone else that a person can do so is a sinner.** (This particular sin will show up as a condemned philosophy in the third volume of this document.) He then said that one has to be even more righteous than the people who were supposedly the examples of righteousness of the time, the writers and teachers of the laws, and the religious rulers (scribes and pharisees), to have access, on ones own, to the kingdom of heaven (See Matthew 5:17-20).

Jesus Pronounced Judgement On All Humanity As Sinners

Then Jesus unloaded on the crowd and told them that none of them were righteous and to recognize their sinfulness, and to be sorry for it. **He said that even being angry was as bad as murder, that sexual lust without love was as bad as adultery, that dissolution of a Godly** marriage was a sin, (and he repeated this particular admonition, not just in the sermon on the mount but at other times as well (See Mark 10:2-11, and Luke 16:18)). He also said that vowing to perform anything one might not be able to deliver is a sin, and that vengeance (the Old Testament rule of an eye-for-an-eye) is now also a sin (See Matthew 5:21-38). And that all these sins are condemnable offences.

Jesus Told What it would Take to <u>Not</u> Be A Sinner *(without an intercessor)*

He followed this by telling the crowd what they needed to do instead. If someone hits you, don't hit back. In fact, offer to allow him to hit you again (turn the other cheek). If someone steals from you give him more than he takes. If someone forces you to perform a task, do more than demanded (walk the second mile). Be generous to someone in need and loan to one who asks for a loan. Show honest love, and pray for not only those who love you but also those who hate you, for they are also children of God, and all living are treated the same by him. **"For he (God) makes the sun to rise on the evil and on the good, and sends rain on the just and on the unjust"** (See Matthew 5:45b). Don't brag that you are a good person and don't make a show of doing good. Pray earnestly but don't make a demonstration out of prayer by doing it in public, and don't make a show out of it by piling up repetitious words and empty phrases (See Matthew 5:39-6:8). *That is, one must be perfect, <u>but this is an impossible task</u>.* **(Except that he later offered himself as a blood sacrifice as a substitute and intercessor for the inevitable sins of humanity (the Passover lamb).**

Jesus taught that believers must even love one's enemies

In Matthew 5:43-46 Jesus said something that most likely went against all conventional wisdom, and the teaching and traditions of people in general, and specifically the Jews. This was to love one's enemies and to pray for them. Throughout the Old Testament are records of numerous individuals, people groups, and nations who committed horrendous crimes against the descendants of Abraham. The people of Israel were taught "eye for an eye and tooth for a tooth". Even in Jesus' time the Romans were considered hated oppressors. And even today, we as Christians are facing Islamic terrorism, aggressive atheism, bigotry, attempts to subvert our freedoms both within and without, oppressive government regulations, and crimes of robbery, rape, and murder. But Jesus said to love all of those who perpetuate these attacks, (a very difficult assignment) because they are also God's creation, in order to be perfect per God's example. *However, I don't think that Jesus meant for his followers to be unprotected victims. In Matthew 10:16, Jesus told those who he was sending out to witness of him that they should be as wise as serpents and as innocent as doves, even in the midst of wolves. In the midst of potential danger, hate, anger, bigotry, and violence, Jesus taught just to use common sense, and trust in God. We now live in a world, and a society full of judgement and anger. (The worst, I think is the assignment of bad intention for any act that might offend someone.) Mistrust is rampant, and being "as innocent as doves" specifically says not to judge others, or not to become bigoted toward certain societal elements, or not to assign nefarious* *motives, but just to recognize and avoid being hurt by slights or even overt attacks. This is often a very hard to think this way. But an angry attitude is in direct opposition to having a heart for God.*

Jesus told believers to not make a show of ones righteousness

Jesus told his followers not to make a production out of practicing one's righteousness, because that would indicate that the person doing so, was seeking the admiration of men rather than God. And he said that this is particularly true when giving to the needy. He said to do it in secret (See Matthew 6:1-4).

Jesus offered an example of the Right Way To Pray

Then he gave an example of the right way to pray. He taught his listeners this right way as follows (also known as the Lord's Prayer) (See Matthew 6:9-14):

"Our Father in heaven, hallowed be your name
Your kingdom come
Your will be done, on earth as it is in heaven.
Give us this day our daily bread,
and forgive us our trespasses,
as we also have forgiven those who have trespassed against us
And lead us not into temptation, but deliver us from evil."

This prayer also appears in an abbreviated form in Luke 11:2-4. In this prayer, several things can be noted. The first thing is that God is praised, honored, and respected <u>before</u> anything else is said. Second, it expresses a desire for his kingdom and his reign to appear on earth. Third, it acknowledges and accepts the idea that <u>God's</u> will (and not ours) is going to be done. However, it does allow and acknowledge that those offering a prayer can ask for daily physical needs, and for forgiveness of wrongs that the one praying has committed against someone else. **But, there is a caveat that the person praying must <u>first</u> forgive anyone who has wronged him or her.** It also tells us that we must ask God to protect us from earthly evils and also temptations to do evil (See Matthew 6:5-14). This prayer is simple and straight-forward with no embellishments. Please also note that the model prayer is not a prayer to Jesus, but to God. *(I am sometimes concerned that we often offer our prayers <u>to Jesus</u> when we should instead be praying directly to **God** <u>through our belief in and acceptance of Jesus</u> (in the name of Jesus). This may be considered a small thing but it, I think, goes against Jesus' words and is a common mistake that we often innocently make.)* To support this concern, please see John 16:23-24.

Tradition has added a significant embellishment to the Lords prayer "for thine is the kingdom and glory forever", but that is not in the prayer that Jesus taught. *(Even though this addition is beautiful I do not personally think it is of value if one has, as Jesus taught, honored, praised and shone respect for God in the beginning of a prayer. However, when asked to pray the Lord's prayer, in reverence, I will include it.)*

(Also I believe Jesus taught this prayer not as <u>the</u> prayer, but as a model of how we should pray; to first acknowledge God's power, glory, and control of our lives, and that his will always comes first, before we ask for anything for ourselves, and also that, when praying, we should acknowledge that there are always temptations out there, and that we, as sinners, are not immune from committing them, even as Christians and believers in Christ.) We can see this in the lesson of the wrongful prayer that Jesus used as a bad example, in Luke 18:11 **"The Pharisee, standing by himself, prayed thus: God, I thank you that I am not like other men, extortioners, unjust, adulterers,...".** *(What do you, the reader, think about how this prayer compares to the one Jesus taught? I see nothing wrong with thanking God as a purveyor of gifts to the one praying, or for praying for others, even though these were not included in the Lord's prayer. However, I do not accept the idea of using prayer to state that one is better than others and to condemn or belittle others as it appeared that the Pharisee was doing.)*

Jesus Taught How To "Fast" (as an Act of Worship)

Unlike several other religions which include fasting as a frequent and important part of worship, fasting was rarely mentioned in the Old Testament. And it certainly was not mentioned as a weekly or even monthly ritual. However, by the time of the coming of Christ, it had some-how become an important ritual in the Jewish faith to use fasting to set apart and identify those who were considered important persons in the Jewish faith. It was practiced at least once and sometimes twice a week, and it involved a total abstinence from food for that day. And in fact, there was an effort to proclaim publically who was fasting. So after teaching how to pray he discussed "fasting". First of all, fasting was intended to be practiced to mourn a loss or to honor God. Jesus did not condemn its practice, but he did condemn the show of it. But he did not insist that it was a requirement of faith. So fasting has fallen from a necessity. And it has, over time, been corrupted first by organized religion to be practiced only on Friday (the day of the Crucifixion) as the proper day for fasting, then limiting such to avoiding only meat, and then later by declaring that fish is not meat, (so is acceptable for consumption during so-called fasting), and then by dropping fasting altogether as a form of worship. *A restaurant near where I live now offers all-you-can-eat fried fish on Friday nights. I am thus afraid that fasting as a form of worship is not any more a valid practice.* But Jesus, because it was being practiced at the time as a form of worship, said to do it in secret instead of making a show of it, because it was intended to be a form of individual worship of God, not a public demonstration of piety. *Further, fasting is not the same as dieting, because dieting is done to better a person's self, where fasting is to honor God.* However, Jesus, in another of his teaching, provided a caveat about fasting that it should be considered by believers (See Mark 2:18-22). *But I am still pondering this scripture, because, when Jesus taught that fasting was not appropriate when he was present, did he mean physically in person or in ones heart? Let the reader decide.*

Jesus Told the Crowds to Consider the Eternal, not in addition to, but instead of the Temporal

He continued his sermon by saying that one should value that which is eternal, not temporal, because this will direct your heart. **"Do Not lay up for yourselves treasures on earth, where moth and rust destroy and thieves break in and steal, but lay up for yourselves treasures in heaven, where neither moth or rust destroys and where thieves do not break in and steal. For where your treasure is, there you heart will be also"** (See Matthew 6:19-21). And don't try to split your loyalties between the eternal and the temporal, because this will result in serious and debilitating internal rational and emotional conflicts. And also, don't let worry and anxiety control your life, but trust God to provide for your needs as they arise. Then Jesus ended this line of thought by saying in Matthew 6:33 **"But seek first the kingdom of God and his righteousness"**, **and your life will be happy and fulfilled** (*without the need for material gain*) *(paraphrased)*.

Jesus then advised to not judge others, but also to not buy into another's destructive ways

Then he listed two "Don'ts". Don't pass judgement on other's perceived shortcomings. **Instead make sure you are not guilty of the same faults you might think you see in others.** And also don't waste time trying to help those who understand only violence and filth, (Jesus used dogs and pigs as examples.) because they could place you in real danger of being dragged down with them. *As an example of that danger, I had a friend once who was active in my church. He was married and had a responsible job as a city attorney. He decided to make it his mission to help save the prostitutes he encountered in court. But he ended up in an adulterous relationship with one of those he was trying to help, and lost both his career and his marriage.*

Jesus said to pray for God's help and expect an answer

Jesus said **"Ask, and it will be given to you; seek and you will find; knock and it will be opened to you"** (See Matthew 7:7). However, this message is full of caveats. **First of all, remember in the Lord's Prayer we can ask, but we are also told to acknowledge that <u>God's will</u> supercedes,** and thus his answer may not be as specifically asked for. For example, in Genesis in the Old Testament, Abraham prayed to God that Sodom not be destroyed if there were any righteous people there. But instead God took Abraham's righteous nephew, Lot, out of the city, and then destroyed it. Also, Job, in the book of Job in the Old Testament, prayed that his problems be removed from him. Instead, God required that first, Job needed to acknowledge God's omniscience and omnipotent power and control, before he was given back what he had lost. Some diseases appear miraculously cured by prayer, but sometimes God's answer is instead to give peace of mind to the person in-pain or dying, and support those grieving a loss (please refer to Matthew 5:4 in the Beatitudes). We must remember that life-troubles and physical death are due for all of us. And it is often how God helps us handle these things that is the answer to our prayers. But, Jesus further taught that God's answers to prayer are not in direct opposition to what is asked. He offered these examples. **"Or which one of you, if his son asks him for** *(edible)* **bread, will he give him a** *(an inedible)* stone, or *(worse yet)* **if he asks for a** *(an edible)* **fish, will he give him a** *(deadly)* **serpent"** (See Matthew 7:9-10). Also, there is another place in the Bible where it was said **"And we know that for those who love God, all things work together for good, for those who are called according to His purpose"** (See Romans 8:28). *Unfortunately, we often don't, on the surface, recognize the good that will come out of loss and suffering, there just may be a greater long term blessing. So, although this quote is not specifically about prayer, I think it applies as an explanation for the unexpected answers to those who pray to God.*

Then Jesus gave some specific rules to live by

First, Jesus pronounced what is called the Golden Rule, **"So whatever you wish that others would do to** *(help and honor)* **you, do also to them, for this is** *(the essence of)* **the law and (the** *admonitions of)* **the prophets"** (See Matthew 7:12). Then he told his listeners to do what is right, not what the crowd does, even though the way of the crowd (the wide way) is easy *(everyone does it)*, and the right way is hard and road is narrow. And also he said to be vigilant to recognize false teachers. They can be recognized by the often disastrous result of their teaching. *(They can often be quite charismatic and believable, but one must think about the terrible outcomes some recent such teacher's messages, such as Jim Jones, Charles Manson, Adolf Hitler, etc.)*

Jesus then gave a dire warning to so-called Christians who do not listen to God

Jesus was very firm about the possibility there will be those who even call on the name of God, give lip service to belief in the Lord, and do **"mighty works"** in God's name, who will not be allowed into paradise, because they did what **they** thought was good and proper, **but did not listen to, nor obey the will and desires of God** (See Matthew 7:21-23).

Jesus final admonition, use good judgement and common sense .

Jesus said to build one's house on the solid ground (the rock) *(belief in a higher power and purpose, wisdom, compassion and empathy, and full knowledge of eternal truths, absolutes of right, wrong, justice, mercy, etc.)* **which does not change over time, as do popular opinion, changing values, whims, and fads. If one does not build on solid ground (builds instead on** *changeable* **sand), the house is guaranteed to disastrously fall** (See Matthew 7:24-27).

The end of the Sermon on the Mount as recorded in Matthew

And when Jesus finished his teaching with a statement I referenced earlier, **"All who heard him were astonished, because he was teaching them as one who had authority, and not as the scribes."**

The Sermon on the Mount as recorded in Luke

The gospel of Luke also records a sermon preached by Jesus that corresponds to the sermon on the mount documented in Matthew. It contains a condensed version of the beatitudes that was documented in Matthew (See Luke 6:20-23). And it also contains an expansion of Jesus words about various sins and ways to better, more righteous, living (See Luke 6:24-36). In addition, it gives a more complete version of what Jesus taught about the considerations and consequences of passing judgement on others (See Luke 6:27). It also repeats Jesus' admonition to build one's house (life) on a solid foundation. One item in Luke's version not included in that of Matthew is an interesting discussion on the kind of fruit born by good and bad fruit trees (See Luke 6:43-45). This item I will discuss later in connection with doing God's will. *My own opinion is that these particular sermons of Jesus in both Matthew and Luke should be studied together as one sermon.*

Jesus' Additional Teaching

But wait, there is more. A well known twentieth century radio commentator, Paul Harvey, was often quoted as saying "Now for the rest of the story". Although Matthew tells of Jesus' words during only one "Sermon on the Mount" where he preached to 5,000 men plus women and children, there was at least one more mass sermon gathering, as described later in Matthew and in Mark. Again several thousand were gathered to hear Jesus (See Matthew 15:32 and Mark 8:1-15). Also, Matthew says in 4:17 that Jesus began to preach in the area around Capernaum and **"throughout all Galilee teaching in their synagogues proclaiming the gospel of the kingdom"** (See Matthew 4:23a). He also preached in Synagogues in Judea as well, stating **"I was sent for this purpose"** (See Luke 4:43-44). In doing this he gained a huge following before he spoke to the crowds in "Sermon on the Mount". The gospels also tell the Jesus taught in the area east of the Sea of Galilee, called the Decapolis. He also had several brief, direct encounters with the Religious leaders, (Saducees, Pharisees, and members of the Sanhedrin) in Jerusalem. And he even taught in the Temple itself.

Statements by Jesus' of his Divinity

Some persons question Jesus' as the Son of God. He often called himself the **"Son of Man"** (a term also used by both Ezekiel and Daniel in the Old Testament) indicating that he was a flesh and blood human. But he also emphatically stated a number of times that he was also the **"Son of God"**. Even so, there are numerous doubters. For instance people of the Muslim faith respect Jesus as a great teacher, but do not accept his deity. And, apparently, there are those in western civilizations who are also doubters. However, on a number of occasions, as recorded in all four gospels, he told his listeners that he was the Christ, the Messiah, the **Son of God**, his father, (including in the Sermon on the Mount as noted above) (See Matthew 5:17). Matthew also records this in Matthew 7:21 where he said **"Not everyone who says to me, Lord, Lord, will enter the kingdom of heaven, but the one who does the will of <u>my Father </u>who is in heaven."** Then in Matthew 18:10, 14, and 35 Jesus also used the term **"my father"** or **"my heavenly father"** when referring to God. Also, there are at least three statements by Jesus in Mark where he talked about being the **Son of God**. The first is Mark 8:38 where Jesus said **"For whoever is ashamed of me and my words in this adulterous and sinful generation, of him will the Son of Man also be ashamed when he comes into the glory of his father and the holy angels."** A second is in Mark 14:61-62 where in his defense before the Sanhedrin, when asked if he were **"the Christ, the son of the blessed"**, he said **"I am, and you will see the Son of Man seated at the right hand of Power, and coming in the clouds of heaven."**

In Luke 10:21-22 it is recorded that Jesus prayed to God, saying **"I thank you, Father, lord of heaven and earth, ... ; yes Father for such is your gracious will. All things have been handed over to me by my Father, no one knows who the Son is except the Father, or who the Father is except the Son and to anyone to whom the Son chooses to reveal him."** Then in Luke 22:29 Jesus, in talking to his disciples, said **"and I assign to you as my Father has assigned to me, a kingdom,".** And again in Luke 22:69 during his defense before the Sanhedrin, Jesus is quoted as saying **"But from now on the Son of Man shall be seated at the right hand of the power of God".**

The book of John presents the most statements by Jesus that he was the **Son of God**. One such is contained in a extensive statement by Jesus that he is not only the Son of God but also the judge of humanity and the giver of eternal life, and states that Moses of the Old Testament predicted him **(See John 5:19-47). See also Deuteronomy 18:18 in the Old Testament. See also John 6:27, 32, 40, and 57).** See also John 8:54 which says **"Jesus said 'If I glorify myself, my glory is nothing. It is my Father who glorifies me, of whom you say, He is our God.'"** Also, see John 10:25, and again in John 10:36-38 Jesus said **"do you say of him whom the Father consecrated and sent into the world, you are blaspheming, because I said that I am the Son of God ? If I am not doing the works of my Father, then do not believe me; but if I do them, even though you do not believe me, believe the works, that you may know and understand that the Father is in me and I am in the Father."** Then in John Chapter 11 is the story of the death of Lazarus. Lazarus' sisters ask Jesus to come to heal him before he died. Jesus said in verse 4 **"This illness does not lead to death. It is for the glory of God, so that the Son of God may be glorified through it."** Actually, Lazarus was pronounced dead and was buried before Jesus arrived. **However, Jesus brought him out of the tomb and back to life.** (See the later section in this volume about Jesus' miracles.) Also, see John 14:1-3, John 14:6-7. John 15:1, and John 17:5 for Jesus' statements on being the Son of God.

And Jesus in John 4:24-26 also revealed and stated firmly to a Samaritan woman that he was the Christ. And, in doing so, he also demonstrated that his message and sacrifice was for all, not just the Hebrews. As I previously indicated that the Samaritans were not originally descendants of Jacob, but were transplanted into the territory of Israel by the Assyrians and were an ethnic group despised by the Jews. The referenced scripture tells of a Samaritan woman at a water well who **"said to him (Jesus), 'I know the Messiah is coming (he who is called the Christ). When He comes, he will tell us all things.' Jesus said to her, 'I who speak to you am he.'"** *(In doing this he witnessed to her and honored her by revealing who he really was.)* (See John 4:25-26). **In this example, to me, the primary lesson is that disciples of Christ must not be prejudiced or bigoted in choosing to whom to witness, and that Christ's saving grace is**

available to all. *And that this is one of several examples of Jesus' teaching that he was the promised Christ and that his message and his sacrifice were for all humanity, not just the Jewish people.*

Statements of others that Jesus' was the Son of God

In Matthew 3:16-17 Matthew states that after Jesus was baptized by John the Baptist, a voice from heaven (God) said <u>**"This is my beloved son, with whom I am well pleased."**</u> Then in Matthew 14:33 after Jesus came walking on rough water to a boat containing his disciples and calmed the waves, **"those in the boat worshiped him, saying, 'Truly you are the Son of God'."** Then also in Matthew16:15-16 Jesus asked his disciples **"But who do you say that I am"**, **"Simon Peter replied 'You are the Christ, the son of the living God'"**. Then while Jesus was on the cross, he was reviled by the chief priests and scribes because they acknowledged that they had heard him say **"I am the Son of God".** Mark began his Gospel by writing **"The beginning of the gospel of Jesus Christ, the son of God."** Then Mark and Luke both repeat in Mark 8:28 and Luke 9:20 the confession of Peter in Matthew 16:25-16 that Jesus is the **Christ, the Son of God.** Mark also in Mark 9:7 related that, as Jesus, Peter, James, and John were leaving a meeting of Jesus with Old Testament prophets, **"A cloud overshadowed them, and a voice came out of the cloud. "saying 'this is my beloved son. Listen to him'".** **Also, at the end of the account of Jesus raising Lazarus from the dead, Martha, sister of Lazarus, said to Jesus in John 11:27 "I believe that you are the Christ, the Son of God". Then there was a significant statement by the Roman Centurion who participated in Jesus' execution, where at the cross he said "Truly this man was the son of God." (See Mark 15:39)**

Jesus defined the kingdom of God (Heaven)

One of the things he said was that the Kingdom of God (Heaven) was not some far off place in the universe but was right now, right there among the people (See Luke 13:18-21 and 17:20-21). In fact in Luke 17:20-21, when asked by the Pharisees when the kingdom of God would come, he answered them **"The kingdom of God is not coming with signs to be observed, nor will they say, 'Look here it is! or there!' for behold, the kingdom of God is** *(right now)* **in the midst of you."** He also described the Kingdom of Heaven in other interesting terms in Matthew 13:31-33 as a thing that grows and spreads. *(To me this says that the Kingdom of God is not even a physical place on earth with national boundaries, and also <u>not</u> someplace far off in space. It instead resides in the hearts of individual believers, and thus knows no boundaries, time, nor dimension. Further, it has no beginning or end and it spreads as believers carry its message. It just is.)* **And Jesus offered a strong invitation to enter that kingdom in Matthew 11:25-30, which ended with the statement "Take my yoke upon you, and learn from me, for I am gentle and lowly in heart, and you will find rest for your souls."** *Interestingly enough, Jesus did not in this statement connect the "Kingdom of Heaven" with "life after death", as we often do today. He instead presented it here as a place of action and emotional rest rather than as a reward for a life of faith.* Jesus also in Matthew 20:1-10 described the Kingdom of Heaven as a place of equality among those belonging to it. On the other hand, John the apostle spoke often of the Kingdom of God as an eternal resting place for believers who's physical body had died. *I believe both are true in that the Kingdom of God transcends both time and death.* And also in Matthew 19:29, Jesus told the twelve disciples the following: **"...everyone who has left houses, or brothers or sisters or father or mother or children or lands, for my name sake, will receive a hundred fold and will inherit eternal life ".** In other words, anyone who has given up of the temporal to follow Jesus will have life everlasting. Thus, Matthew, just like John, acknowledges the God's kingdom is eternal and that there is a place there for all believers.

Jesus insisted that God be <u>first</u> in believers' lives

When he was approached by wealthy young man, who asked what he might do to be saved, Jesus saw through his love for his wealth over love for his creator. So, even though Jesus had compassion on him, he told him that he needed to be willing to give up all his wealth and possessions and follow him, in order to achieve his desired salvation. Unfortunately, the young man went away, apparently refusing to do so. (See Matthew 19:16-21). This is also consistent with one of Jesus' parables about the man who gave up all he had to gain access to eternity, **"a pearl of great value"** (See Matthew 13:44-45). *This however appears not to be a condemning of wealthy per se, because as we will see later that Jesus body was buried in a tomb of a wealthy believer, Joseph of Arimathaea, per that believer's choice.* Also, to my thinking, many of the wealthy are often self sufficient both materially and intellectually, and have a more than normal difficulty not only giving up their material possessions but also their mental, intellectual, and self-sufficiency successes. Unfortunately pride and ego are the twin brothers of material wealth.

Jesus pronounced that government taxation is legal

He was also confronted by the scribes (the lawyers of the day), *(who obviously didn't like the Romans).* They tried to trap him into making a treasonous statement, by asking if it was right for the Jews to pay taxes to Rome. Jesus asked for a Roman coin and then asked who's image was on it. They of course said, Caesar's. And of course, the Romans, even though they were a warlike people, had brought peace and civility to Judea. So Jesus told them to **"Render to Caesar what is Caesar's and to God what is God's"** (See Matthew 12:13-17). *(My comment; I believe this was a sign that Jesus supported the idea that church and state could coexist as equals, one of the foundations of the American legal system, and also that obeying the laws of a temporal government was an acceptable practice even by Jesus' followers.)*

Jesus let Jewish elders know that they shouldn't question his authority

Then the chief priests and elders of the temple challenged the authority of Jesus and his teaching by asking who gave him the authority to teach. Jesus responded by asking them a question about the baptism of John the Baptist, **"Did John's authority come from God or man?"**. They, for political reasons, said they didn't know, so Jesus told them that they then didn't need to know his authority either (See Matthew 21:23-27). This might have sounded like a flippant answer, except that the priests and the elders had refused to believe what Jesus had already announced, that he was teaching under his <u>own</u> authority as the Christ, the son of God.

Jesus offered life after death to believers in him

In John 3:14-15 Jesus told the Pharisee, Nicodemus, **"And as Moses lifted up the serpent in the wilderness (See Numbers 27:5-9), so must the son of man be lifted up, so that whoever believes in him may have eternal life."** In John 5:24 Jesus said **"Truly, truly, I say to you, whoever hears my word and believes him who sent me has eternal life."** In John 6:27 Jesus said **"Do not labor for the food that perishes, but for the food that endures to eternal life, which the son of man will give to him."** In John 6:40 Jesus said **"For this is the will of my father, that everyone who looks on the son and believes in him should have eternal life, and I will raise him on the last day."** In John 6:47-51 Jesus said **"Truly, truly, I say to you, whoever believes has eternal life. Your fathers ate the manna in the wilderness, and they died.** *However***, this is the bread that comes down from heaven, so that one may eat of it and not die. I am the living bread that came down from heaven. If anyone eats of this bread, he will live forever."** In John 6:54 Jesus said **"Whoever feeds on my flesh** *(my words and actions)* **and drinks of my blood** *(accepts my death as a sacrifice one's personal sin)* **has eternal life, and I will raise him up on the last day."** In John 8:51 Jesus said **"Truly, truly, I say to you, if anyone keeps my word, he will never see death."**

Jesus explained that life after death will be radically different than life on earth

Then Jesus was confronted by the Sadducees. As one might already know, the Sadducees were members of one of the leading religious parties in Judea and had representation in the Sanhedrin. Even though they were religious leaders, they, as a group, did not believe there was such a thing as life after material death. Apparently, they felt it could not be, because they only conceived that such an after-life could only be just like life and social order before material death, and that this would raise some impossible dilemmas. Their shallow view was quickly and effectively refuted by Jesus, who pointed out both, that life after death would be quite different, and also gave some additional examples by the words of their own prophets (See Matthew 22:23-33 and Mark 12:18-27). Also, the apostle Paul later more specifically amplified Jesus' statements about life after death in 1 Corinthians 15:35-38 and 40.

Jesus dealt with more issues including his origins

Jesus had the most to say about the ways the temporal religious leaders (the Pharisees) thought and acted in attempting to represent themselves as models of Godliness. He gave some explanations of how they should and should not act as examples of piety, and gave some very pointed and specific examples of some of their shortcomings. **But he also answered their questions with wisdom and profound knowledge of God's intent in providing the law to the Hebrew/Jewish people, and to mankind in general. In several places in the book of John, where Jesus spoke with and** refuted the complacency of the Jewish leadership in their beliefs that, as the chosen people, they were privileged and were the only privileged people. One needs to read in John 6:25-7:52. And also Jesus declared openly that he was the Son of God, and predated both Moses and Abraham. See John 8:12-59. And again see John 10:1-38.

Jesus pronounced the core of the commandments of God

One of the Pharisees asked Jesus **"in order to test him, 'Teacher, which is the great commandment of the law?' And Jesus said to him, 'You shall love the Lord your God with all your heart and with all your soul and with all your mind.'"** But then Jesus added another commandment as well when he said **"And a second is like it: You shall love your neighbor as (you love) yourself** *(assuming you love yourself)*.**"** Then he concluded this by saying **"On these two commandments depend all the law and the prophets."** (See Matthew 22:35-40)

This declaration by Jesus is more than just a statement of the law. First, it is a synopsis, in two statements, of all the Ten Commandments given to Moses on Mount Sinai almost two thousand years before. Second, the first of Jesus statements is actually a quote from Moses' book of Deuteronomy 6:4-5. Third, it demonstrated that Jesus was not a teacher of a rebellious new philosophy, but a knowledgeable supporter the very faith that should have been the basis for the Pharisaic belief system. Fourth, his statement supported God's principle that human love should not be one-dimensional (love of God), but should also, secondly, include others of his creation. Then Jesus went on to find fault with a particular Pharisaic act that demonstrated that the Pharisees' belief system was too one-dimensional, in that he took the Pharisees to task over a specific rule they used to justify breaking the fifth commandment, **"Honor your father and your mother"**, in that they were allowed to declare that they could give to God what they otherwise would use to take care of their parents (See Matthew 15:3-6). Fifth, Jesus placed the love of God first, before love of fellow man, in the same order of the statements of the ten Commandments. And sixth, Jesus, in the form of his presentation, made the commandments of God not just rules to live by, but rather preferred desires of the heart. And he further explained and amplified his second commandment by saying **"A new commandment I have given you, that you l love one another; just as I have loved you, you also are to love one another. By this all people will know that you are my disciples, if you have love for one another"** (See John 13:34-35).

Jesus expressed concerns about the Pharisees' leadership examples

First, Jesus pointed out the problem with the prayer of a Pharisee in the temple, that I presented in comparison with the Lord's Prayer above (See Luke 18:11)

Second, after Jesus stated the "Greatest Commandments" including the words "Love your neighbor", a Pharisee who wanted to justify himself asked Jesus **"and who is my neighbor"**. Jesus told him the story of a Jewish man who was attacked and severely beaten by robbers, who was lying helplessly in the road and passed by or ignored by both a Jewish priest and a Levite, but was rescued by a person who was of an ethnic culture despised by the Jews, a Samaritan. Then he asked the Pharisee **"Which of these three, do you think, proved to be a neighbor to**

the man who fell among robbers?" (See Luke 10:29-36) The Pharisee was forced to confess that the neighbor was the one who helped the man. *(I believe there are three important lessons in this scripture. First, the Pharisee, appeared wrapped up enough in his own selfish self-importance that he questioned Jesus' "Second Commandment" statement. Second, Jesus intimated that the "Kingdom of God" knows no ethnic, national, or racial boundaries. Third, this story says that a neighbor is someone who cares and will go out of his way to help another.)* But Jesus didn't stop there. He followed this lesson by telling the Pharisee to **"Go and do likewise"** (See Luke 10:37). *That is, don't just go around showing off your piousness, do something for others.*

Third, Jesus had some specially critical words for the Pharisees' show of this piousness. Jesus did this because he recognized that the Pharisees, as a group, represented the leadership and models for righteous living under Mosaic Law. But they were also humans, and were often falling far short of that ideal; just as today, preachers, pastors, priests, and ministers of the word, as well as other public figures (such as politicians and entertainers) that people look up to, also often fall short because they are also human, and subject to human frailties. Unfortunately, the Pharisees went around in public, wearing the robes of their office, and often enjoying, too much, their position of respect and as role models assigned to them by the general populace. As indicated above, Jesus used as an example the Pharisee's "holier than others" prayer in the Temple, as discussed above. Jesus also noted that the Pharisees seemed more concerned about the rituals of their worship (such as ritual hand washing and circumcision), than heartfelt honor and respect for God. He spoke about this when a Pharisee invited him to dinner (See Luke 11:37-44). And this time he also lumped the Lawyers (Scribes) in with the Pharisees as having the same or similar problems as representatives of the faith (See Luke 11:46-52). He also pointed out that as humans, the Pharisees could be two faced and hypocritical, because what they were in private might be very different than what they were in public (See Luke 12:1-3). And the whole of Matthew 23 also contains the same or similar concerns by Jesus about the Scribes and Pharisees.

Jesus' other concerns with Pharisees and other earthly leaders

Of course, the flip side of all the above condemnations was Jesus' statements that <u>all</u> men, no matter what their earthly status, even the leaders, must acknowledge that they are sinners, incapable of perfection on their own, as exemplified in the prayer by the tax collector in Luke 18:13.

Thus, Jesus found fault with the examples set as a group, by the Pharisees. However, there are at least two examples of Pharisees who individually believed in Jesus. One was Nicodemus, who was not only a Pharisee but also a member of the Sanhedrin. He came to Jesus individually, and was profoundly taught by Jesus in the well-known third chapter of John in verses 3-21 *(This particular lesson is a must for anyone seeking God's kingdom),* and he assisted in Jesus' burial. A second **"member of the council"** and a wealthy man who believed in Jesus, was Joseph of Arimathaea who offered his own tomb for Jesus burial when he was crucified (See Matthew 27:57-60, Mark 15:43-46, Luke 23:50-53, and John 19:28-42).

Jesus taught further, that simple faith is a necessity

In opposition to the rules and regulations, and intellectualism, scepticism, or law minutia of the Jewish leadership, Jesus taught that simple, unadulterated, un-compromised faith was to be not only greatly preferred but also the only real key to entering the kingdom of God, when he said **"Let the children come to me, and do not hinder them, for to such belongs the kingdom of God. Truly I say to you, whoever does not receive the kingdom of God like a child shall not enter it"** (See Luke 18:16-17 and also Matthew 18:3-4 and 19:14).

Jesus taught to try to avoid sinning at all cost

Unfortunately, there was a heresy in some early Christian churches that proposed that believers should sin greatly to demonstrate the miraculous redemptive power of Jesus' salvation. However, Jesus forcefully taught that his followers should try to avoid sinning altogether, even to the point of symbolically cutting off a part on one's body if it causes him or her to sin (See Matthew 18:7-9). Another wow. Thus Jesus taught that belief in him should be the antithesis of a desire to commit sins, and that as a result of putting God first before all else, there would be no such desire.

Jesus taught that there are two states of life after death, Heaven and Hell, and that Christ is the only way to avoid hell on physical death

In several places in the New Testament, including Matthew 18:8-9, where Jesus taught that there are two states of life after physical death, and that belief and acceptance of Jesus as the Christ is the only way to heaven (the kingdom of God) (state of joy and happiness). He clearly stated this in John 14:6, where he said **<u>"I am way, the truth, and the life. No one comes to the Father (God) except through me."</u>** Wow again. This is one of the most controversial teachings of Jesus for society today. It frightens and turns off many people, who say that they or others they know are good people, and, if there is a life after death, why can't "good" people have access to the kingdom of heaven, even if they don't believe in the Christ. Many people say they have no religious faith, and even some pseudo-Christian religious faiths say there are many paths to heaven. The followers of Mohammed also believe they have the only way. Also, there are a number of other religions in the world representing almost one half of the world's population, which have proposed guides and standards which offer access to "Jannah", "Nirvana", or "Avalon" or some other place of happiness after death. Many ask why should they believe this particular statement of Jesus. **<u>Maybe it is just because he said so.</u>** *It really appears to me that if one believes the Old Testament prophesies of the messiah, the teachings of Jesus, and the proofs of his divinity and fulfilment by him of the Old Testament prophesies through his miracles, how can such a one <u>deny</u> that this statement by Jesus that he is the only way to avoid eternal punishment for one's sins committed while on earth, since he stated clearly that it is.* Think about it. Jesus, himself asked repeatedly for full acknowledgment of his teaching and full commitment to believing and living the way that he taught.

Jesus proclaimed that he had come to minister to more than the house of Israel

Old Testament prophets and Jewish tradition seemed to indicate that the Christ would come to minister and be an earthly king to the Jewish people only. And some even today seem to think this. However, Jesus repeatedly taught and gave examples that he had come to save, not just the Jewish people, but all the people of the earth. One example was that a Canaanite woman from Phoenicia who pleaded with Jesus to cure her daughter. At first Jesus tested her faith by stating that he had come for the Jewish people. However, she said something very profound that proved her faith that she could ask for his healing power as well, so that Jesus healed her daughter (See Matthew 15:21-28 and Mark 7:24-30). Also, I have already given the examples of the Samaritan woman to whom Jesus revealed that he was the Christ, which led to acceptance by many Samaritans; and also the story of the good Samaritan who showed kindness to a stricken Jew, and who Jesus said was a brother. Also, see in Matthew 8:5-13 where Jesus healed the servant of a Roman soldier because of the soldier's faith, even though he was not a Jew. And again in Luke 13:29 Jesus said **"And people will come from the east and west, and from the north and south, and recline at the table of the kingdom of God."** Also in John 10:16 Jesus said **"And I have other sheep that are not of this fold. I must bring them also, and they will listen to my voice. So there will be one flock and one shepherd."** Thus, Jesus proclaimed that he came not just for those of historical birth as descendants of Abraham, but for **all** who believe in him. And then there is the "Great Commission", one of the last statements made by Jesus before he left the earth. He told his disciples to **"go into all the world (or all nations) and make disciples"**. He did not say to go to the Jews or the sons of Abraham, but to the world, and he didn't even mention any limitation about race, ethnicity, or national origin (See Matthew 28:19 and Mark 16:15).

Jesus taught that what defiles a person is what comes out of his mouth, not what goes in

Once, Jesus was accosted by some Scribes and Pharisees, who accused him of being a bad person because he and his disciples were breaking a "Tradition" of hand washing before eating. He countered this by telling those accusers that they were doing worse by breaking the "Commandment" to honor their parents (See Matthew 15:1-9) as cited above. Then he continued this train of thought by explaining to his disciples **"Do you not see that whatever goes into the mouth passes into the stomach and is expelled? But what comes out of the mouth proceeds from the heart, and this defiles a person. For out of the heart come evil thoughts, murder, adultery, sexual immorality, theft, false witness, slander. These are what (*morally*) defile a person. But to eat with unwashed hands does not (*morally*) defile anyone"** (See Matthew 15:17-20). Also Mark repeated this teaching in Mark 7:5-23.

Jesus also taught that belief in him and proclaiming him might not be that easy

Jesus warned his followers that to be his disciples might mean that they would need to give up their material possessions and their former lives if those lives in any way interfered with their mission to follow Jesus (See also Matthew 10:37-39). He had some pretty harsh words for his followers in Matthew 8:19-22 where he told them they might have to give up comfortable living and even loose touch with their families, and that members of their own families might turn against them (See Matthew 10:35-36). In Matthew 10:17-22 he also warned that there were men who would seek to punish those, even under the law, for proclaiming Christ, and that this could happen even within immediate families. He later told his disciples that there would be sacrifice to the point of losing one's individual identity in taking on the burden of Jesus mission and purpose (See Matthew 16:24-26). As previously cited, when a rich young man asked Jesus what it he still needed in his life to be offered eternity. Jesus told him he had to give up all his earthly possessions (as a sign of where his priorities were), and show concern for others by giving the proceeds to the poor (See Matthew 19:16-21 and Luke 18:16-22). Also, in Luke 9:57-62, Jesus warned potential followers that, in order to follow him, they might have to give up any aspect of comfortable living and family ties, and that they could not look back on their former lives. Then in Luke 14:25-33 he told potential disciples that they really needed to count the cost of becoming one of his disciples, because they must be willing to turn away from family and all that they have, and even to be willing to give ones own life. *Thus, what Jesus told them could be a really heavy burden to bare.* An example of this was when the mother of the disciples, James and John came to Jesus to ask the her sons rule with Jesus when he came into his kingdom, he told her and them that they would face many obstacles, and also that such a decision was up to God, not him (See Matthew 20:20-28). In fact tradition says that James was one of the early martyrs and John spent much of his later years in prison.

Jesus warned his followers to be prepared for serious problems

Jesus said **"Behold, I am sending you out as sheep in the midst of wolves, so be wise as serpents and innocent as doves . Beware of men for they will deliver you over to courts and flog you in their synagogues, and you will be dragged before governors and kings for my sake"** (See Matthew 10:16-18). And he said of his message that it would **"....set a man against his father, and a daughter against her mother, and a daughter-in-law against her mother-in-law"** (See Matthew 10:35). Also, when **speaking about his return to earth and was asked when that would be, Jesus told his disciples "And you will hear of wars and rumors of wars. See that you are not alarmed for this must take place, but the end is not yet. For nation will rise against nation, and kingdom against kingdom, and there will be famines and earthquakes in various places. All these are but the beginning of the birth pains. Then they will deliver you up to tribulation and put you to death, and you will be hated by all nations for my name's sake."** (See Matthew 24:6-9).

Throughout the last 2000 years there have been far too many to count examples of this persecution. Believers have been insulted, punished, jailed, and even executed for their faith. This is happening even today in parts of the world. There have even been devastating wars fought not only between believers and non-believers, but also between groups of believers with different concepts of Jesus' teachings. But it appears that Christianity still exists and there are still believers throughout the world.

But Jesus also offered some very important benefits and peace-of-mind to his followers in their lives on earth <u>and eternal life thereafter</u>

In John 3:36 John the Baptist told his own disciples **"Whoever, believes in the son (*Jesus Christ, the Messiah*) has eternal life...."** In Matthew 5:3-16 (the Beatitudes) Jesus pronounced blessings on the many and told his listeners that they were the **salt (*flavoring*) of the earth and the light of the world.** In Matthew 10:39b and also in Matthew 16:25 Jesus said **"Whoever loses his life for my sake will find it."** In Luke 12:6-8 Jesus said **"Are not 5 sparrows sold for two pennies? And not one of them is forgotten before God, why even the hairs of your head are all numbered. Fear not; you are more valuable then many sparrows. And I will tell you that everyone who acknowledges me before men, the Son of Man also will acknowledge before the angels of God."** In Mark 10:29-30 Jesus said **"Truly I say to you, there is no one who has left house or brothers or sisters or mother or father or children or lands for my sake and for the gospel, who will not receive a hundredfold now in this time, brothers and sisters and mothers and children, ..., and in the age to come eternal life."** (However, he did inject in this statement that there will be persecutions as well.) Then in John 8:31 **"If you abided in my word, you are truly my disciples, and you will know the truth and the truth will set you free."** Also in John, Jesus told his followers **"I am the door. If anyone enters by me, he will be saved"** (See John 10:9). Then he said **"I came that they (*my followers*) may have life and have it abundantly"** (See John 10:10b). **Also, in a number of places in the book of John, Jesus promised <u>eternal life</u> to those who would follow him. For example see John 3:14-15, John 5:24-25, John 6:47, John 6:51, John6:54, John 8:51.** In Matthew 11:28-30, Jesus said **"Come to me, all who labor and are heavy laden, and I will give you rest. Take my yoke upon you, and learn from me, for I am gentle and lowly of heart, and you will find rest for your souls. For my yoke is easy and my burden is light."**

Jesus taught that to be his follower it was necessary to bare fruit, <u>but that victory would ensue</u>

One fairly startling example was that Jesus caused a fig tree to die when he found no fruit on it (See Matthew 21:18-19, Mark 11:12-14 and Mark 11:20-21). **With this example, Jesus forcefully indicated that a requirement of his followers was that they bare fruit. That they should not only be shining examples of their faith but also lead others to that faith as well. But he also used this as a lesson to his disciples that unquestioned faith could move mountains and that God will forgive these followers for their sins (See Matthew 21:20-22 and Mark 11:22-25).** Luke tells a fig tree teaching of Jesus in a different way. In this story he gave permission for a follower to try to save the tree from being destroyed **(See Luke 13:6-9)**. In this story, the owner was given permission and time to try to resurrect the tree before destroying it. This was a lesson of compassion, love and caring.

Jesus confirmed the existence of, and taught about, the Holy Spirit

In John14:16-17 Jesus introduces his disciples to the third member of God's existence into the recognition of man, the "Holy Spirit". Jesus said **"And I will ask the father, and he will give you another "Helper", to be with you forever, even the spirit of <u>truth</u>, whom the world** (*of people who need physical proof*) **cannot receive, because it neither sees him or knows him. You know him, for he dwells with you and will be in you."** (*And I believe that he chose his words carefully to convey that the Spirit is timeless, before, now and forever.*) But then in verses 18-21, Jesus went on to say **"I will not leave you as orphans; I will come to you. Yet a little while the earth will see me no more, but you will see me. Because I live, you will also live. In that day you will know that I am in the Father** (*God*)**, and you in me, and I in you."** This leaves some quandary, in that Jesus told his followers that both he and the holy spirit would be within them. Is he telling them that he and the Holy Spirit are one in the same? *I believe not. Jesus very clearly said that the Holy Spirit would be the Spirit of "<u>Truth</u>" and that he (Jesus) would be the spirit of "<u>Life</u>". There is a definite difference here. It appears to me that the purpose of the Holy Spirit is to convict a believer to accept the <u>truth</u> that Jesus is the guide for our earthly lives and the giver of and understanding of eternal <u>life</u>. I believe also that the Holy Spirit can be called an "attitude" that guides one's heart and mind to the understanding of what Jesus has taught and what the sacrifice of his bodily life would mean for humanity (if they would only believe and accept).*

First of all, we need to discus what form of being the Holy Spirit is. Older Bible translations have used the term "Holy Ghost". However, the term "ghost" implies that such is the continuing spirit of a person who had died. This is not at all what Jesus implied. Now think of how we apply the term spirit. One might say "That is a spirited horse" to describe a horse with a lot of energy. One might also say "That person has a lot of spirit" indicating the person has a lot of drive to achieve some goal. And also one might say "That's the spirit" as a complement for a valiant effort. In any case, none of these ways of using the term "spirit" indicate a state of being, but rather a force directed toward an achievement or goal. So it might be proper, thus, to say that persons having the Holy Spirit will not only understand the truth of God, but also who have the energy and passion to achieve the specific purposes that God desires of them. Therefore, I believe that a person possessing the Holy Spirit will not just sit on his or her beliefs, but will also actively promote the messages for living of Jesus and also the meaning and significance of his death and resurrection, and try to lead others to believe as well, by all the means of the talents God gave that person. Thus, I see the Holy Spirit is not only a spirit of Truth but is also the energy, passion, enthusiasm, and direction to do what is in God's plan that would guide a believer.

Although I believe that the Holy Spirit existed before Jesus appeared on the earth (i.e. Abraham, Moses, David, the prophets, and the scribes who wrote the words of the Old Testament); in the Book of Acts as Jesus prophesied, the Holy Spirit introduced itself in a dramatic way to the believers, on the day of Pentecost (about forty days after Jesus' resurrection). On that day it caused many to prophecy (about the Kingdom of God), to convince (of the message and salvation of Christ), and to speak in languages other than their own (to provide a path for leading those who did not speak Hebrew or Aramaic, to belief in Christ as well).

But Jesus also had some dire words for those who might not believe in or accept the Holy Spirit into their lives. In Matthew 12:31-32 he said **"Therefore I tell you, every sin and blasphemy (*against me*) will be forgiven people, but the blasphemy against the Spirit will not be forgiven. And whoever speaks a word against the Son of Man will be forgiven, but whoever speaks against the Holy Spirit will not be forgiven, either in this age or in the age to come."** And Mark phrases this condemnation in chapter 3 verses 28-29 this way. **"Truly I say to you, all sins will be forgiven the children of man, and the blasphemes they utter, but whoever blasphemes against the Holy Spirit never has forgiveness, but is guilty of an eternal sin".** This statement is also recorded in Luke 12:10. **Thus, Jesus was emphatic in his condemnation of those who deny the existence of and the power of the Holy Spirit to propagate the truth of the messages of Jesus and of God.** *And as I see it, those who deny the truth of both or either God the creator and Jesus the messenger, and call these things a myth, are eternally condemned and will have no place in God's kingdom. WOW. In modern vernacular, they would have "gone to the dark side", and will spend eternity in the lake of fire.* **Thus, this is the one unforgivable sin.**

JESUS TAUGHT WITH PARABLES

What is a parable?

Webster's dictionary says that a parable is an allegory or comparison, a story in a familiar setting or tense in order to teach a religious or moral lesson

My personal definition is that it is a teaching method used to present a lesson or information in such a way as to make it understandable to the listener by using familiar terms and settings. Jesus usually used it to make a specific point about commitment and service to the kingdom of God, and what would happen to those who refuse to do God's will.

The Bible tells that teaching through use of parables was a practice of Old Testament prophets long before Jesus, and thus not new with him (See Psalm 78:2). But Jesus used them as a tool to convey or emphasize various lessons that he was teaching. Matthew pointed out the Jesus used parables extensively during his ministry (See Matthew 13:34). But Jesus told his disciples that unless a listener has an understanding heart, parables would be meaningless. Thus, he used parables to especially teach those who's hearts were open to understand his words (See Matthew 13:10-17). This message from Jesus is consistent with numerous later scriptures that his message is not intended for all, but only for those who are hearing his words and are willing to follow him. And this teaching method is also consistent with his prophesy of the end-time when Jesus will separate the sheep from the goats. (The sheep were those with the required believing and understanding hearts.) (See the section on Jesus' prophesies below). Basically Jesus' parables are all lessons on how to act as believers in Jesus or what to expect from those believers. Specifically, Jesus used parables in support of his statement and sermons. But they also provided special emphasis in the areas of service, forgiveness, and what it means to be a brother.

Jesus Parables

The parable of the sower and his crop (the true disciple)

This parable is the first one mentioned in Matthew and is quite descriptive of what it means to be a true follower of Jesus. This parable is based on a planter who is trying to grow a crop (See Matthew 13:3-9). In it, Jesus described several types of people who try unsuccessfully to become his followers. The first are those who hear the word but never listen, and never commit. The second are those that have no depth in their beliefs and soon die away. The third are met with problems and adversities and have no roots, so they also soon die away. The forth group are those who are unable to escape their competing earthly habits and priorities, and those priorities choke out their commitment and make them fall away. Then the fifth group are surrounded by a supporting environment, so that they overcome adversity and competing desires, and become, not just followers, but mature witnesses to the kingdom, and producers of more disciples like themselves. But for further thought, take a look of Jesus' own words in explaining the parable to his disciples (See Matthew 13:18-23).

The parable of an evil attack on the sower's crop (crime and punishment)

This parable is more specific than the one above by pointing to an enemy who tries to destroy the planter's crop by purposely planting weeds in the grain fields, and what should be done with the efforts of the planter's enemy (See Matthew 13:24-30). This parable adds the statement of what would happen to those trying to compromise the believers **"Let both (the weeds and the good crop) grow up together until the harvest, and at the harvest time, I will tell the reapers, 'Gather the weeds first, and bind them into bundles and <u>burn them</u>'"** (See specifically verse 30) again a harbinger of the final punishment. For Jesus' own words about this parable, see Matthew 13:36-43.

The parable of the mustard seed (Kingdom growth)

See Matthew 13:31-32. This parable is about growth of the Kingdom of God among humanity. With it he forecasted how the kingdom can be spread beyond all logic. *I believe Jesus told it to encourage his followers to believe that this small group would become a giant movement.*

The parable of the leaven (Kingdom growth 2)

See Matthew 13:33-34. This parable is another way of telling of the inevitability of the growth of the Kingdom.

The parable of the hidden treasure (Kingdom transfer to and spread
by others)

See Matthew 13:44. This is a prophecy about a very important prediction that the path that the kingdom of heaven would take among humanity after Jesus death and resurrection. It could be a little confusing as to why the finder hid the treasure when he found it. Also, he apparently found it in a field that did not belong to him, so that legally he could not claim the treasure as his own. In addition, a part of this parable unsaid could have been that the treasure, though it belonged to the property owner, the owner might have thought that the treasure was of no value to him. So the treasure finder bought the field where the treasure was located. Then he could enjoy the fruits of that treasure. So it appears that this parable was about two things. One was that the finder was not initially entitled to or prepared to enjoy the benefit of the treasure. That is, until he became committed to it and mature enough to be benefitted by it. *To me, this is Jesus telling his followers that the treasure was the Kingdom of God and its offer of salvation, which was initially for the Jews, but that the field ownership and the treasure it contained were destined to pass to others,* **the believers in him, whatever nationality of ethnic origin.** *But those believers first needed to be prepared to be able to properly accept and deal with it.* Matthew relates two specific incidents where Jesus tested non-Jewish people to see if they were prepared to receive his treasure. One was when a Roman officer asked Jesus to heal his servant. Based on the Roman officer's confession to Jesus. Jesus proclaimed **"Truly, I tell you, with no one in Israel have I found such faith"** (See Matthew 8:10). Then Jesus predicted in Matthew 8:11 that **"I tell you, many will come from east ad west and recline at table with Abraham, Isaac, and Jacob in the kingdom of heaven"**. The second one was when a Canaanite woman asked Jesus to heal her daughter. He challenged her to tell him why she was entitled to such a gift because she was not a Jew, by saying **"It is not right to take the children's bread and throw it to the dogs"**. She answered him by saying ""Yes lord, yet even the dogs eat the crumbs that fall from the master's table. And Jesus answered her, " **O woman, great is your faith! Be it done for you as you desire"** (See Matthew 15:21-27). *In a nutshell, faith trumps heritage. And I would add, it also trumps language and skin color.*

The parable of the Pearl of great value *(Full commitment)*

See Matthew 13:45-46. This parable complements the one above, in that what the inheritor of the pearl (hidden treasure) gave up all he had to buy it, no holding back or split loyalties. This of course relates back to the refusal by the wealthy young man who walked away from Jesus, when Jesus asked him to give up all he had and to follow him (See Matthew 19:16-21).

The parable of the net (Final judgement and punishment)

See Matthew 13:47-50. This is a prophecy that there will be an instant at the end of all things when there will be a decision about who can and who cannot enter the Kingdom of God. Here, Jesus uses a fishing example to explain that, just as the good fish will be placed in containers, and trash fish will be thrown away. And thus there will, for certain, be a final judgement between good and evil at the end of time (and that the evil ones will be destined for the **"fiery furnace"**). See also Matthew 25:31-35 for confirmation of this prophesy.

The parable of the lost sheep (All lives matter, even the lives of those who wander).

See Matthew 18:10-14. In this parable uses the image of a shepherd who worked very hard to save one sheep who is lost, even though he has many who were safe already. It ended with a statement that God cares for everyone.

The parable of the vineyard laborers (The reward of eternal life is the same for all who come to the kingdom of heaven)

See Matthew 20:1-16. This is not listed as a parable in my ESV Bible. However, it fits the profile for one. Jesus told the story of a vineyard owner who had a crop of grapes that needed to be picked in one day, and he needed workmen to get it done. So he went out in the morning to hire laborers. And he hired several for a "dinarius" (a denomination of money of the time). Seeing that the job would not be done by the end of the day as hoped, he went out three hours later and hired more for the same dinarius pay. He then hired more at three hours and 6 hours later with the offer of the same pay. When it came time to pay them all, he payed them each one dinarius. Those who went on the job earlier complained, because those who came later were paid the same. The vineyard owner told them that they had all agreed to the pay offer when they were hired, and that he, as the vineyard owner was entitled to make the rules. **God offers eternal life to all who come to his kingdom, even though some might come to the kingdom earlier and some later. What more do they need.** This might also be compared to the parable of the prodigal son below, with respect to the loyal son (See Luke 15).

The parable of the two sons (one who said he would work and didn't, and one said he wouldn't but did)

See Matthew 21:28-32. This parable is a lesson on words vs. works. Jesus taught that the second son, who said he would work and didn't, failed to do God's will, while the first son who said he would not, but did what was asked of him, and was blessed. This was obviously, a parable that taught that words don't count if there is no commitment behind the words. And also works mean something even though they may not at first be promised. I see one of the messages of this lesson was that the so-called favored ones (the Hebrews) had less chance of entering the kingdom than the sinners who had turned their lives around.

The parable of the *(rebellious)* tenants (God's judgement on those who do not accept him)

See Matthew 21:33-43 and Mark 12:1-11. This is the story about a vineyard owner who leased his vineyard to a group of tenants, with the expectation that he would profit from their efforts to take care of his property. But the tenants decided that they owed the owner nothing and drove away the owner's servants, and even killed the owner's son. Of course, the owner was God. The vineyard was his Kingdom. The tenants were his chosen people. **The owner's son was obviously Jesus (another prophesy of his death at the hands of the chosen).** This was another admonition to the Jews that the Kingdom would be taken away from them and given to others. Then Jesus followed this with a warning and threat in verse 44, that compares his words to a stone that would destroy anyone who disobeys.

The parable of the wedding feast (God's punishment for both the deniers and the unprepared ones)

See Matthew 22:1-14. This parable is about a condemnation of those who would turn down an invitation to the wedding feast for the king's son. An also it is a condemnation of any who showed up for the feast unprepared. The king of course is God, the son is Jesus, the wedding was the joining of Jesus to his church, and those who refused the invitation to the feast are those who refused to honor God or Jesus, and the unprepared one was the person came to enjoy the fruits of the Kingdom without a commitment to Jesus. See also the paragraph above about the rich young man and the parables above about the treasure and the pearl.

The parable of the ten virgins (being prepared or unprepared for the Kingdom)

See Matthew 25:1-13. This parable is about 10 hypothetical virgins who were to be married to a bridegroom. This parable has to do with readiness to enter Christ's kingdom, but it also has intimations of the final judgement at Jesus's second coming. It tells about five who came to the wedding prepared to join with the bridegroom, and five who were not. The five who were not, asked for help from those who were but were turned down. *This, to me, says clearly that salvation is a personal matter between God and individual humans, that acceptance of or commitment to Jesus cannot be traded or shared with another. This does not mean that one should not witness to or pray for another, but rather that salvation is a personal matter and cannot be bought or sold.*

The parable of the talents (proper use of God's gifts)

See Matthew 25:14-30. This parable is about three servants who were given different degrees of resources and capabilities, how those resources were used, and the result of misuse. It first indicates that not all people, though created equally, are not blessed with the same talents or life skills. Despite this fact, the story is not about the differences but the use of those skills. It tells of how two who were given multiple abilities, used them for the benefit of the one who gave them and were rewarded for it. But it is also about one who was given only one talent and did not use it as was expected by the master who gave him the talent. He did not loose it, but master received nothing of benefit for it. What was expected was that the master's wealth (his kingdom) would be expanded by that talent and it was not, so the person was punished for his lack of action. This is a lesson in using whatever talents one has for the benefit of the Kingdom of God, to show belief and trust in Him.

The parable of the crop producing seed (a process beyond human understanding)

See Mark 4:26-29. This parable tells of how a human can plant without any real effort and yet grow a crop for harvest without knowing or understanding how it happens. So even though he does not understand the process, he can be nourished by it. Thus, it is not necessary for a human to understand the processes and will of God, to find the benefits that God provides. A lesson in trust and belief (see also the book of Job in the Old Testament).

The parable of the good Samaritan (he who does good for another is a blessed, **and a brother,** even if he is from a different ethnic group)

See Luke 10:25-37. (This parable was described earlier to tell a different but complementary story about discimination.) This parable first tells about a Jewish person who was attacked, beaten and robbed on a desolate road between Jerusalem and Jericho. As he lay severely injured, bleeding, and possibly dying beside the road, two fellow Jews happened upon him. One was a temple priest who lead religious services and one was a Levite who's job was to care for the temple. Both should have been people who set examples and cared for others particularly of their faith. But both passed him by and continued on their ways, leaving him there to suffer. We are not told why they didn't stop and help. Maybe they were afraid of also getting attacked. Or maybe they just didn't care, or just didn't want to get involved. Then a Samaritan man came along, saw the injured man and stopped to help. (Samaritans, as you know, were a group of people looked down on and discriminated against by the Jews, considered low class and worthless, like people of African lineage have been in America in the past and even some today.) He sterilized and bound his wounds, and then took him to an area hotel (the nearest thing to a hospital of the time), and asked the manager to look after him. He also gave money to the manager for his care, and told the manager that he would pay any additional costs when he came back. This is an example of love and caring for a fellow human that transcended race and ethnic boundaries. And Jesus asked the person he was telling this story to, who was a lawyer, **"which of these three, do you think, proved to be a neighbor to the man who fall among robbers?"** The lawyer said **"The one who showed him mercy"**. I think all of us would have given the same answer, even though the priest and Levite were sons of same Abraham as the injured man, and the Samaritan was not. Also, I think it is appropriate here to include another of Jesus' quotes in Matthew 25:41-46 about the judgement at his second coming. The reader should look it up. And there is a positive command at the end of this parable to **"go and do likewise"**.

The parable of the rich fool (earthly treasures are temporary, and worthless in the eternal)

See Luke 12:15-31. This is a parable about a successful farmer who was able to raise a bumper crop, and instead of giving the excess to the poor and needy, decided to simply build bigger storehouses (more luxurious) to store (and show) his wealth. But he died. And that wealth gave him no immediate nor eternal benefit. Also, God's mission was not helped by the farmer's decision, and neither were the needs of the poor and hungry. Not a good way to exist.

The parable of the barren fig tree (a lesson in second chances)

See Luke 13:6-9. An owner of a fig tree decided to destroy it because it was producing no fruit. His servant asked the owner to let him fertilize and loosen the soil around it to determine if it can be saved before it was cut down. A lesson in giving a person a second chance to love God and do good. Like the servant did, kept on trying to help. Fruit may yet come.

The parable of the lost coin (finding a lost valuable is worth the effort)

See Luke 15:8-10. The parable is about a lost coin. The owner will search until she finds it, and rejoices when she finds it. Jesus compared this to a lost sinner. And this parable is similar in its message to the parable of the lost sheep, and is described in both Matthew and Luke above.

The parable of the prodigal son (a strayed son redeemed, and another jealous)

See Luke 15:11-32. This is the story of a younger son who took his inheritance early and wasted it on riotous living, and then returned home confessing his sins and asking his father to treat him only as a servant. But he was welcomed home with joy and celebration. It was also the story of the loyal older son who was jealous of his father's good treatment of the younger son, but who was consoled by his father and was recognized for his loyalty. It is a story of equal salvation for all believers, the ultimate gift. This parable is similar to the parables of the lost sheep and the lost coin. **However, it goes a big step further in demonstrating God's love for humanity, in that the son who strayed was not just lost, but he actually squandered half his father's fortune. Even so, when he realized what he had done and returned to his father, he was received with joy.**

The parable of the dishonest manager (a shrewd debt collector)

See Luke 16:1-12. *Personally, I have some trouble understanding the lesson of this parable, because it shows that a dishonest man was praised by his employer for what I think were dishonest acts.* The steward's employer had already threatened to fire the steward for wasting the employer's wealth. So the steward made friends with some of the people who owed debts to the employer by reducing the amounts of the debts they owed. The employer praised the steward for his shrewdness to apparently establish new friendly contacts who might employ him in the future. *However, if I were the employer, even though it doesn't say so in the Bible, I would have fired him anyway on the spot.* But there may be another take on this one. In the Old Testament, Jacob was a shrewd and devious man. However, apparently God saw past Jacob's dishonesty, and saw his intelligence and desire for success, and built a nation from his progeny. At the end of this parable Jesus taught that one cannot serve two masters because of conflicts of interest (paraphrased). *Otherwise, I am still not sure of Jesus intention in teaching this parable.*

The parable of the rich man and Lazarus (the decisions we make on earth will make a very momentous impact on us for eternity)

See Luke 16:19-31. This parable is a serious warning tho those who, during their lifetimes on earth only enjoy their wealth and pleasure, with no thought for the hereafter. Lazarus (a fictional character, not the brother of Mary and Martha) was very poor and ill. When he died, he went to be with God in heaven. The rich man lived his earthly his life amid pleasure and possessions with no thought about his eternal soul. He died and was transported to hades and torment. He looked up and saw Lazarus in heaven and asked for help from him. But this was impossible due to great chasm between them. So the lesson here is very clear. Believe in and honor God the creator and follow Jesus while on earth, or the consequences will be devastating. **No do-overs**

The parable of the persistent widow (be strong in prayer and do not lose heart)

See Luke 16:1-8. This parable is about a widow who went before a judge to get a judgement against an adversary. The judge was an uncaring person, and had no desire to help her. However, she was so persistent in her pleading that he decided to give her justice to just stop her bothering him. Jesus ended the parable by contrasting what a caring God would listen and do for the repeated prayers of a believer. So pray without ceasing.

The parable of the ten minas (if one is responsible with small amounts greater rewards will be given)

See Luke 19:11-26. This a variation of the parable of the talents (see Matthew 25:14-30) with the same message. Jesus taught that there were two servants who were each given 10 small amounts of money by a powerful employer who people feared. The first respected his employer and made money for him with sound investments. The second feared the employer more than he respected and hid the money away. The first was rewarded for his success in using what he had been given. The second was condemned for not doing so, and received the punishment he feared. The lesson of this parable is that God will appreciate those who work for him and believe in and respect him, even if he is to be feared.

Another parable of the fig tree (as a fig tree leafs out so will there be signs of Jesus' return)

See Luke 21:29-36. Before the second coming there will signs of its arrival. So don't let earthly pleasures blind one from being prepared for it. But stay awake and pray for strength in God.

Mini parables (familiar terms used to teach a lesson)

My definitions of parables was the use of familiar situations to teach eternal lessons. Although they are not really allegories as normally associated with parables, Jesus used them as teaching tools. One of them was his comparison of the road to salvation as **a narrow gate and a hard path** compared to a **wide gate and easy path** to desolation and destruction (See Matthew 7:12-14). Another was his statement of the difficulty of following him, was like the struggle that a wealthy person might have as compared to trying to pass through the **"eye of a needle"** (See Matthew 19:24). Both of these were warnings to his followers that commitment is necessary and the path might be difficult. But interestingly, when his disciples became concerned as to who could be saved, Jesus told them in Matthew 19:26 **"With man this is impossible, but all things are possible with God"**. An example of this might be when Joseph of Aramathia (a rich man) gave up his tomb for Jesus' burial. Another is what I call a mini-parable where in John 10:9 Jesus says **"I am the door. If anyone enters me he will be saved"**. This one clearly states that Jesus is the way to forgiveness and salvation. And when Jesus talked about people's concerns and worries, he said look the **birds of the air** and **lilies of the field** to allay their concerns (See Matthew 6:26-28). Then in Matthew 5:40 Jesus said that if anyone wins a lawsuit against a believer and takes his **tunic**, he should also give him his **cloak** as well. Also in Matthew 5:41 there is a reference to a **mile**. Unlike the English mile of recent times, 5280 feet, this was a distance established by the Roman army on the move. It represented the distance of 2000 paces. However, it was roughly the same distance of the modern English mile. Apparently, it was a practice of Roman army foot soldiers to force local people into carrying their packs for a mile to relieve their load. Jesus used this practice to illustrate how a believer should do more than asked **(walk a second mile)** to prove ones lack of anger at, but instead, love for fellow man.

Jesus taught with Actions

Jesus attended several Passover celebrationss, very important trips in his ministry

On such trips to Jerusalem for a Passover feast (before the one where he was crucified), Jesus went through Samaria, teaching and healing along the way. On these such trips, he had two extremely important encounters. **On one he encountered a Samaritan woman to whom he specifically identified himself as the longed-for Messiah (See John 4:10-26). On another he met with the Pharisee, Nicodemus, to whom he explained the plan of salvation (see John chapter 3).**

Jesus selected twelve disciples to perpetuate his mission

Jesus knew his time on earth would be limited, so he selected twelve disciples to be his inner circle of followers, to learn from him and continue his mission after he was gone. The number twelve is significant in that the people of Israel were descended as tribes from the twelve sons of Jacob. *Although there were two pairs of brothers among the chosen, it's as if Jesus were selecting one to represent each of those twelve tribes. But the choices he made were not random. They were chosen for specific purposes. The first one he picked was Andrew, a fisherman, in the sea of Galilee, who was previously a disciple of John the Baptist. Andrew is most noted for introducing Jesus to his brother, Simon, who became the strongest and most outspoken of Jesus' followers. Jesus renamed him Peter, the Rock, (I think, because Jesus saw in him a solid, dynamic individual, who, even with a lot of rough edges, would turn out to be a primary initiator of the continuation of Jesus' message, like a boulder rolling down a slope). Then he picked two other brothers who were also fishermen, who were known for their strong opinions and avid attitudes. They were later called the "sons of thunder" (see Matthew 5:9). All four of these men were apparently so impressed by Jesus that they immediately left their fishing boats and nets to follow him (see Matthew 4:18-22). John was the longest lived of the disciples and in his older age, was the most prolific writer among them, credited with a gospel, three letters, and the book of Revelation.*

Shortly after Jesus had selected his first four disciples and after he had gathered thousands of followers (see Matthew 4:25), he began selecting others for his inner circle. The next one to be called was Matthew *(called Levi in Mark's gospel, possibly because he might have been of the linage of the tribe of Levi).* Matthew was a collector of taxes. Tax collectors were considered low-lifes by the general populous, akin to law breakers (apparently because they had a reputation of making themselves rich through the fees they earned, or through skimming, and also because they collected taxes for hated Rome). Matthew was an ideal choice for several reasons. First, he was the best educated and most financially well off of the twelve, and best able to read and write. Second, he had an ordered, business mind, as seen from the organization of his gospel. Third, he was good at keeping records and documenting what he had seen and heard. And fourth, he was a good example of someone who was considered a sinner by many, who became a follower of Jesus, and who's sins were forgiven.

Jesus' sixth choice was Philip, who, like Andrew, had previously been a disciple of John the Baptist. Philip will be seen in volume three of this document to have a special talent for serving and for one-on-one witnessing to individuals both as a deacon and during his travels. Next was Bartholomew, who was an intelligent man and was impressed by Jesus' exceptional powers of observation. After him was Thomas, a pragmatist, who proved to be a strong witness by requiring and receiving physical proof of Jesus' resurrection. Thus, each of these men added special views of Jesus. Also added were Alphaeus and Thaddaeus. Unfortunately, we know very little more about them, except it is assumed that they were dedicated followers.

But the last two, Simon the Cananean and Judas Iscariot, were especially interesting, in that they were of the activist political party of the "Zealots". *These two men were most likely attracted to Jesus because they believed that he would become a warrior king who would throw off the hated*

Roman rule and establish an eternal "earthly" Jewish kingdom. It will become apparent later in this document that Judas tried hard to force Jesus to conform to what Judas had envisioned the Messiah to be, versus what Jesus taught. Thus, Judas played a pivotal role in debunking the idea that Jesus' kingdom would be worldly one, **by betraying him**. *And I believe that Jesus picked him particularly for that purpose. (Maybe Jesus selected Simon the other Zealot as a backup, just in case Judas didn't come through.)*

But also, the personality types of those selected were remarkable because they seemed to represent the summation of the personality types and social statuses of the human race. One was a blusterer, who spoke out his thoughts without first thinking them through. This was Peter, who was a prime candidate to be lead by the Holy Spirit to boldly speak out the truth of Christ. Two others were called the "Sons of Thunder" because they would not hold back when challenged. These were James and John. There were also two men, Andrew and Phillip, who demonstrated empathy for others, and whose personalities were attuned to leading other individuals to become believers in Jesus through personal interaction. Then there was Bartholomew, a thinker and intellectual. Matthew was a business man, good at planning and organizing, also apparently fairly wealthy. Others were loyal people of honor who attempted and reasoned to be true followers. Then there were two who were strong in support of their country and culture. However, one of those was not only a zealot, but had a big ego. He, Judas Iscariot, thought he was a strong enough to bend Jesus' mission to fit his image of what he envisioned the Christ should be. He is almost always roundly condemned. But, interestingly, was a key figure in helping to facilitate one of Jesus' primary missions on earth, his death as a sacrifice for our sins.

But there is a primary lesson here that Jesus taught with his selections. This was that his message was not for a select few, but for all walks of life; the rich, the poor, the educated, the uneducated, the emotional, the rational, those with leadership potential or desires, those contented to be followers, the thinkers, the doers, the rebels, etc. No one class or life style was excluded.

Jesus drove the money changers from the temple

At the time of Jesus, there were people who were making money and lining there own pockets by taking advantage of those who had come to the temple to worship. They were allowed to practice their businesses right in the temple complex and in the temple itself. These included sellers of animals and grain for the Old Testament sacrifices. They were successful because worshipers often came to the temple without items to sacrifice, expecting to buy them on arrival. But they came with different types of currency, most of which was not acceptable for the purchase of sacrifices and for other spending money while in Jerusalem. So there were money changers who would trade currency, charging service and convenience fees for the exchange, which on occasion could have been exorbitant. Thus, these business persons were not directly involved in worship, and basically were parasites, praying on the pilgrims. Apparently, Jesus recognized this, and particularly singled the money changers out for extra punishment as examples of those took advantage of others. He not only drove them out of the temple, but also overturned their money changing tables, assumedly scattering their money (their lively-hood) all over the temple floor, to be picked up by anyone there (See Matthew 21:12-13, Mark 11:15-17, Luke 19:45-46, and John

2:14-16). This was a pretty brazen act. And the temple priests, I am sure, didn't like it, possibly because they were getting a cut of the profits. But apparently Jesus was not arrested for doing this, because he was doing God's work by cleansing the temple of "robbers" as predicted in Jeremiah 7:11.

Jesus allowed his disciples to pick grain on the Sabbath even though this act was considered a sin under Jewish law at the time

By the time of Jesus, the Hebrew leaders had enhanced the Mosaic laws with numerous amendments that made them more and more specific and restrictive. There were specific rules about how far a person could travel and about the harvesting grain on the Sabbath. The scribes and lawyers pointed out that Jesus and his followers, thus, were law breakers because they picked heads of grain and ate them as they walked through the fields as they followed Jesus. This gave Jesus the opportunity to make two specific pronouncements about these rules, their strictness, and their universal enforcement. These pronouncements lead to some his greatest revelations about the relationships between God and man. One such was that **"the Sabbath was made for man, not man for the Sabbath" (See Mark 2:27).** Also in the same lesson, Jesus pointed out that several of the select and respected people in the Old Testament, including King David, broke this law, and that the priests and Levites were doing the same in the current age. And in doing so he also announced that he was **"Lord of the Sabbath" (See Matthew 12:1-8 and Mark 2:25-28).** And he also attacked the Kosher food and eating rules that, in their breaking, were held more sinful than ranting, cursing, lying, etc., by stating **"It is not what goes into the mouth that defiles a person, but what comes out of the mouth that defiles a person" (See Matthew 15:11 and Mark 7:14-23).** (*There will be more about acceptable food consumption in Part III of this document.*). Jesus also performed several healing miracles on the Sabbath, again a sin under Jewish law.

Jesus showed respect for his mother

This was an action by Jesus to obey the fifth of the Ten Commandments. That is to **"Honor your father and your mother"** (See Exodus 20:12) Even though Jesus disappointed his parents as a twelve year old when he stayed in the Jerusalem temple after a pilgrimage without their permission (See Luke 2:41-51), he demonstrated an act of honoring his mother when she requested that he help at a wedding feast that they were attending. (*Apparently, by this time in Jesus' earthly life, his earthly father was not in the picture. Most likely, he had died. It appears also that his mother knew of her son's special powers.*) He, at first, told her **"Woman, what does this have to do with me? My hour has not yet come." (See John 2:4).** However, he did what she asked, even though he had a concern that he was not yet ready to carry out his earthly mission. In doing so, he performed his first recorded miracle, that of turning water into wine (See John 2:6-10), thus honoring his mother's wishes. Later in his ministry, his mother and his brothers came to him while he was teaching and asked to speak to him, but he used this request as teaching tool by telling the crowd that not just his blood relatives were his mother and brothers, but all who believed in him as well (See Matthew 12:46-49) This may at first appears to be a rejection of his family. But to me it is a statement of inclusion instead, indicating an expansion of his family to include all who believed him. The proof that this was not a rejection, is indicated by Jesus when he called from the cross to ask his disciple John, to take care of his mother (See John 19:26-27). This assumption is also refuted by the fact that two of his younger half brothers, James and Jude, became pillars of his church and authored two New Testament books, after Jesus was crucified and ascended.

Jesus gave at least three commissions to his disciples to go and teach his message to others, giving them training and experience with witnessing

Commission 1. At one pont in his ministry, Jesus directed his inner circle of the twelve disciples to go out without him and preach his message. He instructed them to go only to the "lost sheep of the house of Israel" and tell them that the "kingdom of heaven" that they had been waiting for, as told to them by the prophets, was now here. He told them that, as a demonstration of this that he was giving them the power to perform healing miracles. He also said to not take any money or extra clothing with them and not to ask for pay or donations. But he told them that there would be opportunities for them to stay as guests in homes of believing "worthy" people. But he also told them that there also will be people out there who will not just not believe them, but who will hate them and try to punish them, and even possibly to try to kill them. And if this happens, just go on to the next town, for there is no end of towns in which one can witness. And to have no fear for God will be with them (See Matthew 10:5-33). The Bible gave no after-action report of this witnessing trip.

Commission 2. However, at another point, Jesus sent out seventy two of his followers. This time he didn't send them only to the Jews, but instead, he did not place ethnic or geographic limits on where they should go. However, he gave them similar instructions and healing powers, and told them that there would be severe punishment for those that didn't receive them. When these people returned, there was joy among them, reporting that **"even the demons are subject to us in your name"**. And Jesus praised them for their successes (See Luke 10:1-20).

There is a couple of important lessons here in comparing these two temporary evangelical episodes. The first one was to the chosen people, but who, because of their longstanding belief in the savior as an earthly king for the Jews only, would have a tendency to reject the real savior, the messenger of their God; whereas the general population would be more impressed with the miracles, and the message, because they didn't have those preconceived and ingrained ideas of exclusivity. This rejection of the Messiah by the Jews became obvious by both the killing of Jesus and the later opposition to the teachings of the apostles.

Commission 3. And then there was the third and most important and far-reaching of Jesus' direction to send out his followers, to go out as witnesses for his message and his salvation. This is commonly known as the "Great Commission". *I mentioned this item before, but I thought it was appropriate to list it again here.* This sending-out was not during Jesus' time of teaching, but rather after he had been condemned and executed, and then returned to life. Again, he broadened the scope of the charge to his followers, to not just go out temporarily, but to make it their life work to be his witnesses starting in Jerusalem, and then the country of Judea, and then Samaria (not Jews but neighbors whom the Jews held in contempt), and then to the whole world (See again Matthew 28:18-20 and Mark 16:15-16).

<u>And this, I think Jesus did for a very important reason, in that he does not expect all who believe in him to just to be happy and spirit filled, but to be witnesses for him and about him, where-ever we live or travel in life. And more than that, to seek out the lost, where-ever they might be, and to teach them of Jesus and his salvation.</u>

JESUS TAUGHT WITH MIRACLES

Jesus proved his power and authority by performing miracles, and he also used these miracles as another teaching tool. *Like his words and actions, his miracle working deserves a separate section in this document, because these miracles were many and well documented in all four gospels.* Probably the most common miracles he performed were healing people of both physical diseases and mental disorders. But he also performed several miracles where he bypassed the laws of nature. And in at least three cases he actually brought people back from the dead. But these miracles were not an end in themselves. Instead, they were powerful teaching tools to demonstrate his authority over nature, disease, and death, and to help people to listen to his teachings about his divinity. And they also supported and emphasized his instructions about ways of living and worship. Also, several of his miracles were to care for people who were clearly not of the lineage of Abraham, supporting his statements that his salvation was for all people, not just the Hebrew race.

For order in the process I will take these miracles first in the order in which they were described within the first gospel where they appear, taking one gospel at a time, and then, by type of miracle within that gospel. But if they are described in more than one gospel, I will cite in that description all the additional references in succeeding gospels. And, thus, I will not repeat them, unless there are noticeable differences in their descriptions. In describing each miracle, I will also try to describe the setting and who benefitted from it, how they reacted to it, and what was the lesson that Jesus used it to teach.

<u>Miracles according to Matthew</u>

Even before Jesus preached the Sermon-on-the-Mount, he preached and taught in synagogues all over Galilee and began healing illnesses along the way. And he healed all types of diseases both physical and mental, gaining a lot of recognition and drawing a large following all the way from Jerusalem to Syria as a result (See Matthew 4:23-25). However, none of these healings were described in detail until the following:

Jesus' first physical disease healing miracle

This miracle occurred when Jesus was coming off the mountain where he had just finished his "sermon-on-the-mount". He was approached by a person with leprosy. This was a disease that was fairly common in India and the middle east. It was a slowly progressing, terribly disfiguring disease, that caused obvious ugly skin lesions. And it made one not feel pain, so that they didn't feel infections from cuts or other skin damage, so that parts of one's body, particularly the extremities, could turn black, die, and eventually fall off. And in the course of time, it was almost always fatal. It was caused by a bacteria introduced initially by the bite of a particular type of mosquito. Recent strides in modern medicine have come up with cures. However, even with modern medicine, a cure can take up to a year. However, in Jesus' time there was no medical cure at all. Since it was somewhat communicable, people who had it were cast out of their families and communities, and were not employable in trades. The "good" people avoided those that had it. Thus, those with it had to live separately in poverty, sometimes in groups where they could support and take care of each other. It was an awful disease.

As indicated above, by the time of this event, people knew that Jesus had the power to heal diseases. The leper showed respect for him and asked that he be healed. **Jesus reached out and touched him, and he was immediately healed.** Then Jesus told him to go see a priest and show him that he was healed, and make an offering for his healing, as commanded by Moses according to Jewish law, **showing respect for the Law of Moses (See Matthew 8:1-4). For another description of this event, see Mark 1:49-45 and Luke 5:12-16. But in Mark's and Luke's telling, instead of going to a priest, the leper started telling everyone he met that he had been healed by Jesus. This created a problem for Jesus in that he would now be mobbed by people wanting to be healed without respect for the lessons Jesus was teaching.**

The lesson in this healing, Jesus used no incantations nor offered any prayers. He just touched the leper, showing that his own presence and power were sufficient. But there was another aspect to this miracle. The leper respected and trusted Jesus and believed that he could heal him.

Jesus' second physical disease healing miracle

The center for Jesus' early ministry was Capernaum, a relatively large community in Galilee. Jesus was on his way there, when he was approached by a Roman military officer, who asked Jesus to heal his servant. In this case, unlike the previous miracle initiated by Jesus' physical touch, Jesus did not even go to see the servant. Instead he healed the servant remotely. But the reason was that the Roman soldier, even though he was not a descendant of Abraham, believed in Jesus and his power (See Matthew 8:5-13 and Luke 7:1-10). **And this was because of his own belief and not because of his heritage, his servant was healed**

The lesson here was twofold. First, this miracle happened because a powerful warrior showed complete belief, respect, and trust in Jesus, even though he was not a Hebrew. Second, this indicated firmly and early-on in Jesus' ministry that he had come into the world to offer salvation to everyone, not just the Hebrews. (And there was another critical point made here. It was that Jesus' salvation for the Hebrews was not automatic, but required belief in him, the same as for any other person.)

Jesus' third physical disease healing miracle

This miracle happened when Jesus visited the house of his disciple Peter. Peter's mother-in-law was sick in bed with a fever. Jesus touched her and she was immediately healed. And she got up and served him. Then that very evening, neighbors started bringing both physically and mentally ill to him, and he healed them all with just a word. And in this case he did it in fulfillment of a prophesy in Isaiah (See Matthew 8:14-17 and Luke 4:38-41).

One lesson in this miracle is that Jesus not only had the power to heal an infectious disease, far better than modern antibiotics could do, (Please remember there were no antibiotics in Jesus day, and even today antibiotics may take days or even weeks to conquer a disease. And even then, the disease would normally cause noticeable weakness, and require a period of rehabilitation.) Instead, Peter's mother-in-law rose out of a sickbed to serve Jesus, as if she had never been sick. So this was more than just a healing. It was truly a miracle.

Jesus' first nature-controlling miracle - he calmed a storm

Jesus' next miracle, as recorded in Matthew, demonstrated that he could not only control human disease but he could control nature as well. Jesus and the disciples were in a boat on the Sea of Galilee. A storm came up and threatened to swamp the boat. His disciples became quite afraid, and woke Jesus, who was sleeping. He first rebuked them for not having enough faith. Then he rebuked the storm and calmed the sea (See Matthew 8:23-27 and Mark 4:35-41). Wow.

Jesus proved that he had the power to heal mental diseases as well as physical (demon possession)

In the next miracle situation, Jesus was faced with two men who were controlled by something that had taken over their minds. This event took place on the east side of the Sea of Galilee in an area that almost two thousand years before had been assigned by Joshua to the Hebrew tribe of Manassah. However in Jesus' time it was not considered Jewish territory, and those living there were not necessarily Hebrew. And also, these two men were living in a grave-yard and were apparently subject to dangerous, destructive behavior, because noone would come near them. **Jesus, however, approached them**, and in their torment they recognized that he was the "Son of God". What Jesus did for them was what we now call "exorcism". This was the process of causing an evil, destructive spirit to leave a person, identifying and treating it as a separate entity, not a mental disorder. Today, exorcisms are sometimes still practiced, but are often considered funny science or hoaxes. However, this event is documented in detail in Matthew 8:28-34. Something special here was that these evil spirits that possessed the men spoke to him and said "Have you come to torment us before the time." (*The meaning of this statement about "before the time" I will reserve for another author or another exposition.*) Jesus did not answer this. Instead he commanded these evil spirits to come out of the men. The spirits begged him to allow them to enter a herd of pigs in a field nearby. (*Under Mosaic law, pigs were considered unclean animals, and the Hebrews were forbidden to eat their meat.*) So Jesus did what they asked, and the evil spirits came out of the men and entered the pigs. Then the pigs immediately bolted, and ran headfirst into the Sea of Galilee and drowned. The herdsmen ran away in fear. And apparently the people of the area were not believers in the Mosaic law, and were witness to the destruction of their livelihood. So they pleaded for Jesus to leave the region (See Matthew 8:28-34 and Mark 5:1-29).

But in Mark's description he provides more detail about the healing, and also Mark said that there was one man being healed instead of two, as documented in Matthew. Mark also told that after the man was healed, he begged Jesus to let him go with him. But Jesus told him no, but instead to **"Go home to your friends and tell them how much the Lord has done for you, and how he has had mercy on you."** This is the first account of Jesus telling someone else **(who was even a gentile)** to witness about him to others. Again, as indicated in Matthew, this was in a territory that was not part of either Judea or Galilee, but rather an area populated primarily by gentiles.

There is a powerful lesson here, in that Jesus directed someone to witness about him to others, even though the man was not part of his inner, Hebrew, circle. This is a strong call for all Christians to not just be beneficiaries of Jesus' grace, but also to be witnesses about Jesus, no matter their race or where they are from, and to whomever they come in contact. There are several more lessons in this miracle. One is that, with all our modern medical and psychological sciences, human knowledge still falls far short in healing mental diseases. Jesus recognized that the mental disorder that controlled these men was an infection that could be treated as a separate entity that had a life outside the bodies of the those affected by it, just as viruses and microbes, (which of course were not known about at all in Jesus' time). But even more, this particular disease was a separate sentient being that could actually communicate with Jesus. Something for we have no concept even with our level of science today. And it again proved that Jesus' omnipotence and omniscience was far beyond anything we understand even today, thus providing further evidence that Jesus was truly the Son-of-God.

Another lesson was that Jesus took another step toward supporting proof of his statement during the sermon on the mount that he came <u>to fulfill the law, not abolish it</u> (See Matthew 5:17). This was that he confirmed the declaration in the law of Moses that pigs were unclean animals, by facilitating the destruction of a herd of them.

*As I indicated in the introduction, I will point out that there were other accounts in both **Mark 5:1-20 and Luke 8:26-39** of either this or a very similar event. In both Mark and Luke there are far more details than in Matthew. However, there was a noticeable difference between the Matthew account and in the two other accounts, in that the ones in Mark and Luke were about <u>one</u> deranged (possessed) man instead of two. Perhaps Matthew was describing one man with two or more distinct and independent personalities. In modern times we call this schizophrenia. But because of this difference, I have treated each as a separate event. But I also recognize a couple of circumstances that could have caused diverging accounts of the same event. The first was that both the books of Matthew and Mark were records of first hand, eye witnesses, but they apparently did not record this event until at least thirty years after it occurred, and Luke's was written even later. Second, Matthew's view was a desire to record facts, while Mark was* more into actions, and Luke's account was at least second hand, and recorded probably forty five years after its occurrence. But also, Luke's account, even if second hand, indicated he was more interested in details. So I will have to leave the justifications for these differences up to the reader to decide if these differing descriptions were of the same miracle, or two similar ones. In any case, all three accounts demonstrated the same thing, Jesus' ultimate power, something that he wanted his followers to recognize.

Jesus proved that he could heal a paralyzed person

Jesus next miracle recorded in Matthew is described this way. After Jesus had returned to Galilee after crossing the Sea of Galilee, he met a group of people who brought a paralytic to him on a bed, because they had faith that Jesus could heal him. This time, Jesus didn't even touch him. **He just told the man that his sins were forgiven.** However, there were some scribes who witnessed this who felt that Jesus was a liar and a charlatan, because they believed that Jesus did not have the power to forgive sins. So to prove his power, he told the man to get up and walk, **which he did**. And again, like Peter's mother-in-law, the man needed no time to recuperate or regain his strength (See Matthew 9:1-8). This miracle is also described in Mark, except that while Matthew's report specified no specific location, Mark's report said that this miracle occurred when Jesus had returned to a home in Capernaum while he was teaching there (See Mark 2:1-13), and also in Luke 5:17-26, but where Matthew pointed out that the Pharisees scoffed at the event, Luke pointed out that many others were greatly awed by it.

This was the first miracle where Jesus identified that he could <u>forgive sins</u>. And further, this miracle was carried out in another unique way, again proving that is was his personal power, not an incantation, trance, or magic wand that did the healing.

Then there was a double miracle, including a life returned from the dead

A Jewish government official approached Jesus and told him that his daughter had died, and he stated that he believed that Jesus could bring her back to life. **WOW**. Jesus went with him to do just that. But on the way, a woman with a bleeding disease, approached him from behind and touched the hem of his robe, with faith that this would heal her, and it did. When Jesus reached the official's house he found a mourning ceremony in progress. He told all the mourners to go away, and said the girl was **"...not dead but sleeping"**. Then he took her hand and the girl got up (See Matthew 9:18-25 and Mark 5:21-43). In this instance, Mark gave more detail. In Mark we learned the name of the Jewish official who's daughter had died, "Jairus". And we learned that he was a ruler of a local synagogue. We also learned the name of the girl who died, "Tabitha".

The lesson here was again the lesson that these people were healed because of their faith, not because of their heritage. Here also was a demonstration that Jesus proved he had more knowledge about life and death than all the people who were witnesses when Tabitha stopped breathing and her heart stopped beating, including her own desperate father (they all laughed at Jesus when he said that she was only sleeping). And in the case of the bleeding

woman, this incident showed that even the clothes that touched Jesus body had the power to heal while Jesus was wearing them.

Jesus proved that he could restore sight to the blind

While Jesus was walking, he was approached by two blind men, who asked that Jesus restore their sight. After verifying that they really believed in him and his power to restore their sight, he touched their eyes and they could see, another WOW. They were so ecstatic, that, even though Jesus told them not to make an issue of their healing, they told everyone, spreading widely his fame as a healer (See Matthew 9:27-31).

There were two lessons in this event. One was that Jesus could give sight to the blind who believed in him, and it seems obvious that Jesus knew it was more important that people believed in him as the Son of God, than to recognize his power to heal physical problems, because he told them to keep the healing quiet.

Jesus healed a person who could not speak, a physical deformity

The scripture says that the man in question was mute, meaning that he could not make a sound. If a person is unable to speak but still make sounds, this problem is usually associated with deafness, but the scripture does not say this. A deaf person can just not say coherent words. But sometimes a person cannot speak or even make sounds because of a physical deformity in his mouth or throat or maybe a mental disorder. This latter diagnosis appears to be the situation here. The man was apparently unable to make a sound. Matthew said that it was a demon that kept him from speaking. When Jesus cast out the demon, the man was able to speak in words, not just sounds. But there were Pharisees that witnessed this miracle, who denied Jesus power as the Messiah, because they couldn't accept him as such. Instead, they said that if he could cast out demons, he must be a demon himself (See Matthew 9:32-34). ***Boy, were they wrong.***

One lesson here was that Jesus could recognize the cause of the problem, and took appropriate action. But another lesson was that the religious leaders of the time were determined to deny who Jesus really was. There even appear to be a lot of people in this world today who still apparently hold this view. *I wonder that if Jesus reappeared on earth but without the fanfare that Jesus himself predicted at his second coming, how many educated, powerful people would adamantly refuse to believe who he was, even with the miracles he could perform, probably quite a few.*

Jesus healed a second type of physical deformity

This account began when Jesus visited a local synagogue on a Sabbath day. There he found a man who had a physically deformed (withered) hand. He was likely a member of that synagogue and known to other members, including the fact that his hand was deformed. And this situation appeared to be a setup, because those in the synagogue apparently knew of Jesus' power to heal, and they challenged him to heal the man's hand on the Sabbath, supposedly breaking a Jewish law that said that no labor could be conducted on the Sabbath. Jesus said to them **"Which one of you who has a sheep, if it falls into a pit on the Sabbath, will not take hold of it and lift it out."** Then he said: **"Of how much more value is a man than a sheep! So it is lawful to do good on the Sabbath."** Then Jesus told the man to stretch out his hand, and the deformed hand was instantaneously made whole **(See Matthew 12:9-14, Mark 3:1-12 and Luke 6:6-18)**. But here Luke reemphasised the fury among the orthodox that Jesus would perform even a healing act on the Sabbath, when the Lord had set aside the Sabbath as a day of rest, **even after Jesus told them that doing good was an exception to the rule.**

This event had several lessons. One was that Jesus had the power to not just cure a disease, but could correct a significant, recognizable, physical defect. A second lesson was that he had the power to heal, <u>by his word only</u>. (This principle is basic to Christians and Christianity everywhere.) A third lesson was that he clarified the law of Moses in that it permitted doing good on the Sabbath. And it also confirmed, in other words, a statement he made as recorded in Mark 2:27 that "<u>The Sabbath was made for man, not man for the Sabbath.</u>"

<u>Other miracles recorded in Matthew</u>

After Matthew left the synagogue where he cured the man with a withered hand, he went about healing others, to the point of empowering Matthew to point out a prophesy of Isaiah 700 years earlier that had intimated that Jesus was the promised Messiah, by describing his power, his persona, and his virtues, and also that this Messiah would be a blessing to not just descendants of Abraham but to others as well (See Isaiah 42:1-3 and Matthew 12:18-21).

And as I pointed out in Part I of this document, there is an interesting difference between this passage in the book of Isaiah and as quoted by Matthew. In Isaiah, the word used to describe non-Hebrew people was "nations". But Matthew, instead of "nations" used the word "gentiles". To me, this was a clear message that Matthew was saying that Jesus came to reach out to individuals, not political entities, again supporting the idea that Jesus did not come to earth to become an earthly, military conqueror. And this quote also confirmed that Jesus' ministry and salvation was not just for descendants of Abraham.

Jesus spoke to, and fed, 5000 people at one time

Matthew recorded two instances where Jesus was able to feed teaming crowds with very small food donations. The first was after Jesus had spent the day speaking to 5000 men and their families near the shore of the Sea of Galilee (a miracle in itself that all were able to hear him), he was able to feed them all with a small donation of only five loaves of bread and two fish, and even Philip, Jesus' disciple, questioned this . But the people were filled and there were a number of baskets of food left over (See Matthew 14:13-21, Mark 6:34-44, Luke 9:10-17, and John 6:1-15). How could this be?

One lesson here is that the power of Jesus word fills the soul. And the people ate and were satisfied without a lot of material abundance. Please see Deuteronomy 8:3b in the Old

Testament for these words spoken by Moses "...man does not live by bread alone, but by every word that comes from the mouth of the Lord."

But there is an extra lesson taught in Luke where Luke stated that Jesus prayed to God, his father, and thanked him for the miracle he was about to perform, a lesson to all of us that when we sit down to eat, we should thank God for the food we have before us.

Also, in John, three new pieces of information were introduced. First, to put this miracle in perspective; when asked, Philip said that it would cost at least 200 denarii (thousands of dollars) to feed that many people, but they did it with a free donation. Second, Jesus gave thanks to God before he started breaking the bread. And third, the perception of the greatness of the miracle among the people was so profound that if Jesus had not immediately gone into hiding, the crowd would have forcefully taken him and declared him king. *(I guess that the crowd was enamored by someone who could give them free food, "A desire for a Welfare State".)*

And another lesson here was that a few, under guidance of Jesus, can accomplish far more than anyone could imagine, even if they don't fully take into account Jesus' power and grace. Even Phillip, one of his disciples, didn't take that power into account, but who I am sure was taught a significant lesson by this miracle.

Jesus walked on water again (and again overcoming laws of nature)

The situation here was that after Jesus had fed the 5000, he sent his disciples ahead of him in a boat on the Sea of Galilee, while he went up on the mountain to pray. The boat was a long way from shore and was being battered by the wind and waves. Suddenly, they saw Jesus walking on the water toward them. At first they were quite frightened. But Jesus identified himself and told them not to be afraid. But Peter (who often spoke without thinking) said "if it is you, command me to come to you on the water". So Jesus told Peter to come to him. And Peter did. Maybe Peter was testing Jesus power over nature. However, the situation reversed. It became not a test of Jesus' power, but of Peter's faith, because Peter began to sink. And Jesus chided Peter for his sudden lack of faith and then rescued him. And then the storm let up (See Matthew 14:22-33, Mark 6:45-51, and John 6:16-21). Mark stated that Jesus had not intended to come to the boat, but had intended to walk on right by it. And that this is until he saw that they were frightened because they thought they had seen a ghost. So he stopped to reassure them that it was he, and told them to not be afraid. Also, Matthew claimed that the disciples worshiped Jesus and declared that he was **"truly the son of God". However,** Mark said that **"their hearts were hardened" (a differing opinion?).**. Why the difference I have no idea. Maybe there was a difference of opinion among the disciples. Mark indicated that they were troubled over the feeding of the five thousand. However, **in any case, this was definitely a miracle where Jesus proved again that he had power over nature.**

The Lesson here again was that Jesus possessed unimaginable power, not only over people's illnesses but over nature itself, as well as time and space.

This miracle is the second instance involving a storm on the sea. The boat containing the disciples was foundering as before. But this time, the theme of the story was not about so much as Jesus' power over nature, but rather a lesson in faith and trust. It was specifically about Peter's still imperfect faith in Jesus. But, like Peter, we all need to overcome our doubts. Remember, when we pray the Lord's Prayer, we need to trust implicitly in God's power, and have implicit trust in his love and judgement, as we say "Your will be done".

Another healing in non-Jewish territory, most likely not a Hebrew

After Jesus and the disciples had crossed the Sea of Galilee, they came ashore in the same area where Jesus had previously healed a violent man and sent his demons into a herd of pigs. After that event, the people there had asked him to leave. However, the word must have since spread widely about his healing powers. So they put aside their fears and welcomed him, and brought him many people to be healed. They also expressed their humility and belief in his power, by asking only to touch the hem of his garment. "And as many as touched it were made well." (See Matthew 14:34-36 and Mark 6:53-56)

Remember again that this area was not part of Judea or Galilee, and the people there were not necessarily descendants of Abraham (the same as the Roman soldier they were healed by faith, not because of their heritage. This is a lesson to all of us to know that Jesus is our saviour no matter where our ancestors came from. *But even though they believed in Jesus' power to heal, I am not sure they believed that he was the Messiah, the son of God. I will leave it up to the reader to decide.*

The lesson here was that this represented a second example that Jesus healed because of faith, not heritage, and even for someone who's race was condemned by Moses in the Old Testament. (The first example was the faith of a Roman soldier, who's race was looked down on by the people of the New Testament.)

Jesus healed a daughter of a <u>non-Hebrew</u> woman (faith vs. heritage)

The background for this miracle was that Jesus, in his travels again went outside Jewish territory into what is now Lebanon, where he encountered a Canaanite woman. She pleaded with him to heal her daughter who "was possessed by demon". In this Bible passage Jesus made two statements that seem to contradict what is proposed above. He first said to his disciples **"I was sent only to the lost sheep of the house of Israel"**. But she continued to plead with him. So then he said to her **"Is it right to take the children's bread and throw it to the dogs?"**. (These words could have been statements of common beliefs among the Jews, just to confirm her faith in him.) And she did confirm her belief in him, as well as demonstrating both humility and wisdom by saying to him **"Yes, Lord, yet even the dogs eat the crumbs that fall from the master's table"**. In this statement she also confirmed her sinfulness and again that she accepted Jesus as her Master. Thus, Jesus said **"O woman, great is your faith! Be it done for you as you desire"**. And thus, her daughter was instantly healed (See Matthew15:21-28 and Mark 7:24-30). Mark described the believing woman as a "Syrophoenician" instead of a "Canaanite". Either way, she was not of the children of Abraham, further proof that Jesus came to save everyone, not just the Jewish people. And as in Matthew, Mark confirmed that the healing was because of the faith of the little girl's mother.

Jesus fed 4000 (again with very little resources)

Jesus was again near the Sea of Galilee, and he again preached. However, this time he was surrounded by people who were seeking healing from various diseases. He had compassion on them and healed them all. And they all recognized he was healing in God's name, and they glorified God for their heeling. The crowd consisted of 4000 men, plus women and children. At the end of the day Jesus saw that they were hungry and he fed them and satisfied them all with only seven loaves of bread and a few small fish. And they had seven baskets of scraps left over (See Matthew 15:29-38 and Mark 8:1-9).

One lesson here was that by this time the people recognized that the healing came from God. And also, that there does not need to be riches and physical abundance to satisfy when the heeling of body and soul comes from God.

Jesus healed a boy with epilepsy

Jesus was approached by a man who begged for healing for his son, who he said often fell into fircs and water, and he confirmed that he had asked Jesus disciples to heal him and they could not. It was likely that his disease was epilepsy. We now know that epilepsy is caused by a congenital physical brain deformity. So unlike leprosy or a withered hand, this deformity could not be seen itself, but only the symptoms. In Jesus day it was thought to be caused by a demon. He told the disciples that their inability to heal the boy was because of their lack of faith. Then he healed the boy, correcting the physical flaw in the boy's brain (See Matthew 17:14-20, Mark 9:14 and Luke 9:27-43).

The lesson here, emphasized in Matthew, was that Jesus could even heal physical problems that were not visible to humans. Also, he intimated that even strong, proven believers such as priests, pastors, witnessers and soul winners, and others (including his own disciples) with strong faith and commitment, all of us are human, and all with flaws and doubts, and thus not perfect in the eyes of Christ, and are sometimes incapable. But we must remember that he came to save those very people, along with the rest of us who often struggle with our faith.

However; Mark gave far more detail about the reasons why the disciples were unable to heal the boy. The first was characterized by a statement of incomplete faith by the father of the boy, who cried out to Jesus **"I believe, help my unbelief"**. Then, after the boy was healed, the disciples asked Jesus in private why they couldn't heal him. Jesus told them **"This kind *(of demon)* cannot be driven out by anything but prayer"**.

To me, there are two lessons here taught in the Mark account not mentioned in Matthew. First, complete faith is required by the person asking for a miracle. And second, it appears that the *disciples were trying to heal by their own fallible faith, instead of <u>asking</u> God <u>(through prayer)</u> <u>for the power to do it, a seemingly minor but very important distinction</u>.*

Jesus restored the eyesight of two <u>more</u> blind men.

This is the second event of Jesus healing the blind, but this time with a different outcome. Jesus was on his way to Jerusalem for the last time before his crucifixion. He had just passed through Jericho beginning his long climb up into the high country where Jerusalem was located. A huge crowd of people were following him. Two blind men were sitting by the road. Matthew does not say how the knew who he was how they knew that he was a descendant of king David, but as he passed by they started crying out "Lord, have mercy on us, Son of David". The crowd tried to quiet them, but they kept on saying the same thing. And Jesus stopped and called out to them, saying **"What do you want me to do for you?"** They were probably beggars, depending on people to give them money because of their blindness. This was most likely their livelihood, and they would have depended on these gifts in order to live and feed themselves. But they didn't ask for money. They asked to be healed of their blindness. Jesus touched their eyes, and immediately they were able to see. And they immediately got up and started following him. Matthew doesn't say what the crowd thought, but they probably didn't expect this healing and would have been amazed (See Matthew20:29-33).

Mark and Luke record what appears to be the same event as Matthew. However, in Mark's and Luke's telling, there appears to be only one blind man instead of two (See Mark 10:46-52 and Luke 18:35-43) . And there is another difference in that Mark gave the name of the man who was healed, "Bartimaeus". The telling of the rest of the event and the lessons to be learned are essentially the same, with the healed person joining in with the group going up to Jerusalem with Jesus. All three tellings said that this miracle was seen by many.

There are several messages in this event. The first was that the blind man (or men) knew who Jesus was and of his power, without being able to see him. Can we, as sighted people, be able to recognize this? There most likely were many who traveled that same road daily. How did they know who he was, out of the crowd? A second is that they didn't ask for something that would satisfy their immediate needs so that they could go on with their existing lives. Instead, they asked something that would radically change their lives. They asked for physical sight. But the most powerful message in this event, was that they received sight into the salvation of Christ, and didn't just go away celebrating their good fortune like others who Jesus had healed before, but rather they began following him. May we all when we discover the salvation of Jesus not just go out with joy, but follow him like they did, up a steep mountain road that led to Jesus' ultimate sacrifice as the lamb of God.

Recap of the miracles of Christ according to Matthew

It is very interesting that although Matthew records a number of Jesus' miracles. Each one was different with different circumstances, different outcomes, and different lessons to teach us. Also, the methods and results were often different. Most of the miracles were about

healing people of various maladies. Of those, one such was the healing of a visible physical infection. One was the healing of an invisible internal infection. One was the healing of a mental disorder. One was the healing of a visible physical deformity. One was the healing of an internal invisible physical disorder. One was about the healing of a paralyzed person. Although a couple of them involved the healing of eyesight, each had a different lesson to be taught. And one was the actual bringing to life of someone who had died, and mourners were already preparing for a burial. Some involved Jesus' physical touch. One involved only a command. And a couple involved a healing without Jesus even seeing the person being healed. And at least one only involved the touching of Jesus' garment by the one being healed. A couple were based specific statements of faith by the persons asking for the healing miracle. And all healings were instantaneous without need for recuperation time or therapy. And several of the healings were of people not among the children of Israel or even sons of Abraham. In fact in one instance, Jesus informed his followers that such a heritage was no guarantee of any benefit, and several times he indicated that he was on earth to bring salvation to all people.

Other miracles involved overcoming the laws of nature. One was that he could be heard at one time by a crowd of possibly up to 10,000 people without benefit of any modern voice amplification system. Another was that he was able to feed eight or ten thousand people at one time with only a couple of loaves of bread and a few small fish. Twice he was able to calm a violent storm, and in one instance he was able to walk on water.

Every one of the individually described miracles in both Matthew and Mark had a lesson by which Jesus taught about his power, his persona, or his purpose on earth, or how, or what it means to be a believer.

None of Jesus' miracles involved incantations. magic wands, trances, or hallucinogenics. He didn't have to pray to God for power to perform these miracles, <u>because he was God on earth and had God's power within him.</u>

<u>So, now with miracle specifics that appear only in Mark</u>

Jesus healed a deaf man

(See Mark 7:31-37) This miracle again occurred outside of Jewish territory east of the Sea of Galilee, and on a man apparently not of Jewish heritage. And unlike the healing of a mute man in Matthew, this man could make sounds but could not speak coherently because of his deafness. Mark described in detail how Jesus went about healing him. And when he finished, the man could both hear and speak plainly. Then Jesus charged the man and the people who witnessed this miracle not to talk about it. However, he could not help himself, and widely spread the story of this miracle.

There were at least two lessons in this miracle. One was that again Jesus demonstrated that his will and power extended beyond salvation for the Jews. And a second was that he did not desire that people talk about these healing actions without recognition that the person performing this miracle was the Messiah.

Jesus healed a blind man in Bethsaida

(See Mark 8:22-26) The setting for this miracle is Bethsaida, a town located at the mouth of the upper Jordan river where it enters the Sea of Galilee. It is on the boundary between the Jewish west side of the sea and the gentile east side. This is a healing event that seems to be of special interest, because the man was brought to Jesus by a community, not him asking for healing himself, and also the method by which Jesus healed the man was different than the technique he had used in other blindness restoration miracles. *This could be assumed to be because the man had a unique type of blindness.* Mark describes in detail the way Jesus gave site to the man, using his spittle as well as touching his eyes. And when the man told Jesus his eyesight was not completely restored, Jesus touched his eyes a second time to fully heal him. But before Jesus healed him, he took the man away from the crowds and healed him in a private setting, not in public. And he told the man to go home, not back to the town.

I suspect that there were two reasons for Jesus to tell the man not to return to the town where he and the healing miracle would be recognized. One could have been that Jesus was concerned that he was receiving too much publicity for his healing miracles separate from faith in him as the Messiah. The other could have been because the unique method he used would have been tried by others with no result (because it was due to Jesus' healing power rather than technique), and the possible danger of infection to the person being treated when an unclean person tried to heal him.

Jesus cursed a non-fruit-bearing fig tree and it withered

(See Mark 11:12-14 and 11:20:25) This miracle is another startling example of the power of Jesus over nature, in that he used his power to actually kill an unproductive fig tree. One day it was alive and covered with leaves, and the next day it was withered and dead. This miracle may offend many of believers in Jesus, and cause them to question his image as the epitome of love and compassion. However, it is a graphic proof that Jesus expects all believers in him as the Christ, the Messiah, to be **"doers of the word and not hearers only"**. So we need to be warned that Jesus, as the Son of God, has the power to give and take away, and that we need to be productive in his kingdom here on earth.

Interestingly, when his disciples asked him about this event, he gave a very positive answer, talking about the power of prayer, and saying that if one fully believes in the effectiveness of prayer, it can move mountains. But he ended his words about the power of prayer with a word of advice, saying to them "And whenever you stand praying, forgive, if you have anything against anyone, so that your Father who is in heaven may forgive you your trespasses". In other words, don't expect your prayers to be effective unless your hearts are pure.

116

Recap of the miracles of Christ according to Mark

In most cases, the documentation in Mark of Jesus' miracles is a duplication of those events in Matthew. However, there are some differences, such as Mark's description of the healing of one insane person on the east side of the Sea of Galilee instead of two, as stated in Matthew. To me that might be attributable to variations in scripture translations over time, or a way that Matthew described a person with a split personality. Also, in Mark's description of the "walking on water" event, Peter's problem with belief was left out, and Matthew said that the disciples praised Jesus. Whereas in Mark they did not. (Maybe Matthew was awed, but maybe Mark was reflecting a possible contrary opinion [Judas]). Another difference is that Mark's descriptions of some of Jesus' miracles seemed more personal, because Mark mentioned several of those healed by name, whereas Matthew did not. Two miracle event descriptions were specifically unique to Mark. One was the direction of a gentile to go to his own people a tell of Jesus. Another was the condemnation of the unproductive fig tree. Both of these were strong lessons that believers in Jesus were expected not to just worship him, but also to witness for him.

Special Note: A *proposed reason for more than one gospel*

It is noted that both Matthew and Mark were written about the same time, about thirty years after Jesus was crucified. (Actually, Mark may have preceded Matthew by about five years, which would have made it the first gospel to be written.) Matthew, was written by one of Jesus' twelve disciples. The other was written by John Mark, one of Paul's disciples. However, the tenor of Mark's gospel strongly reflects an intimate personal witness to the events, as indicated by the names of some of the people who benefitted by the miracles. Tradition says that the person who is telling about Jesus through Mark was Peter, one of the inner circle among the disciples who may have been more often present when the miracles happened. This assumption seems quite valid; first, because of the action oriented tenor of the gospel like Peter, and second, the intimate detail of the events.

But moreover, Jesus' presence on earth was so profound and astonishing that it just wasn't possible for one writer to fully document and interpret all that occurred. And as we see by the sometimes different descriptions and interpretations of the same events by the two authors who were both intimate acquaintances of Jesus, that even though the two men were being guided by God in their authorship, their personalities and their memories could sometimes result in such differences. And in these differences, we must recognize that Jesus was not a creation of an individual author, but rather the primary, and only, subject of all four of the gospels, and was beyond the ability of any one author to describe.

Then there was Luke. He was a Greek, trained in logical processes, thus presenting Jesus in a different light. And he was able to provide some data not included in the Gospels of Matthew and Mark He became a companion of Paul during one of Paul's missionary trips. Andt he was not present in Israel during the time of Jesus' ministry. However, because of his scientific, analytical approach and his apparent research skills, he was able to accurately determine and document the story of Jesus' life and message. This can be noted by his approach, in that he laid out his gospel in time sequence order, from birth to death and resurrection. He most likely introduced his gospel about ten years after those of Matthew and Mark.

John, like Matthew was one of the original twelve disciples. Finally, about twenty of thirty years after the other three gospels were written, John wrote his gospel, where he added two elements to the previous gospels. One was that he "filled in the blanks" by telling the story of Jesus in a more personal, intimate light, and also setting it in a far more spiritual environment, emphasizing Jesus' heavenly persona. Thus, the gospel of John could almost tell the whole story of Jesus on its own.

Jesus' miracles as uniquely recorded in Luke

The gospel of Luke was most likely written at least ten or twenty years after Matthew and Mark. Luke was a gentile, the only one of the four gospel authors who was not a Hebrew. Moreover, he had not been present in Jewish territory at the time of Jesus' earthly ministry. Rather, he was a Greek disciple of Paul, who became a companion of Paul during Paul's later ministries, and went with him on several of his missionary journeys. It appears from his style of writing that he was trained in the Greek logical processes. Tradition says that he was also medically trained and was Paul's doctor, possibly treating Paul for what Paul called his "thorn in the flesh". Luke actually wrote two books of the New Testament. His second book was a chronological record of the "Acts of the Apostles" from just after Jesus' crucifiction until the end of the lives of those first generation apostles. Both books indicate that even though he was not present during Jesus earthly ministry, and not always present in Judea during the first several years afterward, he did an outstanding job of collecting first hand information about Jesus' life and about the early growth of the Judaen church, including the miracles performed during that time.

Jesus' first miracle recorded in Luke - Jesus' words alone had power

(See Luke 4:31-37) In his early ministry Jesus was driven out the town of Nazareth because he had stood up in the synagogue there and declared that he was the messiah. After this he went to the nearby town of Capernaum, where he continued his ministry in their synagogue. During one of his sermons there, a man stood up and challenged Jesus' authority in a loud voice. Jesus commanded the angry spirit in him to "be silent and come out of him". The man immediately collapsed on the floor without being touched. The others present were amazed at the power of Jesus' words.

The lesson here was that Jesus' words carried unimaginable power, (see John 1:1), enough power that physical touch and force were unnecessary.

Jesus gave a huge fish catch to Peter, James, and John

(See Luke 5:1-11) This, I believe, is the miracle that caused Peter, James and John to become full time, committed followers of Jesus. Peter, at the time, was called Simon. *He actually didn't acquire the name Peter until later when he made a full confession that he believed that Jesus "**was the Christ, the son of the living God**" (See Matthew 16:16). Jesus told him at that time that he would henceforth be called Peter (the Rock) instead of Simon. (Many believe that Jesus was referring to* *the person, Simon/Peter as the rock. However, I believe that what Jesus was referring to was the absolute belief/acceptance that was expressed by Peter as the rock on which Jesus would build his church, not Peter the person.)* At the time of the event described in Luke 5:1-11 Jesus was standing on the shore of the Sea of Galilee and saw two fishing boats beached on the shore at the end of the day. One belonged to Peter, and the other belonged to James and John. They had been out fishing that day but had caught nothing. Jesus first climbed into Peter's boat and used it as a platform to teach followers who had congregated there. Then he asked Peter to put his boat back in the water for a catch. At first Peter argued with him, saying that they had been out all day and caught nothing. However, Peter did as Jesus asked and immediately caught so many fish in his net that the net was in danger of breaking. James and John then launched their boat to help drag the net to shore. All three were greatly astonished at the size of the catch. Jesus then used this miracle to tell Peter, James, and John that if they followed him, he would make them **"fishers of men"**. They immediately walked away from their boats and became full time disciples of Jesus. (The calling of Peter, James, and John is also described in Matthew 4:18-20. However, neither Matthew nor Mark mentioned the miracle that caused them to give up their professions to follow Jesus.)

The lesson here was that Peter, James, and John just didn't all-of-a-sudden decide on their own to follow Jesus. Instead Jesus gave them a miraculous reason to do so. <u>May we as believers see the miraculous power of Jesus through the eyes of Peter, James, and John to fully accept him as our saviour.</u>

Jesus healed many who came to hear him

(See Luke 6:17-19) This also seems to be another telling of a time when Jesus taught and healed a vast multitude of people, not only from Jewish Judea and Galilee, but also from gentile Tyre and Sidon, cities now in Lebanon. However, the emphasis here seems to be on the healing aspect of his ministry, because the multitude crowded around him just to touch him for his healing power of both physical and mental problems.

A lesson here is again that Jesus made no distinction with respect to heritage. But also, unfortunately, that people sought Jesus' power often without knowing him or taking him and his message into their hearts. <u>We often take for granted the fact that the society we live in, is almost entirely based on trust and love that exists because of Jesus' teachings.</u>

Jesus raised a man from the dead

(See Luke 7:11-17) As Jesus was approaching a town, he encountered a funeral procession of a young man, he obviously was recognized by the whole town as having died. And the townspeople were headed out to dispose of his body. In this case Jesus didn't ask for belief in him, but instead simply determined to demonstrate his power and felt sorry for the mother who was a widow and had lost her only son. Jesus stopped the procession and simply said to the man **"young man, I say to you, arise"**, and he did and started speaking. The community reaction was shock and awe. And they glorified God, calling Jesus a "great prophet".

One lesson here was that Jesus could not only cure but also again had the power over physical death. A second lesson here was that sometimes the proper response for we Christians is to at least show compassion for those who are hurting.

Jesus healed a woman with a deformed back, <u>on the Sabbath</u>

(See Luke 13:10-17) Jesus was teaching in a synagogue on a Sabbath when he noticed a woman who had a severely deformed back so that she was bent over and could not stand straight. "And he laid his hands on her, and she was immediately made straight." She started glorifying God. But the synagogue ruler was very upset, because he felt that it was a sin to heal on the Sabbath. Jesus answered him by calling him a hypocrite, and gave the same justification as he did in another synagogue when he had healed a man with a withered hand (See Luke 6:6-18). With his justification, all those who had condemned him were put to shame, and all the people rejoiced.

Jesus healed a man with dropsy, also <u>on a Sabbath</u>

(See Luke 14:1-6) Again Jesus healed someone on a Sabbath and this time at a house of a ruler of the Pharisees where he was being carefully observed by those present, and he justified his action just as before (that healing is not prohibited on the Sabbath) . **It appears to me that Luke, as a doctor, wanted to emphasize that healing of physical problems was a high calling, superceding some pointless Jewish rules, supporting Jesus' statement elsewhere that the Sabbath was made for man, not man for the Sabbath.**

Jesus healed ten lepers

(See Luke 17:11-19) On Jesus' way to Jerusalem for the last time, he entered a village along the along the border between Galilee and Samaria. There he encountered ten lepers. They all asked to be healed. Jesus did not touch them, but told them instead to go to the local priests and show themselves. And while they were on the way, they were healed. Of the ten, only one of them went back to Jesus to thank and praise him. And it turned out that he was a Samaritan. **Jesus noted this and pronounced that is was not one's heritage, but his faith that healed him.**

Also, a lesson. If we are a recipient of a miracle, no matter how insignificant or rationally explainable, we must always remember to recognize God as the source of that miracle and to thank, honor and worship him for it.

<u>Jesus' miracles uniquely recorded in John</u>

Changing water into wine

(See John 2:1-11) As noted earlier, Jesus attended a wedding ceremony with his mother in the city of Cana in Galilee. This appears to be Jesus' first miracle recorded in the Bible. At this time he had already picked some of his disciples, probably Simon (Peter), Andrew, James, John, Philip, and Nathaniel, who accompanied him to the wedding. Apparently, either there were more guests or they were bigger drinkers than expected, and the host ran out of wine. And it appears that Mary was already familiar with Jesus' powers, so she asked him for help. After voicing some concern that he was not ready, he did what she asked in a miraculous way, turning several large jars of water into wine.

The lesson here is obvious. He gave us an early example of obeying one of the Ten Commandments, "Honor your father and your mother". But there was another lesson here, in that in Jesus' time and place, water was often tainted with disease causing microbes. By changing it to wine made it pure and safe to drink.

Healing of the Jewish official's son

After this he returned to Cana where John records a second miracle **(See John 4:46-54)**. There he was approached by a Hebrew official, who begged Him to heal his son, who was gravely ill. Jesus sent him on his way, assuring him that his son would live. It turned out that the child's fever broke the very hour that Jesus told the official that his son would live. So the official and all his household believed in Jesus. It appeared that the Jewish official had been unsure of Jesus' healing power, but came to believe when he saw his son actually get well. Also, this is another example of Jesus healing without even seeing the person being healed. But it was instead because of a request by a person who had a hope in Jesus, and who became a believer when he saw the miracle.

The lesson here was that it is possible to find Jesus' love and grace by even those who are not fully committed to him, so that those may see his full power and glory and become fully committed to a belief in him, thus turning believers into "true" believers.

Jesus healed an invalid

There was a pool just outside Jerusalem's Sheep Gate, called the pool of Bethesda, who's waters were believed to have had healing powers. But those powers could happen only when the waters were effervescent. There were a lot of ill and lame people lying around the pool waiting for the bubbles. When this happened, all of the people there tried to get into the water at once. And some were not able to. Jesus was again visiting Jerusalem, and saw a paralytic who had been there for 38 years waiting to get into the water when it was bubbling so he could be healed **(See John 5:2-9),** Jesus saw him and had pity on him. The man complained that there was noone who would help him into the pool. Instead of helping him into the pool, Jesus said "Get Up. Take up your bed and walk". And the man was immediately healed, and picked up his bed and walked away. However, Jesus had healed the man on the Sabbath, and orthodox Jews of the time thought healing or carrying anything on the Sabbath was a sin. **(See John 5:10-18)** Jesus told them he was doing God's work. So his detractors decided that this was the ultimate blasphemy, and thus decided that Jesus must die.

There is a lesson here, that with God's power, Jesus could perform miracles any time any place. But it also appeared that he was baiting his own people to decide that he was the

ultimate sinner even though he was not, to make sure he was to be the sacrifice for the sins of others.

Jesus healed a man blind from birth, again healing a not just a disease, but a physicao defority

(See John 9:1-41) Jesus healed several blind men. But this healing was unique in several ways. One was that the man had not become blind, but was blind from birth, indicating a significant birth defect. A second was that the disciples assumed that his blindness was the result of some sin that he or his parents had committed. Jesus told them that this assumption was not true. But rather that his blindness and his healing were to further demonstrate the **"the works of God"** and also to show that he, Jesus, was the **"light of the world"** (see also the story of Job in the Old Testament). Then he went about a unique procedure to heal the man and restore his eyesight. First, he spat on the ground and made some mud with his saliva. Then he put the mud on the blind man's eyes and told him to go to go to the pool of Siloam in Jerusalem and wash the mud out of his eyes there. **He did as Jesus directed, and his sight was restored.** He then returned to wherever he had been begging on the street as a blind man. Some of the people who knew him before were shocked and awed by his sudden capability to see. Others refused to believe that a miracle had taken place and assumed that this was a different person. But the man assured them that he was the same person who had been blind. They first asked where Jesus was and he said he didn't know. The people then took him to some pharisees, who at first refused to believe he has been blind, but then changed their minds and asked who did this to him. And it turned out that Jesus had healed him on the Sabbath. So some of the pharisees decided that Jesus was of the devil because they said he broke a law of the Sabbath. Others still didn't believe the man had been healed until they talked to his parents, who assured them of his previous blindness. Then they told him to give God the glory, but not Jesus. When he refused, they tossed him out of the assembly. Later, Jesus found him and explained that he was the Messiah, the Son of Man (see Daniel Chapter 9). And the previously blind man believed in him and worshiped him. Then he rebuked the pharisees for their unbelief.

There are several lessons taught by this miracle and the followup actions. First of all, the man healed was blind from birth. This meant that his blindness was most likely caused by a birth defect, not by disease or aging. Therefore, his blindness had a much more severe source. This means that Jesus' miracle here was more that just healing, but instead a basic change in the man's physical makeup, a more remarkable proof of Jesus' power.

A second lesson is that the healing was not by a standard process, but was by a process that Jesus tailored specifically to the man's need. This demonstrated Jesus' remarkable knowledge of the human condition, and again demonstrated that it was his personal power, not a process, that did the healing.

Third, the miracle required not only faith but also action by the man being healed. He had to go someplace and take a specific action for the healing to take place, the washing off of the mud at the pool of Siloam.

Fourth, even though the blind man's acquaintances were presented with first-hand visual proof of his healing, some didn't believe that the person in front of them was actually healed (maybe even a different Person?). When they took him to the governing authorities, the people who were considered earthly wise and religious leaders (the pharisees), these so-called authorities also doubted the miracle. And they asked for more information about Jesus, not to believe in him but to find some flaw. And they discovered that Jesus had performed this miracle on a Sabbath, so even though they may have recognized the miracle, they condemned Jesus, because they decided he "broke the Old Testament rule about working on the Sabbath". And they also condemned the miracle by deciding that Jesus was "of the devil". This again showed blind subservience to an interpretation of a rule, without considering the valid exception to the rule that produced a marvelous outcome. And so, they also condemned the man who was healed. *This type of attitude has unfortunately been repeated over and over again throughout the history of Christianity, where good things have been condemned because they didn't fit a preconceived human assumptions. One example of this was that a man, William Tyndale, was burned at the stake for translating the Bible into English. Another example was that Galileo was tossed out of the church and jailed because he declared that the earth was not the center of the universe.* We now accept both the English Bible translations and Galileo's discovery. *How much other new knowledge or discoveries are Christians condemning today because they don't fit traditional assumptions?*

Another lesson was that Jesus cared enough about the man to later follow up with him. *This is an example that teaches that we, as Christians, need to follow up with new converts, or Christians new to our communities of believers, or believers who have experienced a traumatic event; to befriend, to nurture them, and include them in our assemblies.*

Jesus raised Lazarus from the dead, <u>a very important event</u>

(See John 11:1-44) Sisters Mary and Martha, who were friends and followers of Jesus, lived in the town of Bethany in Judea about two miles east of Jerusalem. Lazarus, their brother also lived nearby. They must have become friends and followers of Jesus during one or more of his trips to Judea. Lazarus became ill, and the sisters sent word to Jesus, with the news that Lazarus was ill, and they asked him to come, having faith that Jesus could heal Lazarus. But Jesus was most likely in Galilee at the time (several days walking distance from Bethany). Also, Jesus waited a couple of days to start his trip to Bethany. I suspect that he knew that he could not arrive in Bethany before Lazarus would die. And before he started, he made a very interesting statement. He said **"Lazarus has fallen asleep, but I go to awaken him"** (See John 11:11). How did he know that Lazarus had died? And by the time he arrived in Bethany, he found that indeed Lazarus had not only died but had already been buried in a cave.

Martha went out to meet Jesus and chided him for not being there in time to heal Lazarus. But she did have enough belief in Jesus and his teachings that she said, as documented in John 11:21- 26, as follows: "Martha said to Jesus, Lord, if you had been here, my brother would not have died". (Even though Jesus had already healed someone without being there. But obviously, Jesus had a different teaching purpose.) And Martha continued by saying, "But even now I know that whatever you ask from God, God will give you." And Jesus said to her, "Your brother will rise again". "Then Martha said to him, I know that he will rise again in the resurrection on the last day." Then Jesus said to her, **"I am the resurrection and the life. Whoever believes in me, though he die, yet shall he live, and everyone who believes in me shall never die. Do you believe this?"** Martha said to him, "Yes Lord, I believe that you are the **Christ, the Son of God**..."

Then Martha called Mary to come to meet Jesus as well. And Mary expressed the same sorrow and grief. But neither of them really still understood the extent of Jesus' power over life and death, nor the reason for his assumed delay in coming to them. Nevertheless, Jesus recognized and empathized with their grief and was moved to tears (See John 11:35). They took him to Lazarus' tomb. And during this time, several of the people with them kept asking themselves why had Jesus not shown up in time to keep Lazarus from dying, again recognizing neither Jesus' purpose nor the extent of his power. When they arrived at the grave, Jesus asked them to remove the stone from the grave opening. Martha, being the practical one, said "By this time there will be an odor", assuming that decay had set in. But Jesus said to her **"Did I not tell you that if you believed, you would see the glory of God?"**. Next, Jesus prayed to his father, God, that they would believe more fully in him, Then, Jesus cried out with a loud voice **"Lazarus come out"**. **And he did**, still bound with the cloths that they had wrapped him in for burial. Then Jesus commanded those present to unwrap him and let him go. **WOW**.

There are five primary lessons in this event. The first was Jesus' ability to know about events without being told (i.e Jesus uncanny foreknowledge about Lazarus' death). The second was that even if we Christians believe in the ultimate power of the Christ and have come face to face with him, we still have trouble comprehending it. The third was Jesus' caring and empathy for grief and loss. The forth was a demonstration of Jesus' ultimate power over life and death. The fifth was that this event was a remarkable pre-view for Jesus own death and resurrection.

Side note: This trip to Bethany and then on to Jerusalem was Jesus' last visit there that ended in Jesus' crucifixion, only a few weeks later. The frightful end outcome of this trip was actually forecast after a discussion among the disciples about the deadly danger of going back to Judea. This discussion was ended by the disciple Thomas, who said about Jesus just before Jesus started his trip "Let us all go so we can die with him". One may also notice a particular similarity between Lazarus' tomb and Jesus' tomb. Both were in a cave who's entrance was covered by a stone.

The aftermath of the resurrection of Lazarus

Apparently the word of Lazarus' miraculous resurrection almost immediately reached the Judaic ruling body, the Sanhedrin. It generated a lot of discussion among the members about the impact of Jesus' power and influence on the future of Judea. The pharisees were not only afraid of losing their position of power and authority, but were also afraid that the Romans would use the turmoil that Jesus was creating in disrupting "the normal order of things", to take over full control pf Judea and eliminate the local government. They decided, in counsel, that a drastic step was required. **In** fact, Caiaphas, the chief priest, pronounced a lethal decision, when he said ".. It is better for you that one man should die for the people, not that the whole nation should perish." (See John 11:50), pronouncing, before-hand a death sentence. B*ut we shall see that this was God's plan all along. And we shall also see in Part III of this document, that about forty years later, the nation of Israel was actually destroyed by Rome, the very event that the Sanhedrin was trying to prevent. And in the process, the Roman army razed the temple, the center of Jewish worship, to the ground and slaughtered the last holdouts at Masada. And it was not because of Jesus, but because of the unwillingness of the Jewish power structure to accept Jesus as the promised Christ, the Messiah.*

But the condemning of Jesus to death was not enough for Ciaphas because he felt that even if Jesus were put to death, Lazarus' resurrection would still bare witness to Jesus' power and authority. So he decided that Lazarus should be put to death as well (See John 12:9-11). Unfortunately, the Bible does not indicate if this additional execution was ever carried out.

A summation of Jesus' miracles as recorded in the Gospel of John

John actually recorded a smaller number of Jesus' miracles than the other gospels. However, John generally described them, the procedures Jesus used, and the results, in more graphic detail than in the other gospels. For someone who set them down in writing, John appears to have had a better understanding of the environment of the events and the lessons to be learned. This, even though John recorded these a number of years after the other gospels were written, indicating a most intimate understanding of Jesus' intent and purpose.

A summation of all the miracles performed by Jesus

First of all, all of them were performed, not for esoteric reasons, but rather to teach several things. One of those things was to help people recognize and respect his absolute power (over nature, disease, birth defects, and physical death) to prove that he was indeed the son of the most high God. A second was to prove that he had an ultimate knowledge of the human condition and the way people thought. A third was to demonstrate the love of God for mankind. Also, he showed that he did not come to earth to heal everyone just for esoteric reasons, or to provide eternal life (See the story in Genesis where God expelled Adam and Eve from the Garden of Eden so that they would not live forever like the angels (See Genesis 3:22-23)), But he came rather to provide a way for a person's essence (soul) to find eternal life in heaven with God. Thus, these miracles were really just another step to provide the eternal to all humans.

Part II Section 6 - Jesus was also a prophet

Jesus prophesied that he would be killed as a martyr, but would rise from the dead three days afterward.

Despite a lot of beliefs about the coming Messiah, even among his disciples, that Jesus was to set up an earthly kingdom, Jesus repeatedly told both his enemies and his followers that his penultimate mission on earth was that he would be sacrificed as the once-for-all pass-over lamb, and also that he would rise from the dead on the third day. All four gospels record the fact that Jesus told his followers and others several times that he would be killed. Matthew documents one such statement in Matthew 12:38-40 when he told some scribes and Pharisees when they asked for a sign of his authority, he said **"An evil and adulterous generation seeks a sign, but no sign will be given to it except the sign of Jonah. For just as Jonah was three days and three nights in the belly of the great fish, so will the Son of Man be three days and three nights in the heart of the earth".** This statement is repeated by Jesus in Matthew 16:4. Then at the "Last Supper" when Jesus was just one day from being nailed to a cross, he told his select disciples that he himself was the pass-over lamb, by offering to them bread that he said represented his body, and wine that represented his blood. **In Mark 8:31 Jesus told his followers plainly that he would be rejected by the elders, chief priests, and scribes and be killed, but would rise on the third day.** Also in Mark 9:30-31 he repeated this to his disciples by saying **"The son of man is going to be delivered into the hands of men, and they will kill him". But he also assured them he would rise from the dead three days later.** Then Jesus said it again in Mark 10:33-34, including assurance of his resurrection after three days, when he was preparing to go to Jerusalem for the last time Mark also writes in his Chapter 14:22-24 of the last supper, and the offering by Jesus of the bread as his body and the wine as his blood, indicating that he himself would be the ultimate pass-over lamb.

Luke documented three occasions where Jesus told of this mission. Once was to the scribes and Pharisees (See Luke 9:22) where he told his disciples that he would be rejected by the **"elders and chief priests and scribes, and be killed, and on the third day be raised".** Then Luke documents in Luke 11:29 that Jesus told crowds of people that what happened to Jonah would happen to him as well. Then in Luke 18:32-33 Jesus told his disciples on their way to Jerusalem for the last time, that **"he will be delivered over to the gentiles and will be mocked and shamefully treated and spit upon. And after flogging him, they will kill him, and on the third day he will rise."** Then on the eve of the pass-over when Jesus was dining with the twelve, Luke tells in Luke 22:15-20 that Jesus offered his body and blood for those who believed in him.

John reported in John 7:33 when Jesus was speaking to a crowd, the Pharisees sent officers to arrest him. **"Jesus then said, 'I will be with you a little longer, and then I am going to him who sent me.'"** John also writes in John 10:11 **"I am the good shepherd. The good shepherd lays down his life for the sheep."** Then in John 12:24 as Jesus was nearing the time of his execution he said about himself **"Truly, truly, I say to you, unless a grain of wheat falls into the earth and dies, it remains alone; but if it dies it bares much fruit."** Then in John 12:27 Jesus said that his soul was troubled as he prayed in the Garden of Gethsemane, asking God to save him from this hour. But then followed this by saying **"for this purpose I have come to this hour."** This particular prayer dialog is recorded to varying degree in three of the gospels (See Matthew 26:36-42, Mark 14:35-36, and Luke 22:41-42.) (John, on the other hand, emphasized the part of Jesus' Gethsemane prayer where he prayed for his disciples.)

Jesus predicted how two specific disciples would act when he was arrested

He predicted that Judas would betray him to authorities (See Matthew 26:21-23, Mark 14:18-20,and John13:21-26). And he predicted that Peter would deny three times that he was a follower of Jesus during Jesus' trial (See Matthew 26:34, Mark 14:29-30, Luke 22:34, and John 13:37-38).

Jesus prophesied that the temple in Jerusalem would be destroyed

Jesus predicted that the Temple, the center of the Jewish faith and earthly residence of God, would be utterly and completely destroyed (See Matthew 24:1-2, Mark 13:1-2, and Luke 21:5-6). This did actually happen in about 70 AD at the hand of the Roman army. *To me this was a dramatic symbol that the center of the belief in God would no longer be in an edifice built by men, but instead be in the hearts of men, **and that the covenant given by God through the law of Moses was being replaced by the new covenant given by God through <u>grace and truth </u>of Jesus Christ*** (See John 1:17). Many Christians I have talked to or heard seem to think that maybe Jesus was talking about himself instead of the temple building in Jerusalem. However, there are several referenced that Jesus made about his death and resurrection that differ from this particular statement. Therefore, I believe that Jesus, in this case, was referring specifically to the temple on the temple mount in Jerusalem, which was rased to the ground by the Romans in 70 AD.

Shortly after this in Luke 21:10-15. Jesus predicted in that there would be wars and persecution. And he told his followers that they would be arrested and brought before kings and judges for judgement. However, this would be a good thing, because it will give them opportunities to witness about the way, the kingdom of heaven, and their faith (See the narration of Paul's arrest and incarceration in Part III).

Jesus prophesied that he would come to earth again

Jesus taught that he would return to earth, but in a different role than of a teacher and sacrifice for sins. This time he would return as a judge and prosecutor. His predictions about his return may be divided into three major parts. One is what would be harbingers of his return. A second is how he would appear to the people. And third, what would he do when he appears. But, he also warned that it would be a vain exercise to try to predict when he would return.

Of course, he appeared to his intimate followers shortly after his death. But he specifically also told his followers that, after he went to sit on the right hand of God, he would return at a later time, "at the end of the age", *which to me really means the end of time, the end of all things. Among theologians there are three views of the end, Pre-millenialism (the view that Christ will return to rule on earth for a period peace before the end of time), A-millenailism (the view that Christ will return concurrent to the end of time), and Post-millenialism (the assumption that the return of Christ will be after the end). The Book of Revelation in the New Testament (which is basically a book of mystic poetry) tends to hint at "Pre", Concurrent with, and "Post" without a clear distinction. However, I believe that what Jesus himself taught in the gospels was that Christ would return concurrent with the end. That is my view.*

Jesus prophesied that salvation and eternal life will be for many who are not of Hebrew heritage

In Matthew 8:11 Jesus prophesied that **"many will come from east and west and recline at table with Abraham, Isaac, and Jacob in the kingdom of heaven"**. Some people may say that Jesus was referring to the return of Jews to Israel. However, it was said in the context of the healing of a servant of a Roman soldier, **because of the faith of that Roman**. Jesus was definitely predicting that salvation would be available to all humanity, not just the DNA descendants of Abraham, Isaac and Jacob. This apparently tended to rankle a number of Jews, even among the believers, who seemed to hold on to the idea that the Messiah would come as an earthly king of the Jews only, who would be destined to reestablish an independent Jewish monarchy on earth.

Jesus prophesied what the end of the age will be like

First what is meant by the "end of the age". I believe it is when time ends and all things stop, the end of time. And, Jesus very graphically described what would happen before then. The gospel of Matthew appears to contain the most comprehensive and most graphic description of what Jesus said must happen before the end comes. Matthew chapter 24 begins in verse 3 with a dialog between Jesus and his followers, thus **"As he sat on the Mount of Olives, the disciples came to him, privately saying, tell us when these things will be, and what will be the sign of your coming and of the close of the age."** Jesus proceeds, starting in verse 4, telling of and warning of the worldwide events that will occur before the end **"See that no one leads you astray. For many will come in my name, saying 'I am the Christ', and they will lead many astray. And you will hear of wars and rumors of wars. See that you are not alarmed, for this must take place, but the end is not yet. For nation will rise up against nation, and kingdom against kingdom, and there will be famines and earthquakes in various places. All these are but the beginning of the birth pains."** Then, starting in verse 9, he turns to more specifics about how these events will affect Jesus' followers by saying **"Then they will deliver you up to tribulation and put you to death, and you will be hated by all nations for my name's sake And then many will fall away and betray one another and hate one another. And many false prophets will arise and lead many astray. And because lawlessness will be increased, the love of many will grow cold. But (*any*) one who endures to the end will be saved. And this gospel of the kingdom (of God) will be proclaimed throughout the whole world as a testimony to all nations, and then the end will come"**. The "end" of course will be when the Christ will return. This prophesy is repeated almost verbatim in Mark 13:3-12. Here he repeats a condition in verse 10 that before the end that **"the gospel must be proclaimed to all nations"**. However, this has not yet happened even though many are trying. Will we know when this happens? Most likely not.

Jesus prophesied the coming of "The abomination"

Then in Matthew 24, verse 15 and Mark 13:14 Jesus becomes even more specific by identifying an individual or power called **"the <u>abomination of desolation</u> as spoken by the prophet Daniel, standing in the holy place (let the reader understand),"** (See Daniel 9:27, 11:31, and 12:11 in the Old Testament) (Also, the apostle John spoke of an individual called the **"Anti-Christ"** in Chapter 2 verses 18 and 22 in the first of his letters later in the New Testament that also may be associated with the **"abomination"**). Then in Matthew 24 verse 16 Jesus told his followers to **"flee to the mountains"**. And then in verses 17-21 he told of the tragedies that will befall those who stay behind. Following this in verses 23-25 Jesus repeated the statement that many false Christs and false prophets will come.

*This prophesy by Jesus has also been misinterpreted by many, who have decided on their own, who was or is the "**the abomination of desolation**" as a harbinger of the end of time. Some recently said it was Adolph Hitler. Others have, over the centuries, named other earthly despots like Napoleon, and Roman emperor Nero, all obviously in error. I think the most suspect would have been when the Muslims built the Blue Mosque on the site of the Jerusalem temple. But of course, the end of time didn't occur then either. We are still waiting. But Jesus said that we will recognize this "**Abomination**", and more often than not, many might be led astray by such an entity. So we need to beware and recognize this imposter. **Also, this imposter might be a general destructive attitude of a multitude of people, not just an individual.***

Jesus prophesied that the timing of the "end" <u>cannot</u> be foretold

I have an opinion about the above prophesies. It is this, that Jesus was not saying that the above happenings were signs that the end was near, because both the man-made and the natural disasters (wars, rumors of wars, famines and earthquakes) have occurred in every century and even in every generation, both long before and ever since Jesus was crucified. However, in every generation someone will rise up and say "These are the signs that the end is very near". But, Jesus himself is quoted in both Matthew 24:36 and also in Mark 32-33 *as stating* **"concerning that day and hour no one knows, not even the angels of heaven, nor the son, but the father only."** *This prophesy is also mentioned in Luke 12:40. Yet men continue to predict the end of times, and even set specific dates, sometimes with disastrous results, like mass poisonings. But Instead of giving a set of circumstances, Jesus said in Matthew 24:42* **"Therefore, stay awake, for you do not know on what day the lord is coming.** And also in Matthew 34:44 Jesus said **" Therefore, you also must be ready, for the Son of Man is coming at an hour you do not expect."** And Luke, chapter 17 also gave examples that indicated when previous destructive events occurred (the Genesis flood and the destruction of Sodom), noone knew beforehand that they would happen.

But Jesus prophesied that his second coming will be quite obvious

Jesus then told his followers there will be no need to look for him when he comes because his coming will be obvious, saying in Matthew 24:27 **"For as the lightning comes from the east and shines as far as the west, so will be the coming of the Son of Man"**. And then he continued by elaborating in verses 29-30 by saying **"...the sun will be darkened and the moon will not give off light, and the stars will fall from heaven, and the powers of the heavens will be shaken. Then will appear in heaven the sign of the Son of Man coming on the clouds of heaven with power and great glory"**. *Double Wow, an appearance far beyond anything we might imagine.*

Jesus prophesied what he will be and do when he arrives a second time

When Christ came to earth the first time, he came to teach how the people should live, and also to die as a sacrifice for our sins. The second time he will come as a **judge**. In Matthew 25:31-35 Jesus said of himself in the third person **"When the Son of Man comes in his glory, and all the angels with him, then he will sit on his glorious throne. Before him will be gathered all of the nations, and he will separate people one from another as a shepherd separates the sheep from the goats. And he will place the sheep on his right, but the goats on the left. Then the king will say to those on his right, 'Come, you who are blessed of my father, inherit the kingdom prepared for you from the foundation of the world'."** And then in Matthew 25:41 he said **"that he will say to those on his left,'Depart from me, you cursed into the eternal fire prepared for the devil and his angels'."** And he also empathized again that his salvation would not be for just the Jews because both Matthew in 24:31 and Mark 13:27 tell that the Christ **"will then send out the angels and gather his elect from the four winds, from the ends of the earth to the ends of heaven." And there will be no escape from his judgement.**

Part II Section 7 - Jesus prepared for his martyrdom

During his earthly ministry, Jesus accomplished a very logical series of activities to assure his martyrdom, specifically as the ultimate and final Passover lamb.

First, he selected group of disciples who he meticulously taught. Some of whom, given the help of the "Holy Spirit", would perpetuate his message throughout the world. And at least one other one (Judas Iscariot) would be an instrument in the carrying out of his earthly purpose of becoming the martyr as the Passover Lamb of God. *(I believe he picked Judas Iscariot as one of his twelve disciples because he recognized Judas' strong conviction that the purpose of the Messiah was to command an army of loyalists to throw off the Roman rule and set up and earthly kingdom, and that Judas would take a decisive action to try to force that role on Jesus, even to the point of betraying him.)*

Second, Jesus developed a strong, loyal following by performing numerous miracles that convinced a huge group among both Hebrews and also others (Greeks, Romans, Canaanites, Samaritans, etc.) with which he came in contact, that he was not just a prophet, but the actual son of the Most High God of the universe, and thus, he deserved their undying awe and respect, and also that he had come to serve and not be served.

Third, Jesus told his followers that he would be killed, but would rise from the dead three days afterward. That, despite a lot of beliefs about the coming Messiah, even among his disciples, that Jesus was to set up an earthly kingdom, Jesus repeatedly told both his enemies, and his followers, that his pen-ultimate mission on earth was that he would be sacrificed as the once-for-all Passover lamb, and also that he would rise from the dead on the third day. All four gospels record the fact that Jesus told his followers and others several times that he would be killed. Matthew documented one such statement in Matthew 12:38-40 when he told some scribes and Pharisees when they asked for a sign of his authority, he said **"An evil and adulterous generation seeks a sign, but no sign will be given to it except the sign of Jonah. For just as Jonah was three days and three nights in the belly of the great fish, so will the Son of Man be three days and three nights in the heart of the earth"**. This statement is repeated by Jesus in Matthew 16:4. Then at the "Last Supper" when Jesus was just one day from being nailed to a cross, he told his select disciples that he himself was the Passover lamb, by offering to them bread that he said represented his body, and wine that represented his blood. **In Mark 8:31 Jesus told his followers plainly that he would be rejected by the elders, chief priests, and scribes and be killed, but would rise on the third day.** Also in Mark 9:30-31 he repeated this to his disciples by saying **"The son of man is going to be delivered into the hands of men, and they will kill him". But he also assured them he would rise from the dead three days later.** Then Jesus said it again in Mark 10:33-34, including assurance of his resurrection after three days, when he was preparing to go to Jerusalem for the last time Mark also wrote in Chapter 14:22-24 of the last supper in his gospel, and the offering by Jesus of the bread as his body and the wine as his blood, indicating that he himself would be the ultimate pass-over lamb.

Luke documented three occasions where Jesus told of this mission. One was to the scribes and Pharisees (See Luke 9:22) where he told his disciples that he would be rejected by the **"elders and chief priests and scribes, and be killed, and on the third day be raised".** Then Luke documented in Luke 11:29 that Jesus told crowds of people that what happened to Jonah would happen to him as well. Also in Luke 18:32-33 Jesus told his disciples on their way to Jerusalem for the last time, that **"he will be delivered over to the gentiles and will be mocked and shamefully treated and spit upon. And after flogging him, they will kill him, and on the third day he will rise."** Then on the eve of the pass-over when Jesus was dining with the twelve, Luke tells in Luke 22:15-20 that Jesus offered his body and blood for those who believed in him.

Also, John reported in chapter 7, verse 33 in his gospel that when Jesus was speaking to a crowd, the Pharisees sent officers to arrest him. **"Jesus then said, 'I will be with you a little longer, and then I am going to him who sent me."** He also wrote in John 10:11 **that Jesus said "I am the good shepherd. The good shepherd lays down his life for the sheep."** Further, in John 12:24, as Jesus was nearing the time of his execution, he said about himself **"Truly, truly, I say to you, unless a grain of wheat falls into the earth and dies, it remains alone; but if it dies it bares much fruit."** Then, in John 12:27, as Jesus prayed in the Garden of Gethsemane, he said that his soul was troubled and asked God to save him from his execution. But then he followed this by saying **"for this purpose I have come to this hour."** This particular prayer dialog is also recorded to varying degree in all of the other gospels (See Matthew 26:36-42, Mark 14:35-36, and

Luke 22:41-42.) (John, on the other hand, emphasized the part of Jesus' prayer in the Garden of Gethsemane where he prayed for his disciples.)

Fourth, Jesus disrupted the accepted order of business in the temple by driving out money changers, thus alienating priests and other temple caretakers who were responsible for maintaining order in the temple complex, and who might have been profiteering from these businesses.

Fifth, Jesus went out of his way to make enemies of the leaders of Judea, insulting the priests by saying that he was the promised Messiah, and insulting the Pharisees, by accusing them of misleading the people with overly specific rules, for setting bad examples of righteousness, and for teaching rituals instead of the truth of God. In this way he was telling the truth, but also assuring the undying hatred and fear of him by those leaders, thus guaranteeing that they, as a group, would have a strong desire to condemn him and to assure his death.

Sixth, he also set up the timing of his sacrifice by traveling to Jerusalem for the celebration of the Passover, assuring that he would be put to death at the Passover. And that the anger and fear by the Judaen leaders was so strong that those feelings hid from them the fact that he was fulfilling a powerful and meaningful Old Testament prophecy. Added to this was the overarching hatred of the Romans by many Jews, which made them believe that the purpose of the Messiah was to overthrow the Roman rule and set up an "eternal" earthly Hebrew kingdom, instead of introducing the Godly, heavenly kingdom that Jesus taught.

Seventh, after he was arrested and was brought before the high priest, Jesus challenged him to justify why he was arrested, questioning his authority, infuriating him.

Eighth, when he was taken to the council of elders, where the high priest acted as prosecutor, who demanded that Jesus say who he was, Jesus caused a near riot among the priests by telling them that he was Christ, the Messiah, the Son of God (See Mark 14:60-69), a declaration that they clearly could not handle. This of course caused these leaders to generate condemnations among enough citizens to perpetrate a riot among the general population when Jesus was brought before the Roman governor, so much so that the Roman governor gave in to their demands (See John 18:38-40).

Part II Section 8 - The events of the last Passover week, up to and including the Lord's Supper

Jesus visited Jerusalem for the last time the week of his crucifixion. The first thing he did was to send his disciples into a nearby village to borrow a donkey. He was to ride this donkey into Jerusalem as a fulfillment of an Old Testament prophesy (See Zechariah 9:9).

Jesus entered the city on the first day of the Passover week on the donkey, to the high acclaim of his followers, who laid palm fronds in his path. Then he spent the next three days in the

holy Jerusalem temple, cleansing it of profiteers, healing the sick, and teaching his message. (A synopsis of his message there was best documented in John 13:31– 16:15. On the fourth day, he and his inner circle of disciples found a large room above a stable in which to hold a Passover meal. They prepared this meal on the fourth day according to the Old Testament tradition and then gathered there to eat the meal traditionally called the "Lord's Supper".

WHAT HAPPENED AT THE LORD'S SUPPER

The Passover lamb was to be prepared on Thursday so that it could be eaten on Friday, the day of the Passover. Thus, Jesus and his disciples did not eat together on the Passover day as many often assume, but instead on Thursday, the Day of Preparation. Jesus carried out several very important actions during this meal. This sequence of events during the Lords Supper are enumerated as follows.

The ritual of foot washing

The first significant act that Jesus performed at that dinner was to wash the disciples' feet. This act was important in several ways. First of all, he and his disciples had just walked for several days on dusty roads from Galilee to Jerusalem, and then had spent several days walking in and around the temple. They were wearing open sandals, not shoes, and their feet would be very dirty. So it was obvious that, if they to were to enter upon a very holy event, they should not participate without being cleansed (See John 13:3-5). Jesus' offering to wash their feet, first of all, was to notify them that this meal was to be very special. And was to be thought as more than just a Passover celebration.

But this act was to serve two purposes. One was to reminding them that he was not royalty to be served, but he was there to serve them. This was a firm and natural fulfillment of his teaching at the "sermon on the mount", that "the meek (*those who serve*) shall inherit the earth". But in the midst of this action, Peter said he didn't think this act of abeyance was proper. However, when Jesus explained to him **"What I am doing you do not understand now, but afterward you will understand**, (See John 13:7) (Also see 1st Corinthians 13:12). Then Jesus told Peter something somewhat of a dire warning, when Jesus said to him **"If I do not wash you, you have no share with me"** (See John 13:6), so Peter's put aside his pride and he relented (apparently a reference to baptism with water).

The second purpose of this act was a call his disciples to also be servants by telling them; **"Do you understand what I have done to you? You call me teacher and lord, and you are right, for so I am. If I then, your lord and teacher, have washed your feet, you also ought to wash one another's feet. For I have given you an example."**

The act by Christians of washing each other's feet is no longer generally practiced. However, the practice still exists. Sam Rayburn, a former speaker of the US House of Representatives, was also a member of a small "foot washing" Baptist church in north-east Texas. And the Catholic pope practices it annually. And Jesus told us we should do it. Of course, today we no longer walk to church, and usually wear shoes instead of sandals. However, Jesus himself told his disciples to do it in acknowledgment of him as our "teacher and lord" but also our servant. Many might assume that the practice has been overtaken by believer's baptism (See Peter's request in John 13:9). So we rarely recognize foot washing as a part Christian worship today. However, it most likely needs to be revived as a form of worship.

As a matter of logistics, the practice of foot washing is not practical among large assemblies. It would be more practical in small groups of believers such as in individual Bible classes. Also, since there is an element of intimacy involved, such a small group might be more appropriate. And it is something to be seriously considered.

The identification of the betrayer

The second thing Jesus did was to announce to those present, that someone in their midst would betray him. Then he actually told John, personally, who it would be, and specifically pointed Judas Iscariot out to John (See John 13:25-26). But like Peter, John apparently did not fully understand what was about to happen, and that it would happen that very night, So he took no action. However, Judas did. He left the table and the gathering.

The commandment to love one another

The third thing Jesus did was to give his disciples what he called a "**new commandment**". He said "**A new commandment I give to you, that you love one another; just as I have loved you, you also are to love one another. By this all people will know that you are my disciples, if you have love for one another** " (See John 13:34-35).

An identification of human weaknesses

Then, Jesus had a verbal exchange with Peter, where Peter exclaimed his undying loyalty to Jesus. But Jesus told Peter that Peter would deny his association with Jesus three times before the following dawn. It appears that Jesus well understood Peter's strong, flamboyant personality, and let him know that there was a critical weakness there, that Peter had yet to control in his own mental and emotional strength. *And, this weakness it will be seen in Peter, even after Jesus' resurrection, until the Holy Spirit got hold of Peter and gave him endurance* (See John 13:38).

And then he had a verbal exchange with Philip, when Philip said to Jesus "Lord, show us the Father". This statement demonstrated the limitation in Philip's perception of him. Philip, even then, after several years as Jesus' disciple, did not understand one of the basic characteristics of Jesus. Even though Jesus had earlier said "**I and the father are one.**" (See John 10:20). It, even at this late stage of his ministry, showed a faith weakness held by many even today that Jesus was only a prophet. Jesus chided Philip into the right path by saying "**Have I been with you so long, and you still do not know me, Philip? Whoever has seen me has seen the father. How can you say show us the father? Do you not believe that I am in the Father and the Father is in me?**" (See John 14:8-10) In this case, Philip's limited understanding of God was the same thing that troubled Job, 2000 years earlier, and us today 2000 thousand years later. *If we want to see God, he can easily be found in both his creations and his **word**.*

The introduction of the meaning and purpose of the Holy Spirit

Then Jesus explained that he would ask his father, God, to provide the "Holy Spirit" to those who love him, as a helper, the "spirit of truth", to be with them forever. And he also said that the world would not know the Spirit because **"You know him, for he dwells with you and will be in you"** (See John 14:17).

The reiteration that Jesus would be gone only temporarily

Following this, Jesus told his disciples at the table that, after a little while, the world would see him no more, but they will see him again (see John 14:19). *To me, Jesus is telling them of his resurrection.*

The prophesy of what lay ahead

Then Jesus followed this, by openly explaining again his mission and purpose, and that they, as his disciples, would face hatred and adversities, but would ultimately be victorious. And that they would have the Holy Spirit to guide and comfort them. During this monolog, the other disciple named Judas (not Iscariot) asked him how they would be conscious of Jesus presence with them. Jesus answered him simply that he would be in their hearts (see John 14:1 through 16:28 and 16:31-33). The disciples then told Jesus that they may have finally understood what Jesus had been telling them (see John 16:29-30).

The "Communion" as a remembrance ritual

Also, near the end of their meal together, Jesus introduced the "Communion Ritual" as recorded best in Matthew 26:26-28. He first took a parcel bread, and after giving thanks, broke it apart and gave the parts to his disciples, and he said **"Take, eat, this is my body"** . And then he took a cup of wine, and when he had given thanks for it as well he said **"Drink of it, all of you, for this is my blood of the covenant, which is poured for many for the forgiveness of sins."**

Then, as described in Luke, after distributing the bread, Jesus said **"Do this in remembrance of me"** (see Luke 22:19). This, of course, began the practice of the Lord's "Communion" in various forms and frequencies throughout the history of the Christian church.

I believe that in distributing the bread, Jesus was really saying to his disciples to take into them-selves (and for all time) the presence, teachings of, and belief in Jesus as the promised Messiah while he was here on earth . And with the offering the wine, he was preparing his followers for the sacrifice that he was about to make as the ultimate (for all time) Passover lamb for the salvation of believers in him.

The Benediction

John followed this by saying that Jesus prayed. The other gospels say that at the end of the meal the disciples sang a hymn.

After the Lord's supper, Jesus' final prayer and the weakness of his disciples

Then they left the house to go up the "Mount of Olives", into a garden called Gethsemane just east of Jerusalem,. When they reached the garden, Jesus told most of his disciple to sit down and wait. Then he took Peter, James, and John further into the garden. He told them that he was very troubled (*I assume because he was very aware of what was in store for him*), and left them there with an admonition to "**watch with me**" (see Matthew 26:38). Then he went a little further, fell on his face, and began to pray. In this prayer he showed three things; his knowledge of his innocense, his humanity, and his reluctant willingness to complete his mission. His prayer was thus. "**My father, if it be possible, let this cup pass from me; nevertheless, not as I will but as you will.**" (See Matthew 26:39). Then he rose up, apparently resigned to the fate of his humanity and returned to where he had left Peter, James, and John. And he found them asleep, a proof that they were not yet ready to carry out the mission that he had planned for them.

Part II Section 9 - Jesus' betrayal, arrest, and trials

Jesus' Arrest

What followed was a startling event that developed in this way. Picture the scene. It was about midnight Thursday night, the night before the Passover celebration. Jesus had wakened his three inner circle disciples (Peter, James, and John), exited the garden, and joined with the other disciples he had left at the garden gate. Immediately, a crowd of people approached them, carrying lanterns, torches, and swords. The crowd was most likely made up of a number of Zealots (strong believers in Jewish tradition), people loyal to the pharisees, and several temple guards. And the group was lead by Judas Iscariot. They had assuredly come to arrest Jesus. But remember this was 2000 years ago. There was no TV nor internet, nor social media, and the people in the crowd obviously knew of Jesus, but most likely many of them had not seen him in person. In order to assure that they arrested the right person, Judas had told them in advance that they would know him because Judas would approach and kiss Jesus. Judas probably approached Jesus with a big smile on his face and a friendly greeting, including a kiss. After some hesitation, during which Jesus assured them that he was the right person, the temple guards started to place Jesus under arrest. Peter, who was armed, most likely with a Roman style short sword, rushed up and swung his sword at one of the temple guards, cutting off one of his ears. Jesus, probably using his most commanding voice, stopped Peter from further carnage. Then he performed a remarkable feat by mending the guard's ear. Following this, Jesus submitted to the arrest, and all his disciples ran away. For Bible references of this event, see Matthew 26:47-56, Mark 14:43-50, Luke 22:47-53, and John 18:2-12. *Critics might find some differences in the event descriptions. However, it must be remembered that these references were written by four different authors, 35 to 70 years after the event occurred.*

Jesus taken to be tried as a criminal

As soon as he was arrested, Jesus was immediately taken to a court made up of members of the Counsel of the priests of the temple, as well as elders and scribes.

The first trial (Before the Priests)

Apparently the conspiracy against Jesus was well organized, because, even though it was about midnight before the start of the Passover, a council of priests of the temple was in session, ready to start Jesus' trial. The group who had taken him into custody, immediately brought him there. *(Remember that the people who took him into custody were temple guards under control of the priests.)* Apparently the scene was quite chaotic, because those priests, scribes, and elders who showed up for this special session were universally in contempt of Jesus, both fearing and hating him. He was placed in the docket, and the members immediately started insulting him and accusing him of all sorts of crimes and blasphemies against Israel and God, and they called several witnesses to substantiate their claims, but found none plausible. At last, a witness came forward who claimed that he heard Jesus say "**I am able to destroy the temple of God, and to rebuild in three days**" (See Matthew 24:60-61). But this was not really true. (*Jesus had actually said that the temple **would be** destroyed, not that he planned to do it. Also, many believe that he was actually talking about **his own body**, not the stone and wood building where the priests served.)* Caiaphas, the high priest, asked Jesus to either confirm or deny this, but Jesus stayed quiet. Then Caiaphas asked Jesus if he were the promised Christ. In so many words, Jesus said that **he was**, and also that he possessed the full power of God. This threw Caiaphas and the whole assembly into a rage. And they started spitting on him, physically punching and slapping him, and demanding that he be executed. This particular trial is described in detail in both Matthew 26:37-68 and Mark 14:53-65.

The second trial (Before Pilate)

However, under Roman law at that time, the authority to execute someone resided with the Roman governor of the province (See John 8:31). At this time the governor of the Roman province that included Judea was Pontius Pilate, a minion of the emperor in Rome. The primary purpose of the governor was to pacify the populace and keep the peace. So after condemning Jesus, the assembly brought Jesus to Pilate at his headquarters in Jerusalem, demanding that he order Jesus' execution. (In order to keep the peace?) (See Matthew 26:57-68, Mark14:53-63, Luke 22;65-71 and John 18:19-28)

So Pilate had Jesus brought in him into his headquarters and asked him, "Are you king of the Jews", *apparently because Jesus' accusers had told Pilate that this was one of Jesus' false claims.* Jesus told Pilate that others said this, but that his kingdom was not of this world. Next, Pilate went out and tried to placate the priests by saying that he found no fault in Jesus. But they continued to demand his execution.

The Third trial (Before Herod Antipas)

Then Pilate determined that Jesus was from Galilee. So in a last ditch effort to avoid pronouncing the demanded death sentence, Pilate sent him to see Herod Antipas (one of the sons of Herod the Great) who was the titular king of the region of Galilee, and who was in Jerusalem for the Passover. However, when Herod tried to interview Jesus he refused to speak, so Herod allowed his men to mock him and treat him with contempt. And then Herod sent Jesus back to Pilate. (See Luke 23:4-11) *(This trial does not appear in the other gospels, but tha does not mean it didn't happen.)*

The fourth trial (Again before Pilate)

Then Pilate tried one more time to avoid ordering Jesus' execution by instead offering to execute Barabbas, a murderer and terrorist. *(For the most complete record of the dialog between Jesus and Pilate, see John 18:33-38.)* But, the Jewish leaders still demanded the death of Jesus and threatened a riot. So, even though Pilate did not want to, he acquiesced to the demands, and sentenced Jesus to be executed. (See Luke 23:13-25 and other gospels). Thus, instead of choosing one who offered peace and life, they chose a terrorist who would only promote death and destruction *(I believe that the choice of Barabbas over Jesus sealed the end of Judea as a nation, the destruction of the temple, and the killing of all the nation's leadership in 70 AD by the Romans.)* .

Intervening note - Peter's denial

During Jesus' trials, most of his disciples had fled. However, Peter made an effort to find out what was happening to him. So early in the morning, he approached a fire around which several of the onlookers were sitting. The people there recognized that he was one of Jesus' followers by his Galilean speech accent. Probably fearing that he would also be arrested, he vehemently denied it. Then a rooster crowed. But the people persisted so he denied it again, and then for a third time, just as Jesus predicted he would, at the meal the previous evening. Then suddenly Jesus appeared, most likely as he was being led from one trial to the next. And he said to Peter in essence, "I told you this would happen". "And Peter went out and wept bitterly" (See Luke 22:62). He was suddenly faced with the fact that he had betrayed his leader and his Lord. *(And thus, Peter again demonstrated he was not yet ready for the role he was destined to play in the early stages of the growth of Christianity.) (This failure of Peter was apparently very important to the gospel authors, because this occurrence appeared in all four of the gospels, see Matthew 26:69-75, Mark 14:66-72, Luke 22:54-62, and John 18:15-18.)*

Part II Section 10 - Jesus' execution and burial

The execution method

(The accepted method of execution at the time for criminals of the state was crucifixion. This was a very barbaric process. The process started with the building a large wooden cross, probably twelve or more feet tall, with a crosspiece longer than the reach of the victim. A hole was dug in the ground for the base of the cross. First, the cross was laid on the ground, and the victim was laid out full length on the vertical part of the cross. Next, his forearms would be bound to the crosspiece by ropes. Then, metal spikes would be driven into his wrists or the palms of his hands, pinioning his hands to the arms of the cross. Following this, his feet would be crossed one on top of the other and a spike would be driven into his crossed feet, pinioning them to the vertical part of the cross. Then the cross would be lifted up, and its bottom would be dropped into the hole that had been dug for it. And he would be left hanging there alive, in excruciating pain, until he succumbed to shock, asphyxiation, loss of blood, or dehydration. And his death might take as much as several days.)

The specifics of the treatment of Jesus

Though the mob demanded that Jesus be killed, under Roman law the process had to be carried out by the Roman soldiers as neutral functionaries. First, the soldiers beat him. The soldiers also, because he had claimed to be a king, fashioned a crown for him to wear. However, it was not made of metal or cloth, but of the branches of a thorn bush. When placed on Jesus' head, it must have immediately brought blood and stinging pain. They also put a fake royal rob on him and mocked him (See John 19:1-3). Then Pilate brought Jesus out, apparently hoping this punishment would be enough. It was not.

Also, an ultimate debasement was to force the victim to carry his own cross to the place of execution. Thus, Jesus was to be forced to carry his cross to his place of death. The route he would have had to follow was from the center of Jerusalem, up a hill outside the city gates, to a place called Golgotha (the place of the skull). And he would have had to do this by wending his way through jeering and grieving crowds. However, a bystander, Simon of Cyrene, was pressed by the Roman soldiers into carrying the cross for him (See Luke 23:26).. *(Cyrene was a small town in Egypt, on the Mediterranean coast, west of Alexandria. He was probably a Jew, in town for the Passover).*

When Jesus reached the place of execution, He was offered sour wine, probably to ease the pain, but he turned it down. He was then stripped naked, lain on the cross and nailed to it per an Old Testament prediction (See Psalm 22:16). (After Jesus was stripped, the Roman soldiers cast lots for his clothing, also as predicted in the Old Testament (See Psalm22:28). Per Pilate's direction, a sign was placed at the top of his cross that said "King of the Jews" in three languages. This was most likely done to state Jesus' supposed crime, that he was accused of questioning the Roman authority, and as a warning to others who might try to do the same. Then the cross was raised to the vertical with Jesus fastened to it, and its base dropped into the hole prepared for it.

The Jewish leaders objected to the sign on Jesus' cross. But Pilate, most likely because he was angry that he had to appease those leaders by executing someone who he believed to be an innocent man, told them "What I have written I have written." (See John 19/31), and refused to change it or take it down.

Jesus' initial prayer from the cross

At this point, Jesus prayed to God for those who were in the process of executing him **"Father forgive them, for they know not what they do"**. And Matthew wrote in Chapter 27, verses 39-42 that those who passed by, including chief priests and elders mocked him, thinking that if he were really the Son of God, God would save him from dying. This was about 6:00 AM.. *(Obviously none of those involved understood that his primary purpose on earth was to be the sacrificial lamb to die for the sins of anyone who believed that he was God's son. Obviously how really confused and lost were they.)*

More of Jesus' statements and prayers from the cross

Two other men were executed with Jesus. Shortly after the bases of their crosses, with the three men mounted on them, were placed into the ground. One of those being crucified with Jesus reviled him. But the other rebuked the first, and demonstrated that he was a believer by saying to Jesus "remember me when you come into your kingdom". And Jesus answered him **"Today, you will be with me in Paradise."** (See Luke 23:42-43)

Then Jesus saw John standing in the crowd with his mother Mary, and asked John take her into his home. (See John 19:25-27)

About 3:00 PM, after Jesus had hung on his cross about nine hours, he made four statements apparently in fairly quick succession. His first utterance was most probably that as reported in Mark, when he said **"My God, my God why have you forsaken me?"**. (See Mark 15:34) This was most likely the moment when God turned his back on Jesus to let him bare the full weight of the sins of the world. Then Jesus said **"I thirst"**, and the soldiers again offered him some wine on a sponge (See John 19:26). Next, probably in order to insure his death, one of the soldiers thrust a spear into his side (as specifically predicted in the Old Testament Zechariah 12:10). Then God apparently answered and reassured him, because he next cried out **"Into your hands I commit my spirit"**, (See Luke 23:46). Then he followed this with the words **"It is finished"** (See John 19:30), **and he gave up his spirit**.

At Jesus' death

As Jesus approached the end, the whole land was covered with darkness like night, from noon until 3:00 PM. Then, as he breathed his last, suddenly, according to Matthew, a significant earthquake hit the area, and all the gospels record that the veil in the temple that divided the Holy from the Most Holy was ripped into, from top to bottom.

This was an extremely important event, because the Most Holy area of the temple, containing the Arc of the Covenant, was considered to seat of God. And it was available only at certain times and only to designated temple priests. The tearing of the veil suddenly opened access to God to all believers, not to just a select few priests And forever after, it symbolized that all believers in Christ Jesus would have direct access to God through him. *Some Christian denominations have since re-established a priesthood hierarchy. However, the ripping of the veil makes this unnecessary.* **Also the fact that it was ripped from top to bottom, not bottom to top, signaled that it was God's doing, not a human act.**

Jesus burial

Then, shortly thereafter, a member of the Sanhedren, Joseph of Arimathea, obtained permission from Pilate to take down Jesus' body and bury it in a rock tomb that Joseph owned nearby. Also, Nicodemus, another Sanhedren member helped with the burial and provided a large amount of embalming spices. They wrapped his body in a clean linen shroud, and placed a large stone to cover the tomb entrance. Then the next day, a delegation of the priests and pharisees obtained Pilate's permission to seal the tomb, to prevent Jesus followers from opening it, stealing his body, and claiming he had risen from the dead as he had claimed he would. Not only did he give them permission but also provided a guard of Roman soldiers around the tomb entrance (See Matthew 27:37-66, Mark 15:42-46, Luke 23:50-53, and John 21:38-42).

Part II Section 11 - Jesus Rose from the dead

OCCURRENCES AT JESUS' RESURRECTION

Initial recognition, by Mary Magdaline

Two or three of the female followers of Jesus had stayed after Jesus had died, and they saw his body being taken down from the cross and observed where he was being buried. They also must have seen that a large stone had been rolled in front of the entrance to the tomb. But they may not have observed that the tomb the next day was tightly sealed and guarded. Thus, they must have assumed that if they went on the next following day they might be able to find someone to roll back the stone, so they could enter the tomb and put spices on Jesus' body. And they went to his tomb expecting to get in. Instead, they found that not only the seal had been broken and the stone had been rolled back, but also the Roman soldiers assigned to guard the tomb were lying of the ground around the entrance unconscious. And also they found at least one unfamiliar man clothed in a white robe (assumed to be an angel?) sitting at the tomb, who told them that Jesus had risen and was not there. They immediately ran to where the disciples were staying and told them what they saw. But the disciples did not believe them, despite what Jesus had told them on three different occasions that he would rise on the third day. Impossible, they still thought.

However, Peter and John decided to investigate, and ran to the tomb. They found it open, and observed that the shroud, that was used to wrap his body was empty, and the face cloth that had covered his face was lying separately, neatly folded. Then they left to tell the others and to ponder just what had happened (see John 20:3-9).

But one of the women, Mary Magdalene, had followed Peter and John back to the tomb, and stayed there after the men had left. She stood outside the tomb crying. She stooped to look into the tomb and saw not one but two angels robed in white, sitting inside. One asked her why she was crying. She said "They have taken away my Lord, and I don't know where they have laid him", *apparently still not believing he was alive.* Then she turned around and saw Jesus standing right behind her. However, she still didn't recognize him. But he then said her name **"Mary"**, and through her tears, she suddenly saw who he was (see John 20:2011-18).

The above sequence of events is recorded in all four gospels, Matthew 28:1:7, Mark 16:1-11, Luke 24:1-12, and John 20:1-18. *One will note that there are some variations in the four authors' descriptions of the event. However, these variations can easily be attributed to the differences in the authors' views and desired emphases, and the fact that they were recorded between 30 and 60 years after they occurred. And these variations do not in any way detract from the basic fact that this event really did occur.*

Jesus' Appearance on the road to Emmaus

Later that same day, two men were walking from Jerusalem to the town of Emmaus, and they were discussing the events surrounding Jesus' crucifixion and also the report of his resurrection. But it appeared that they may have been skeptical about his resurrection. A third man joined them and asked what they were talking about, and they told him. This third man was Jesus himself, but they didn't recognize him. That might have been easy because he was probably emaciated, had three days extra beard growth, and was wearing a different cloak. (Remember that the Roman soldiers had taken what he had been wearing.)

And he began to speak, saying **"O foolish ones, and slow of heart to believe all that the prophets have spoken, telling that it was necessary that the Christ should suffer these things and enter into his glory!"** Then, he explained the Old Testament prophesies concerning him.

When they reached their destination, they invited him to eat with them. He agreed, and when they started eating, the two men suddenly recognized that he was talking about "himself", and he suddenly disappeared (See Luke 24:13-31).

Jesus' Appearance to the disciples in Jerusalem

Then also on the evening of that same day ten of the chosen disciples were gathered together some-place in Jerusalem.,. They were behind locked doors because they were afraid that they might also be arrested and crucified. Not included in this gathering were Thomas and Judas Ascariot (who had by then hanged himself for his treachery). Suddenly Jesus appeared, **physically** standing among them. Wow. The disciples were startled and assumed he was a spirit So he showed them the scars on his hands and the wound where the spear had pierced his side and asked for something to eat. They gave him a piece of fish and he ate with them (proving he was still a live flesh-and-blood human being) (See Luke 24:36-43). Then he commissioned them to go forth and preach of him, and also he breathed on them and instilled the Holy Spirit in them, so that they would also be able to forgive sins. (see John 20:19-23).

The convincing of Doubting Thomas

Thomas, a few days later, joined them, and told them that until he himself saw Jesus in the flesh, he would not believe in the resurrection. So shortly, Jesus showed up again and told Thomas to look at the scars on his hands and to touch where the spear had entered his body. And Thomas was finally convinced (See John 20:24-29). *I think the attitude expressed by Thomas is represented by many today who feel that they have a special wisdom based on their own ego-based personal knowledge and biases, even when presented with a large body of evidence to the contrary. So Thomas just did not believe the testimony of the other trusted people in the group until he saw for himself. This of course is still a stumbling block for many throughout history.*

Author's note - Variations between the gospels

After this point in the account of Jesus' resurrection, the four gospels seem to deviate in their descriptions of Jesus' and his disciples' words and actions. Three of the gospels seem to leave the impression that the disciples stayed in Jerusalem. However, one gospel, John, described a return of some of them to Galilee. The others give the impression that Jesus' ascension occurred almost immediately after his appearance to the disciples. But if one assumes that there is no contradictions between the gospels, there is a plausible time-line that makes all the various stories plausible. So with this assumption let us continue with this account.

Some of the disciples went back to Galilee

Even after the appearance of Jesus in the locked upper room and the proof of Jesus' resurrection to Thomas, Jesus' disciples apparently still did not understand what they were supposed to do with knowledge of Jesus' resurrection, and what mission they needed to carry out. Remember that these men were taught from an early age that the Messiah would come as a conquering hero, who would drive out the hated Romans and re-establish an eternal, earthly kingdom of Israel. Despite Jesus fame, miracles, and proven power, and despite his teaching that his kingdom was "not of this world", he just did not fit that mold. And so they did what familiar to them. Before they had decided to follow Jesus, the leaders of the group of disciples were Galilean fisherman (Peter,

James, and John). So the always impetuous Peter, along with James and John, decided to return to that familiar home and profession. And several of the other disciples, Thomas, Nathanael, and two others, went with them.(See John 21:1-3).

Jesus reappeared to those who had returned to Galilee

This group went out onto the Sea of Galilee at night to fish. But they caught nothing in their nets. Then, just as dawn was breaking, Jesus appeared on the shore within ear shot of the boat, but the fishermen did not recognize him. He asked them if they had caught anything. They said "no", so he told them to throw the net on the other side of the boat. When they did this, their net was immediately filled with large fish to the point where it should have broken, but it didn't. Someone on the boat said "it is Jesus", and they immediately headed. for shore. Peter decided the pace was too slow, so he jumped into the water and swam to shore ahead of the boat. When they reached land, they found Jesus, cooking fish over a charcoal fire. He also had some bread and he invited them to come and eat. Jesus turned specifically to Peter and asked him if Peter loved him more than all else, and Peter said yes. Then Jesus told Peter to feed and tend his sheep, meaning those who followed him. Jesus then also told Peter that this commission was to be lifelong work even to when Peter was very old. Peter then turned to John and said, what about him. And Jesus told Peter not to be concerned because he had other plans for John (See all of John chapter 21). He probably, also reminded them of what he told them before he was crucified, using the example of their futility in fishing before he gave them guidance, and the success afterwards (See John 15:5) .

Due to succeeding events, Jesus must have also directing them to return to Jerusalem.

Jesus' Final visit to his chosen disciples

The gospel of John does not mention this encounter. But the other three do. However, the descriptions in these three gospels vary in the locations where this encounter took place. Matthew related that the eleven disciples traveled to Galilee to a mountain where Jesus had directed them. But that Matthew also indicated that some of them still doubted his identity as the Messiah. And it was there that Jesus gave them the "Great Commission" as follows **"All authority in heaven and on earth has been given to me. Go therefor and make disciples of all nations, baptizing them in the name of the Father and the Son, and the Holy Spirit, teaching them to observe all that I have commanded you. And behold, I am with you always, to the end of time." (See Matthew 28:16-20)**, and that he ascended to heaven there.

Unlike the two previous times he sent the disciples out, he placed no limit on where they should go and witness of and for him. This time it was to "all the world". And he placed no restrictions on how they should go about it.

Mark seemed to indicate that the eleven disciples were still or again in Jerusalem when he last appeared to them. Mark also indicated that some of the disciples still doubted, and Jesus berated them for their **"unbelief and hardness of heart"**. Mark also gave a description of Jesus great commission. However, Jesus was quoted as adding several things that would result from this witness. He said that those who believed would be saved and those who did not would be condemned. He also said the those who witnessed would be able to cast out demons, be able to speak in other languages, be protected from venomous snake bights and poisonous drinks, and be able to heal the sick. (See Mark16:14-18) (See also in Part III the experiences of Paul during his trip to Rome that Paul possessed those powers).

Luke indicated that the disciples were in Jerusalem when he last visited them, and that he gave them the "great commission" there. And that he lead them out to a place near Bethany where he ascended to heaven.

But even though there may be a discrepancy as to where Jesus final ascension took place, **the fact was that he did ascend to heaven**. His responsibility on earth as a human being had ended.

Part II - CODA

And finally:

Jesus, the son and flesh and blood persona of the almighty God of heaven, had been born on earth as a human being.

He had been certified by God as his son when he was baptized by John-The-Baptist.

He identified himself as the Christ, the Messiah, as numerously predicted by Moses and the prophets in the Old Testament.

He demonstrated his unlimited power by performing numerous miracles both against the laws of nature and the healing of human illnesses (including bringing several back to life after they had died).

And he demonstrated that he was the Redeemer for <u>all</u> people not just the Jews, by healing people not of that race.

He taught that love for the all-mighty God was the first and greatest commandment.

He also taught a new way to live and to think that is based on love of one another, even the down-trodden, and ones enemies.

He forecast, planned, and insured that he would be slaughtered as the Passover lamb to take on the sins of all believers.

And he rose from the dead to certify life after death.

Wayne Sherman

He blessed and set forth, with the help of the Holy Spirit, a body of ardent apostles, who were able to take him and his messages to the world.

And, after only about three years of active ministry, he has had greater influence on humanity than any other man in history.

But this is not the end of the story. Part III of this document will explore the lives, messages, successes, and failures, of those commissioned to spread his message to the world during the first century AD.

Part III - THE IMPACT OF JESUS

Foreword

As indicated in the first and second parts of this document, I am a believer in Jesus Christ and his redemptive power, his majesty, and his caring for humanity. And I feel that I can contribute to the knowledge and beliefs of others by expressing my beliefs, and the justifications for those beliefs. Thus, I have written this three part document to that end. This is the third part of three about Christ the Redeemer. In the first part I provided, to the best of my knowledge and research, the data for the predictions of, and prophesies about Christ, the Messiah, in the Old Testament of the Judeo/Christian Bible. In the second part, I have told the story of Christ by delving into his life while on earth, during the first century AD. In it, I believe that I have been able to show Jesus, a Jewish boy, as the real earthly son of the Most High God as predicted in the Old Testament, and that he was set on earth to provide a design for loving and righteous living, and also a path to the eternal life through the giving of his own life, that was denied to the human race because of their nature as flawed (sinful) human beings.

In this part of my book I will attempt to show how the people who were followers of Jesus were so influenced by his guidance, persona, message, and sacrifice, that they were able to build belief in him across the Roman Empire, as the start of a worldwide religion that has become the dominant religious faith in the whole world.

I start this out by the primary use of the New Testament book of Acts of the Apostles (Acts for short), written by Luke. Luke was a companion of the apostle Paul in his later missionary journeys into southern Europe, where Paul was able to introduce Christianity into both the cultures of Greece and the Roman Empire.

Luke was a medical doctor, a Greek trained in the Greek scientific and logical processes. He wrote two books that appear in the New Testament. The first was the book of Luke, a gospel about Jesus Christ, that I used as a resource in part II. And the second was the book of Acts that extended the story, to the growth of Christianity during the next 60 or so years following Jesus' resurection. Since Luke was not present during Jesus' life or in the area where Jesus lived, all of the information he used for his books was apparently based on extensive interviews and research with those actually present in Jesus life. And both his books are logically ordered in historic sequence of events, as would be expected of a scientifically trained mind.

Acts contains a fairly detailed history and actions of several of Jesus' close followers, plus the story and martyrdom of Steven, a strong post-crucifixion follower of Jesus' life and message. However, except in one instance, it does not track the actions of several of the original twelve of Jesus' disciples, James the apostle (John's brother), Bartholomew, Matthew (Levi), Thaddaeus, Thomas, or Simon the Zealot. Of those who are mentioned, I will attempt to provide an honest interpretation of the roles of those selected disciples and their contributions.

There are a number of possible reasons for the omissions of the activities and witnesses of those disciples who were not included in Acts. One is that they were not men of letters, and just did not write anything that would have been included in the Bible. Another possibility is that some of them turned away and did not continue as Jesus' followers. Another possibility is that some met the same fate as Steven, killed in purges of this new religion, in which Saul participated. Another possibility is that some were part of the group of Christians who left Jerusalem to avoid persecution and death. *"Acts" records that Saul was on his way to Damascus to possibly find and prosecute some of those believers when he encountered Jesus (more about this later). Also,* today there are pockets of Christian believers in places like Ireland, Northern Iraq, and even India, who's origins are very ancient and veiled in mystery. And it is possible that these origins could be attributed to apostles not documented in the book of Acts.

The rest of the New Testament except for the book of Revelation is made up of copies of letters written to Christian churches and believing individuals across modern day Turkey and Greece and in the city of Rome, Italy. The last book of the New Testament (Revelation of Jesus Christ, commonly known just as Revelation) was written by the apostle John. This book is made up partly of letters to individual churches, but mostly of prophesies of the future of the world and the kingdom of God. So let us start off from here with more detail of the book of Acts.

Part III Section 1 - The book of Acts, early explosion of Christianity

The gathering in Jerusalem of the devout and their prayers

Acts begins with Jesus telling the disciples, as they witnessed Jesus ascension, to go back to Jerusalem and stay there. He also told them to expect the Holy Spirit to descend on them in not many days. But they still apparently, despite all that he had taught, had expected Jesus to restore the earthly kingdom of Israel. So he more strongly told them that they, not him, would receive the power of the Holy Spirit directly from God himself, to be able to witness **effectively** to the whole world. When the eleven remaining disciples returned to Jerusalem, they gathered in the upper room where the last supper had taken place, along with several women, including Mary (Jesus mother) and two of her other sons (assumed to be James and Jude), where they prayed earnestly for God's guidance

By this time, Judas Iscariot had met an ignominious death, overwhelmed by his treachery (See Acts 1:15-20). So with his death, the disciples determined to replace Judas in the inner circle in order to number them again as "twelve". They used the system of "lots" to pick a man named Matthias (See Acts 1:21-26).. But it will be noted later in Acts that God had other plans. *(Note that "lots" were used in the Old Testament to pick Saul as the first king of Israel, but God had something else in mind when he chose another, David, to replace Saul.)* Matthias was not mentioned again in the scriptures

The Pentecost

After a period of a few weeks, the followers had gathered together at an unidentified public place in Jerusalem. And suddenly there came upon some of those there, something that sounded like the **"sound of a mighty rushing wind"** and appeared like **"divided flames of fire"**. These things came to rest on the chosen ones, giving them each individual other-worldly abilities to speak and understand languages other than their native tongue. And suddenly they were changed in an instant from disciples, (**learners** of the word), to apostles, (**teachers** of the word), with powers **and capabilities that would change the world (See Acts 2:1-4).**

But there were a large number of others who were drawn to the commotion there, who were not touched by these powers. They were astounded and confused by what had just happened. However, some of these were from other middle eastern countries and islands in the Mediterranean Sea who spoke in various non-Hebrew languages, and they heard these supposedly uneducated Galilean people speaking and wittnessing for Christ in their native tongues. But others who did not understand, just assumed they were intoxicated (See Acts 2:5-12).

Peter's assumption of leadership and his first sermon

Remember Peter, the disciple who often spoke without thinking. This is the Peter who had blurted out that Jesus was the Christ, and then failed to be able to walk to Jesus on the water, who denied that he was a follower of Jesus during Jesus' trials, and even after Christ had risen, and had gone back to Galilee to go fishing. But after he was imbued with the Holy Spirit at Pentecost he almost immediately became the leader and spokesman for the chosen group. He began to boldly speak to the crowds who had gathered, and gave a very masterful, soul-winning sermon to those present (See Acts 2:14-36). And then he gave them the path to salvation, "repent and be baptized". And about 3000 people immediately became new followers of Christ (See Acts 2:37-41). And in this sermon, Peter demonstrated a miraculous knowledge of the listeners' Hebrew heritage, something totally unexpected from a relatively uneducated fisherman. As a result, the people were so awed and thrilled by this new revelation that the long-predicted Messiah had come, that they joined together in supreme fellowship and joy, daily attending the temple and gladly inviting all into their homes and sharing meals together. **"And the Lord continued to add daily to their number"** (See Acts 2:42-47).

Author's note

However, in my opinion, some of them made a miscalculation because they apparently didn't comprehend that the timing of Christ's second coming would be on God's schedule and not that of

men (See Second Peter 3:8). So "they sold their possessions and belongings" in order to provide added help all those in need. As a result, many of them faced long term impoverishment, and they themselves would also become needy. Also, many of them would most likely not be prepared for the trauma and tribulation that, as Jesus predicted, would later befall them (See Matthew 10:16-18 and 21-22). However, the congregation of believers in Jerusalem did survive under the undaunted leadership and healing miracles of the apostles and other stalwarts in the faith, as we will see following. For further information on this issue, see below.

The first healing miracle performed by an apostle

Peter and John were among those who entered the temple to pray when at the temple gate they encountered a beggar who had been lame from birth. The beggar asked for money, but Peter said to him **"I have no silver or gold, but what I do have I give to you. In the name of Jesus Christ of Nazareth, rise up and walk" (See Acts 3:6).** Peter then took him by his hand and he immediately rose to his feet, and entered the temple with them, walking and leaping and praising God..

Peter's second sermon

After this miracle, Peter preached a second sermon, building on the above miracle (See Acts 3:12-26). In this sermon, Peter first admonished the people for supporting Christ's crucifiction, but then he emphasized God's forgiveness of sins through faith in Jesus. And again Peter, despite his humble upbringing demonstrated, in this sermon a remarkable knowledge of Moses' teachings and the words of the Old Testament.

Peter and John arrested and released

Peter and John continued to speak in the temple, telling all who would hear them that Jesus was the promised Messiah, and proclaiming that Jesus was the path to resurrection from the dead. This greatly troubled the priests and Sadducees. So they arrested Peter and John, (apparently along with crippled man they had healed) and held them over-night. Then they were brought before a selected group of the priests and were questioned, not about what they were preaching, but how they had healed the lame man. This opened the door to Peter, who chastised those who were questioning them, to declared that the man's healing came through Jesus, and that salvation came through him as well (See Acts 4:8-11).

The judges were obviously confused and troubled that such bold declerations came from men who they considered common and uneducated, but also by the fact that the cripple had been miraculously and suddenly, fully healed. So they released Peter and John, with only an admonition to quit preaching about Jesus, which of course they could not and would not do.

The power of the Lord proved deadly to liars

The policy among the young body of believers was that that they were to share everything in common. But two of the company, Ananias and his wife Sapphira, were among that group.

However, they had sold a piece of property but only gave a portion of the proceeds to the group and held back the rest. Peter found out that they had lied about the gift and confronted Ananias. Peter's challenge was so strong that Ananias immediately dropped dead in front of him, as also did Sapphira when she was also challenged with the same lie. This confirmed the strength of Christ's commission to Peter as the early church leader, and also the seriousness of unity and honesty among the new apostles and disciples.

The apostles arrested again, and again released

John and Peter were arrested again, along with several other apostles. This time an angel opened the cells and released them, and also told them to return to the temple and continue their exhortations. The next day, when the guards were sent to bring the prisoners to the council, they found the prison was locked but that the cells were empty. The guards were then sent to the temple, where they found them and brought them before the council anyway. The council reminded them that they had been told to stop preaching of Jesus as the Messiah. There, Peter, as the apostles' spokesman, openly stated **"We must obey God rather than men. The God of our fathers raised Jesus, whom you killed by hanging him on a tree. God exalted him at his right hand as Leader and Savior, to give repentance to Israel and forgiveness of sins. And we are witnesses to these things, and so is the holy spirit, whom God has given to those who obey him." (See Acts 5:29-32)**

This enraged the council members and they wanted to kill them. But an honored member of the council, Gamaliel, a respected pharisee and teacher, reminded them that others had tried to start up new sects but had failed in time. And he told them that if this was not from God it would fail also. But if it were from God this action would be against God's will and would bring calamity on Israel (See Acts 5:34-39). So this time they again released them from custody but they beat them first. And the apostles again continued their teaching unopposed. And the number of believers continued to grow. And even some priests joined them.

The appointment of deacons

By this time the number of believers had grown to about 5000. So a decision was made to appoint additional people to leadership as servants of the needs of the members, freeing up the apostles to teach. So seven men were selected for this role. Among them were Philip *(who may have been one of the original apostles)* and Steven, an outspoken follower.

The stoning of Steven

In his new leadership role, Steven began preaching strongly in the name of Jesus, citing many Old Testament instances that led to the coming of the Messiah (See Acts 7:2-53). However, he made some powerful enemies in his enthusiasm, and was singled out for punishment. He was accused of salacious statements by false witnesses, and was arrested and condemned to be stoned to death. As he was being stoned, he cried out something similar to what Jesus said from the cross **"Lord, do not hold this sin against them"** (See Acts 7:60).

Part III Section 2 - The book of Acts, spread of Christianity beyond Jerusalem

The introduction of Saul into the story of Christianity

Among those who supported his stoning of Steven, and who opposed the movement, was a zealot named Saul, who held the coats for those throwing the stones (See Act 7:58). Saul was a very interesting person, in that he was a Hebrew who came from Tarsus on the southern coast of what his now Turkey. But he must have traveled to Jerusalem for his education, to be taught by none other than Gamalial, a most esteemed teacher of the law. And he was very driven and bright, especially in his opposition to the new faith, centered on Jesus. He apparently was able to speak fluently in at least four languages; Hebrew, Aramaic, Greek, and Latin. Further, he had been awarded Roman citizenship, a significant honor. And, as we shall see later in this document, when after a miraculous conversion, Paul would become an extremely strong supporter of Jesus as the Messiah. Also, part of his training was apparently that he became a master of the Greek logical processes which he used effectively in his Christian testimonies after his conversion.

Growth of opposition caused the relocation of believers

The number of believers in Jesus continued to grow, even including some priests and Pharisees. However, the opposition to the new group was also growing, exemplified first by the stoning of Steven. Saul became a leader of the group who were persecuting the believers in Jerusalem. A number of them were arrested and thrown into prison. Many others had to leave Jerusalem and move to other cities. But in doing so, they took their beliefs to new fertile ground to spread the truths about Jesus.

The story of Philip - One of those who relocated

Philip relocated to Samaria, where he won over many new converts by curing mental disorders, as well as healing the lame and paralyzed. Included was a popular local magician by the name of Simon, who at first tried to buy the power of the apostles, but was repentant when he realized that it was God-given and not a magic trick that could be bought. Peter and John also visited there and brought the Holy Spirit to the new converts (See Acts 8:5-17).

Later, Philip encountered and brought to Christ a eunuch from the royal court of Ethiopia. This took place on the road south of Jerusalem as the eunuch was returning from a visit to the holy city (See Acts 8:26-39). *This encounter may have been the progenitor of today's strong Christian presence in the country of Ethiopia.* Then Philip moved from town to town in other parts of Judea away from Jerusalem, making many more new converts, until he apparently settled in Caesarea (See Acts 8:40).

Other relocations of the dispersion of believers

Some believers moved to Damascus. Others relocated to the island of Cyprus and also to Phoenicia (Lebanon) and to Antioch, a city now in northern Syria., There the movement prospered, and the members were the first to be known as Christians, and the term "church" was first used to identify a body of believers. Some also relocated to towns throughout modern Turkey, at that time called Galatia, *(as will be verified further in this writing). There are also indications that some traveled as far as territories that are now parts of northern Iraq and Iran, and even India.*

Saul continued his efforts to eradicate the new faith, but a miracle happened

Saul had many believers arrested in Jerusalem. But not satisfied with this, he decided to go to Damascus to root out believers there. However, as he approached the city, there suddenly came a bright light from heaven that knocked Saul to the ground. Then he heard a voice say **"Saul, Saul, why are you persecuting me?** And Saul had the presence of mind to say "Who are you lord? And then the voice said **"I am Jesus who you are persecuting. But rise up and enter the city, and you will be told what to do"**. He did get up but discovered he was blind and could see nothing. Those with Saul took him into the city and left him in an apparently vacant house on the main street of Damascus, where he had nothing to eat or drink for three days (See Acts 9:1-9).

Saul's redemption

On the third day of Saul's dire situation, a vision came to a believer in Damascus named Ananias to go to the house where Saul was, and to lay his hands on Saul to give him back his sight. At first, Ananias expressed fear because of Saul's reputation as an enemy of believers. But through the vision, the Lord said to him **"Go, for he is a chosen instrument of mine to carry my name before the Gentiles and kings and children of Israel. For I will show him how much he must suffer for the sake of my name"**. So Ananias did the Lord's bidding, and remarkably not only was Saul's eyesight restored, but he quickly regained his appetite and strength (See Acts 9:10-19).

Almost immediately Saul started visiting the Damascus synagogues and proclaiming that Jesus "was the son of God". This shocked and surprised the Jews there, and some opposed him, but he confounded them with his superior logic. So some of them decided to kill him. However, his supporters helped him escape by lowering him in a basket through a hole in the city wall (See Acts 9:20-25).

Author's note; Remember in the Old Testament a thousand years before, where the Hebrew elders used "lots" to choose another man named Saul as king, who proved unacceptable to God. So God sent Samuel to find a replacement, David. And as was mentioned before, the apostles used "lots" to choose Matthias as a replacement apostle for Judas Iscariot. Again, God had other plans. He chose the new Saul instead.

Saul returned to Jerusalem, a new man but was rejected

Saul came back to Jerusalem a new man, a believer in Jesus. However, the congregation of believers there also were afraid of him, until a member, Barnabas, interceded for him, being aware of what had happened in Damascus. Saul then started preaching in Jerusalem, but he again made some enemies who wanted to kill him. So the apostles sent him back to his home in Tarsus.

Peter continued his healing ministry

Peter traveled to visit the believers who lived in Lydda, a costal city in Judea. There he encountered a paralyzed man named Aeneas, and he healed him. Then Peter was called to Joppa also on the Mediterranean sea coast where be actually brought back to life a woman named Tabitha. After this, Peter remained in Joppa for some time, living in the house of a believer there, Simon the tanner (See Acts 9:32-43).

Peter was taught that Gentiles could also be Christians

Despite the multiple times that Jesus had told his disciples that he had come as a redeemer for all people, not just the Jews, (and had proved it by healing several non-Jews including Romans), they continued to hang on to the idea that he had come as saviour for them only. Apparently Peter was one of them. So the Lord came to Peter in a vision, an told Peter three times (remember that Jesus told Peter three times to feed his sheep) that **"What God has made clean, do not call common"**. By this time, Peter had left Jerusalem and was by the staying in Joppa, a Judaen town on the Mediterranean coast. Peter's dream perplexed him, until some representatives of Cornelius, a Roman Centurion, showed up where he was staying in Joppa, asking Peter to go with them to Caesarea to witness to their leader. And he did so, led by the Holy Spirit.

When Peter arrived, he found that Cornelius had gathered a whole room full of family and friends eager to hear what he had to say. So Peter preached to them the word of God, and ended by saying "...all prophets bear witness that everyone who believes in him receives forgiveness of sins through his name". And many of those present believed, and received the Holy Spirit, and were baptized. And those who had come there with Peter were confounded and saw with their own eyes, that the spirit could be given to unclean (uncircumcised) people (See Acts 10:34-48).

Circumcision

Maybe here again is the place in this document to explain circumcision. This is a surgical ritual practiced on Hebrew men to set them apart as those chosen by God. This surgery is still practiced today for religious or health reasons. It involves cutting off a natural flap of skin that covers the tip of a man's penis. In Jesus' time it was normally performed by a priest after a male child's birth. The Bible records the Jesus was taken to the temple in Jerusalem for this ritual about a week after he was born. Some believers in Jesus believed that only those men who had been circumcised could become real Christians and enter the kingdom. The above instance and several others in the New Testament (Including Jesus' own statements) proved that this was not true.

Peter returned to the Jerusalem church and confronted the Judaizers

Peter returned to the Jerusalem congregation of believers, and pronounced there that he now fully accepted the idea that Jesus was the redeemer for all people, not just the Jews. However, there was a circumcision-only group within the church that criticized him for not only leading Gentiles to Jesus, but even eating with them in their homes. *This meant that Peter had eaten food not been blessed by a priest (not kosher food). Something that was considered sinful.* So Peter explained to them about the vision he had received in Joppa and the subsequent trip to Caesarea, where he had led many Gentile souls to Christ, and that God gave to them the same Holy Spirit that befell the Jews at the Pentecost. And he concluded with the statement "who was I that I could stand in God's way" (See Acts 10:34-11:17).

Barnabas moved to Antioch

As the Christian church continued grow in Jerusalem, so did its opposition. So believers continued to move away. Barnabas, for one, was sent to Antioch, a city in north western Syria. Then hearing about Saul and his new witness for Jesus/Christ, he went to Tarsus and found Saul and brought him back to Antioch (See Acts 11;25).

Persecution of the church became more violent and Peter was arrested again, but this time was again miraculously set free

The persecution of the church reached as high as Herod the Tetrarch (a son of Herod the Great), the king of Judea, became involved. He had James the apostle, the brother of John, assassinated, and Peter arrested again. Apparently aware of Peter's previous miraculous escape from prison, Herod had him chained and set multiple guards. But the night before he was to be brought to trial, an angel miraculously rescued him from prison again (See Acts 12:1-10). He fled to the house of the mother of the disciple, John Mark, where people were gathered praying for him and were joyous to see him. When Herod found out that Peter had escaped, he ordered the guards to be put to death. However, Herod himself, died shortly after this, dropping dead while sitting on his throne, surrounded by his subjects. *This is the last time Peter was mentioned in the book of Acts. However, apparently, he continued as a leading apostle in the Jerusalem church, and survived the continued persecution of the church there. He also later wrote two letters to the disbursed Jewish Christians which appear in the New Testament.*

Part III Section 3 - Also in Acts, Saul and his mission trips and name change

At this point and forward, the book of Acts concentrates on the travels and Christian witness of Saul, even though there were obviously other missionaries who carried the message of Christ to the world (see a reference below about Apollos as an example). However, it seems

that Saul and his witness were so strong, literate, and effective, that the framers of the content of the New Testament two centuries later, chose the book of Acts, and its concentration on Saul, as the corner-stone of the story of the growth of Christianity in the century following Jesus' crucifiction. (**But please note that abought this time, Saul changed his name to Paul,** apparently to be more acceptable to the Greeks and other Gentiles)

John Mark joined Paul and Barnabas in Antioch of Syria, and started on a mission trip

During the time, John Mark, another beliver in Christ, also came to Antioch of Syria from Jerusalem. Shortly thereafter, the Holy Spirit told those in the Antioch church to send Saul and Barnabas on a trip to visit several cities where other churches were located. And John Mark went with them. They first sailed to Cyprus where they encountered a false prophet named Bar-Jesus who spoke out against them. Saul caused him to be blinded, and won over the head of the Cyprus government to become a believer. But, after some further travel, John Mark left their party to apparently return to Antioch, (and then sometime later returned Jerusalem) (See Acts 13:2-13).

Paul and Barnabas won many souls in Antioch of Pisidia, but got in trouble

Paul and Barnabas then traveled to another city also called Antioch, this time in a district of Pisidia on the southern coast of modern Turkey. There in the local synagogue on a Sabbath, Paul made and impassioned speech, recounting the history of the Hebrew nation, quoting many Old Testament scriptures showing God's promises to Israel, and ending with an explanation that Jesus was the promised Messiah. And he also returned to the synagogue the next Sabbath, where this time almost the whole population of the city had gathered. And this time, he proclaimed that Jesus was the saviour for not just the Jews but all the people of the earth. This greatly pleased the Gentiles, but caused serious anger among some of the devout Jews, and they stirred up some of the city leaders who drove Paul and Barnabas out of the district (See Acts 13:14-50).

Paul and Barnabas continued their trip and then returned to Antioch of Syria .

Despite their setback in Pisidia, Paul and Barnabas continued on their way, visiting other synagogues, and speaking in them wherever they went, proclaiming the good news of Christ. However, they were threatened with stoning in one town, and Paul was actually knocked cold by a stone in another. But wherever they went, they continued to win many souls, both Jews and Gentiles. Then they returned to Antioch in Syria to report their successes for Christianity, including opening the door to Gentiles (See Acts 13:51 thru 14:28).

Paul and Barnabas confronted the Judaizers

Later, some believers from Jerusalem showed up in Antioch proclaiming that people must be circumcised before they could join the church (despite what Peter had preached earlier in Jerusalem). This resulted in a serious debate between them and Paul and Barnabas. So Paul, Barnabas and several others decided to travel to Jerusalem to settle the issue (See Acts 15:1-2). There, several of the Christians who also were Pharisees insisted that circumcision was necessary "in order to keep the law of Moses". After some debate, Peter sided with Paul and Barnabas, saying that salvation comes through "the grace of the Lord Jesus Christ" and not through physical surgery. Then the whole assembly fell silent and listened to Paul and Barnabas as they justified their position that the Gentiles who come to Christ should not be burdened by Jewish heritage practices. They supported this through quotes from Old Testament prophets, including Amos, that refuted this requirement. But Paul did suggest that they should write to the Gentile converts, telling them that they stay away from food offered to idols and from sexual immorality. So the whole council composed the recommended letter and sent it back to the Antioch church, and followed this recommendation by sending out elders, including Barsabbas, Judas, and Silas, from the Jerusalem church to confirm the authenticity of the letter and the position of the Jerusalem church. This led to much joy among the people in Antioch (See Act 15:3-35).

Paul and Barnabas planned a second mission trip but split up

After a time, Paul and Barnabas started planning another trip. However, Barnabas wanted to take John Mark along, and Paul strenuously objected, citing John Mark's failure on their previous trip. So the two spit up and went different directions. Barnabas took John Mark and went back to Cyprus, while Paul chose Silas to go with him. And Paul went with Silas through Syria and then again west along the Mediterranean coast through the province of Cilicia, visiting and strengthening the churches along the way (See Acts 15:36-40).

Author's Note

Please note that there are no more references in the Bible about Barnabas or John Mark (except briefly in Second Timothy chapter four). However, there is an indication that John Mark was the author of the gospel of Mark, considered the first book in the New Testament about Jesus. It is assumed to have been written about twenty years after the last reference to John Mark in the Bible. There is also an indication accepted by many scholars, that the words in Mark are really those of Peter as written down by the gospel author, Mark. This would mean that if John Mark were the scribe (ghost writer) for Peter, as indicated above, he would have, at some point, returned to Jerusalem to become Peter's disciple.

Paul and Silas traveled on to Lystra where they met Timothy

Timothy was already a believer and disciple, and well spoken of. His mother was Jewish and also a believer, but his father was Greek. Paul wanted Timothy to join his travel party, but there was a possible problem with the Jewish people they would encounter, He was of Jewish heritage but not circumcised. So Paul circumcised him, ouch. At this point, Paul not only accepted Timothy into his group but began to mentor him as a future leader. *Timothy later became a church leader and was written to twice by Paul with suggestions about how to manage his witness.* After this, Timothy went with them through other towns and cities in Turkey, where they informed people in the synagogues and churches of the Jerusalem Council decision to allow in Gentiles. In the process, the churches were strengthened and experienced significant membership growth wherever they went. Their next stop was Troas on the north west coast of modern Turkey (Troy of Greek mythology) (See Acts 16:1-8).

Paul called to go to Macedonia (in northern Greece), and was joined by Luke

While in Troas, Paul had a vision of a man calling him to cross into Europe to northern Greece. *At this point the word "we" entered into descriptions of the travels of Paul and Silas, assuredly indicating that the author of Acts, Luke, had joined their party, probably in Troas. Luke was a Greek Gentile, trained in* medicine. *Paul, in one of his letters, complained that he had a "thorn in the flesh" an apparent physical malady that Luke may have helped him with.* So Paul's mission entourage, now at least four people strong, sailed from Troas to Samothrace, and then traveled by land on to Philippi, the leading city and a Roman colony in Macedonia (northern Greece). There Paul met and won to Jesus a business woman of means named Lydia, who asked his party to be her guests there, where he won over all of her household. Thus, Paul carried Christianity to Europe (See 16:8-15).

Problems and events in Philippi of Macedonia

But, while witnessing in Philippi, they attracted the attention of a slave girl who had a spirit of divination and was making money for her owners. She started following Paul's group around, proclaiming "These men are servants of the Most High God". This apparently turned their work as missionaries into an entertainment spectacle. and interfered with their witness. So Paul commanded the spirit to leave her. And when it did, her owners were angry, and had Paul's group arrested on trumped-up charges. They were subsequently beaten, and put in prison, and their feet fastened in stocks (See Acts 16:14-24).

Then, about midnight, while Paul and Silas were praying and singing hymns, the city was hit by a large earthquake that miraculously sprung all the prison cell doors open and released the prisoners' restraints. When the jail warden woke up and discovered that the prison was open, he felt it necessary to kill himself because his prisoners had escaped. But Paul cried out to tell him that the prisoners were still inside. When the warden confirmed this, he brought them out and said to them "What must I do to be saved?". **And they explained the plan of salvation to him, and his whole household accepted Jesus and were baptized**. The jailor then brought them to his home, bandaged their wounds and fed them. And shortly thereafter the city leaders showed up to exonerate them of the trumped up charges, and they apologized for the beatings they received. However, the city leaders asked them to leave town (See Acts 16:16-40).

Paul witnessed in Athens

Paul's missionary party continued to travel through cities in northern Greece, winning souls for Christ, but was also causing ire among some of the traditional Jews there. So they went on to Athens. Paul decided to preach Christ there also. He was able to lead several to believe and accept Christ. However, Athens was a city full of various religions and philosophies, and Paul's message was treated there by many as just another such. In one of his later letters, he expressed the feeling that the visit to Athens was a failure (See Acts 17:16-34).

Paul in Corinth, church/state separation

Then Paul's group went on to Corinth, a major trade city on an isthmus between two parts of Greece. Again Paul encountered some problem with the local Jews. However, he found Corinth a more fertile field for his message than Athens. There, he won over numerous souls, both Jews and Gentiles. and stayed there a year and a half, preaching Christ, first in the local synagogue. There, Paul met Priscilla and Aquila, a Jewish couple whom he brought to Christ. And while he was in Corinth he worked for them in their tent-making business to earn his way. However he was again rejected by the Jews of the local synagogue, so he started a Christian church next door.

Then the local Jews again tried to attack him, this time in civil court, but the Greek judge threw the case out, saying this was a religious matter, not suitable for a Greek civil court, **indicating for the first time in the Bible, the concept of "separation of church and state", which has become one of the foundations of modern democracies, including a provision in the U.S. Constitution.**

Paul's return again to Antioch of Syria via Ephesus

After this experience, Paul stayed in Corinth some time longer, but decided eventually to return to Antioch in Syria (See Acts 18:1-23). However, he briefly stopped over in the city of Ephesus on the way. And Aquila and Priscilla, who had apparently joined his party in Corinth, traveled there with him. *Ephesus was a major port city and educational center on the west end of the Turkish peninsula.* There, he went to the local synagogue and reasoned with the local Jews. *These Jews were obviously more rational and accepting of his message than those in Greece, and were more open to what he had to say about Jesus, because they apparently listened to him without rancor.* They even asked him to stay longer, but he declined, saying that "if God wills" he would return. Prcilla and Acquilla left his party there. He then traveled on to Antioch, staying there for some time (See Acts 18:1-22).

Book of Acts account of Paul's continued mission trips

Paul began his third mission trip from Antioch first by going north through the regions of Galatia and Phrygia in what is now central Turkey, strengthening the Christian churches there, and then traveling back to Ephesus.

Apollos, another missionary for Christ, and help for him from Aquila and Priscilla

However, between Paul's Ephesus visits, a man named Apollos showed up in Ephesus from Alexandria in Egypt. Like Paul, he also effectively, and accurately proclaimed Jesus as the promised Christ. And, like Paul, he was an eloquent speaker. He spoke boldly in the Ephesus synagogue, complementing and supplementing Paul's previous messages there. It appears though, he had a gap in his understanding of the true meaning of Christian baptism. *I suspect that his view was that baptism might have been only the cleansing from sin (as proclaimed in the Essene culture and John the Baptist), and not the proclamation of the believers' introduction into the Kingdom of God.* Aquila and Priscilla were among the Ephesus congregation, having remained there after Paul had left for Antioch. *They apparently helped Apollos to more fully understand that Holy Baptism was not only the cleansing from sin **but also the acknowledgment of the death, burial, and resurrection of Christ**.* But, prior to Paul's return to Ephesus, Apollos had traveled on from Ephesus to Corinth where he again effectively and powerfully refuted the Jews there who had opposed Paul. He did this by opening more clearly to them the Old Testament scriptures that showed that the promised Christ was really Jesus (See Acts 18:23-28).

Author's Note, Who was Apollos?

This reference to Apollos in Acts and one other brief comment in Paul's letter to Titus are the only mentions of him in the Bible. Thus, we have no knowledge of how he came to know Jesus, nor how he knew that Jesus was the Christ/Messiah promised in the Old Testament,. We also don't know who was his teacher, although a Greek teacher named Philo. may have been responsible for his ability to reason and to speak so eloquently, and also he must have had close contact with one or more of the original apostles. Even though his name would indicate that he was Greek, he has been identified by tradition as a Jew. But the fact that he did not have a good understanding of how baptism played into becoming a Christian, indicates that he was not present at, nor had first-hand knowledge of Pentecost. However, his witness was powerful, accurate, and commanding. So the story and identification of Apollos is best understood in that there was a strong, rapid expansion of God's message to the people of the time, through the right people, who could spread the good news of salvation, propagating the miraculous growth of Christianity in the first century after Jesus was crucified.

Paul's experiences on his return to Ephesus

When Paul arrived in Ephesus he found some believers who had not received the Holy Spirit. So he re-baptised them in the name of Jesus and laid his hands on them. And the Holy Spirit came on them, and they began speaking in tongues and prophesying. *As earlier stated, this gift of tongues and being able to witness in another language were very important to the spread of the early church, because of the disparate languages of the area.*

The Paul first spent three months speaking in the synagogue and then in the Christian chrch next door he again . But then he again encountered difficulties with the traditional Jews. There, he spoke boldly of Jesus and a performed a number of healings. So, several traditional Jews tried to heal without invoking Jesus, but rather using witchcraft. But an evil-possessed man overpowered them all, beat them up, and drove them into the street naked. So a number of additional people who had been on the fence about Paul's message now turned into believers. And those who had been trying other ways to heal, confessed and burned their witchcraft books (SeeActs 19:1-20).

Then, having championed over his Jewish and witchcraft dissenters, Paul encountered another group of opposition. It turned out that Ephesus was the center for worship the goddess, Artemis. And a number of tradesmen were making large profits from the manufacturing of images of her and related trade items. And Paul's new following was damaging their businesses. This group stirred up a riot among the citizens, some of whom had no idea of what was going on. The crowd converged on the local center for public meetings and theater productions, a large open air theater. Everyone there was shouting "Great is Artemus of the Ephesians". However, the city manager took the stage and quieted the crowd by saying that he thought that Paul and his group were innocent of wrongdoing, and telling them that any remaining concerns could be handled peacefully in a court of law. And the crowd disbursed. Following this, Paul and his group set sail again for Greece (See Acts 19:23 thru 20:1).

Paul back in Greece

Paul and his group then again spent some time in northern Greece, encouraging the Christians there, and gaining several new converts. Also, while there, Paul's entourage grew by several more disciples. Then they traveled back to Troas (Troy) in Turkey (See Acts 20:1-6).

Paul back in Troas (where he raised a man from death) and then on to Jerusalem

Paul's group spent a week in Troas, preaching there. One of his talks went well into the night, and one of his young listeners went to sleep and fell to his death out of a third story window. Paul immediately went down and restored the young man's life. Then his party left Troas and traveled back to Ephesus where he spoke to the elders of the church there, giving to them another impassioned Christian sermon. But after they had prayed together, he told them sorrowfully that he would not be back, and he prepared to sail back to Syria. His travel group landed in the city of Tyre where he stayed a week, again encouraging the church there. Then, despite some misgivings by his traveling party, he traveled on to Jerusalem (See Acts 19:1 through:20:6 and 20:13 thru 21:15).

Paul in Jerusalem, (where he caused a riot), then on to Caesarea

Paul at first was praised for his witness to the Gentiles by the elders of the Jerusalem church. Then he took great pains to purify himself so he could enter the temple. However, later when he went to the temple, he was arrested, and accused of desecrating it, because his accusers thought wrongly that he had brought some unpurified men into the temple with him. And the crowd even sought again to kill him. But he was rescued by Roman soldiers.

Then, after convincing the Roman soldiers that he was not a terrorist, they allowed him to speak to the crowd. He spoke in Hebrew, recounting his birth and training as a devout Jew, and that he at first participated in the arrest of many Jesus' followers. Then he told them of his miraculous conversion to belief in Christ. But then he told them that the Lord had then sent him to witness to the Gentiles. This caused the crowd to again demand his death.

The Romans then put Paul into protective custody. At first, they were going to flog him to get at the hatred of the Jews, until he explained that he was a Roman citizen. So instead, they dispatched him to stand for a hearing before Felix, the Roman territorial governor in Caesarea (on the Judaen coast). But the Jewish accusers followed him, insisting that Paul was a rabble-rouser and a criminal. However, Paul gave an effective defense before Felix, including the fact that he was both a devout Jew and a follower of Christ Jesus. Felix decided to believe Paul but continued to hold him in protective custody anyway, where Paul remained for his safety, and also possibly so that Felix could learn more about Jesus. So Paul was detained there for two years.

After the two years, Felix was replaced by Porcius Festus, and Paul was required to give his defense all over again (See Acts 21:17 through 26:23). Festus wanted to send Paul back to Jerusalem to stand trial there. Unfortunately, Paul would have faced death there again, so he said "I appeal to Caesar". This meant that he would, of necessity, be sent to Rome for his trial.

God opened a door for Paul to witness to both a Roman Governor and a Judaen King

The above sounded bad for Paul, but the sequence of events actually opened the door for Paul to witness to both high level Roman officials and subsequently to King Herod Agrippa of Judea, who Paul had an audience with before he set sail for Rome. This gave Paul a whole new realm in which to tell of Christ Jesus, which would have far reaching, positive influence in the spread of Christianity.

Part III Section 4 - Paul Sent to Rome as a prisoner

Thus, Paul started on his fourth missionary journey, but this time as a prisoner. He had hoped to visit Rome, but not as a prisoner. However, God often works in mysterious ways. He was put on board a ship among other prisoners bound for Rome. But the ship he started out on was not headed there. So he was transferred to other ships along the way.

On the way Paul had another chance to witness for Christ

One of those ships encountered rough seas, and ran aground and was destroyed on the island of Malta. There, Paul proved he was chosen by God because of two events. First, Paul was bitten by a poisonous snake and the local people expected him to die. However the snake bight had no effect on him, a big surprise to the locals. Then Paul was able to heal the father of the local chief, who was sick of a fever and dysentery, simply by praying over him and laying his hand on him. After this, Paul healed a number of others on the island (See Acts 27:39 through 28:10). . *Malta later became a bastion for Christianity in the Mediterranean Sea, possibly initiated by Paul's visit there*

Paul arrived in Rome and was welcomed by believers there

After staying in Malta for a season, Paul was taken by another ship to Italy and eventually to Rome. On the way to and in Rome itself he discovered a number of believers and truth seekers already there, who found him a comfortable place to live, with only a Roman guard. And Paul was again able to witness to them. However, he again found some dissension among the Jewish leadership there, and he decided again to turn to the Gentiles to expand the body of believers (See Acts 28:24-30).

Details of Paul's stay in Rome

Paul's stay in Rome was apparently fairly lengthy while he awaited trial. It was initially quite fruitful, in that he gained a number of new followers (See Acts 28:16-23), and wrote several of the his letters there that were later chosen to be parts of the New Testament. *Though not in the Bible, legend has it that during his stay he may have been temporarily released, and traveled to and witnessed in Spain. He was apparently later executed in Rome during one of the purges by one of the increasingly virulent and insane Roman emperors.* Toward the end in his second letter to Timothy, he sounded somewhat depressed, probably not realizing what a fulfilling life he had lived and what a tremendous, positive impact he had had on the spread of Christianity (See Second Timothy 4:6-18).

This ends the story of the first century spread of Christianity according to Acts, but it appears that Luke's account in Acts was really only part (however a very important part) of the story,of the remarkable spread of Christianity throughout the Roman empire. *But since those other such historical accounts were not in the Bible, I will leave them to other authors.* However, much more of the first century growth of Christianity is revealed in the letters written to the first century churches and individuals that appear in the New Testament after Acts, as will be seen following.

Part III Section 5 - Letters of the New Testament

After the four gospels and Acts, most of the rest of the New Testament of the Bible is made up of copies of letters written either to various Christian churches or to individual believers across modern day Turkey and Greece and in the city of Rome, Italy. Most of the letters followed a standard format of the time, that began with a greeting which included identification of the author, and ended with personal information and a gracious salutation. All of them included praises, but also criticisms of various unchristian actions or attitudes that had crept into their worship practices. And in several were instructions as to proper practices of worship and living.

Nine of the letters to churches were written by the apostle Paul to specific churches by name; Romans, First and Second Corinthians, Galations, Ephesians, Phillippians, Colossians, and First and Second Thessalonians. Paul also wrote four letters to individuals; First and Second Timothy, Titus, and Philemon. The apostles Peter and John wrote three letters to Christians in general; first and Second Peter and First John. Also, James, Jesus' half brother, wrote one letter to Christians in general. Also, John wrote two letters to individuals. And another of Jesus' half brothers, Jude, wrote letter to an individual. Also one letter, Hebrews, was written by an unidentified author, but which might have been written by Paul. All of these letters appear in the New Testament.

The apostle John also wrote the last book of the New Testament (Revelation of Jesus Christ, commonly known just as Revelation), which is made up partly of letters to seven individual churches, but mostly of prophesies of the future, as they relate to Christianity.

The order in which Paul's letters appear in the Bible are fairly obviously <u>not</u> in the order they were written, (Romans, one of Paul's later letters, appears before Galatians, which was probably Paul's first letter). However, the letters are grouped together by author. All but Paul's letters were probably originally written in Hebrew. Paul was multi-lingual, so I suspect that his letters were most likely written in the language of the letter recipients. Also, the styles of his letters appear to be tailored to the recipients' culture. For instance, Romans seems based in Greco/Roman logical processes, while the Corinthian letters are plain spoken. And his letter to the Ephesians seems to recognize their intelligence and sophistication. But all of them express the sound foundation of belief in Christ. And among other things, they deal with issues (errors and misconceptions) encountered by the new, rapidly growing and multiplying churches.

Errors and misconceptions in the early churches

One of the primary items dealt with in the letters to the churches and individual believers were the several wrong ideas that had crept into the doctrines of the various new Christian churches. The authors of these letters tried to combat these wrong ideas and tried also to refine the basic concepts of worship of Jesus Christ. Expressed below are some of the more prominent concerns, followed by a section on proper attitudes and actions among believers. First, let us begin with the errors and concerns.

Predestination

It is obvious that Christianity began to spread rapidly shortly after Jesus assended. Unfortunately, several misconceptions of this belief in Christ intruded themselves into worship. One was that it was a Jewish sect, meant for Jews only. This idea took two directions. One was that anyone who tried to bring Gentiles into the faith was a gross sinner and worthy of death, ergo attempts on Paul's life. The other direction, insisted on by converted pharisees, was that if a non-Jew wanted to be a Christian, he or she must first become a Jew by espousing to the laws of Moses, separate from belief in Christ as saviour. Among other things, this meant that they should only eat foods blessed by Jewish priests (kosher), and also that the men must become circumcised. Both Peter and Paul preached against this. Paul, in his letter to the Romans, stated that the path to Christianity was through the grace of God via confession of ones belief in Christ as saviour and redeemer, and belief in one's heart in Christ as their saviour, not through works or ritual. Peter in particular found this out in a vision and gave witness to it in his letters and actions (See Acts 10:9-16 and Acts 10:34-47).

And there is also a more modern version of this assumption of predestination, adopted by several Christian denominations, that God preselects those who will be saved, an idea expressed by the man John Calvin. Those who espouse this concept cite Ephesians 1:4-9. However, in context, this scripture is inclusive rather than exclusive, because it refers to the opening of the door for Gentiles to enter the Kingdom, not closing it. In support of this, with the "great commission" Jesus sent his disciples into all the world (not just to the preselected) that all might be saved. Also, Paul, in Romans 9:9 said that the path to salvation is through faith (no mention of preselection). And Paul, in First Timothy 2:3-4, said that God desires all people to be saved.

Christians are no longer sinners

Another misconception was that a true Christian no longer commits sins. Paul countered this by confessing in both Romans and First Timothy that he was a sinner and had continued to be so, even though he was trying not to be. And Paul said that only by the grace of God through Jesus Christ are our sins not recognized and are forgiven (See Romans 3:23-25 and 7:14-25 and First Timothy 1:15). Unfortunately, another and extreme misconception of sinning was the idea that one should increase in sinning so that God's grace would be increased, a horrible idea, and something that Paul preached against. In several of the letters by both Paul and others, it was pointed out that we as humans are all sinners, and that when we accept Christ that we do not become sinless but that instead, our sins are forgiven. And also that in accepting Christ's forgiveness we recognize our inherent sinful nature, and that we should try to reduce our sinning, not increase it. (Interestingly, Paul said that the Law of Moses was important in that it helped us recognize sin and sinning [See Romans 7:7-12].)

The immediate return of Christ

And another early misconception was that Christ's return was imminent, even though Jesus himself said that even he did not know the time, but that it was up to God, his father. Many in the early church in Jerusalem joyously quit their jobs, and sold everything they had to join together and live in worship awaiting his return. These people, over time, ran out of resources and became destitute. Paul stated in one or more of his letters that he was collecting money to help them out. Peter also recognized this misconception in Second Peter 3:8 where he said "But do not overlook this fact beloved, that with the Lord, one day is as a thousand years, and a thousand years is as a day." Even today many believers still say that we are in the end times. But we really don't know this, because the end times are not in our hands or even ours to assume, but in the hands of God only (See Matthew 24:36).

Stoicism

Another problem in the early church was a philosophy called Stoicism. It was based on the idea that the ultimate goal of humans was to live a "virtuous" life, and that this was an end in itself. This idea was propounded by a number of philosophers including the Greek philosopher, Aristotle. Unfortunately, this went against the Christian contention that all men are sinners by nature and could not stop being so on their own. And thus, ultimate virtue is an impossible state, that instead requires salvation by the grace of God through Jesus/Christ, separate from human abilities,. It also seemed to ignore the power of prayer in its ability to create change, a basic Christian principle. Remember that Jesus said **"I am the door. Knock and it shall be opened to you. Ask anything in faith and it shall be given to you."** Paul and others fought against the stoic philosophy, in that it denied a personal God who loves and cares for his creations, including humans.

The practices of the Nicolaitans

In the New Testament book of Revelation, the practices of the Nicolaitans are condemned (See Rev. 2:6 and 2:15-16). The Bible does not say what these practices were, but other writings of the time seemed to indicate that the Nicolaitans were a so-called Christian sect, which apparently involved acceptance of sexual intimacy with multiple partners and sex orgies as normal and sin-free practices, even for Christians.

Complacency and prosperity

Throughout history there has persisted a belief that acceptance of God's grace would guarantee peace and prosperity for the believer. However, Jesus warned that belief in him would result in problems and strife, not prosperity and comfort, and that there will be enemies. To confirm this, Jesus taught that Christians should love their enemies. Also, several letters in the New Testament acknowledged the problems facing the early churches and Christians in general, involved arrest and execution of individuals (i.e. Saul's early persecution, and the execution of Steven the deacon and James the apostle). Also, Jesus taught that destitution and disease would always be a fact of life. And also he taught that that prosperity was not a benefit of belief in Christ, but could actually be a detriment to commitment (i.e. the rich young ruler who turned away when Jesus told him to give away what he had). And also in Revelation, John quoted Christ as saying in his letter to the church in Laodicea that he would **"spit you out of my mouth"** because they were **"lukewarm"** and that they were saying that they were rich and prosperous and needed nothing (See Rev. 3:15-17). *It* *appears that the peace that Christianity provides is an inner peace that God's will is in control, but that physical prosperity is never promised.*

How to act as Christians

In order to counter some of the errors expressed above, the authors of the letters gave several recommendations for proper thinking and actions as representatives of the Christian faith on earth. Below are the most prominent of those.

Love one another

Several of the letters gave instructions to believers on how one should feel, think, and act as Christians while on earth. Love was predominant in such, in that love for fellow-man was a sign and symbol in the recognition of the followers of Christ. However, Christian love is not characterized by common types of love; erotic (sexual) love, possessive love, selfish love, dependant love, masochistic love, or love of animals, inanimate things, or possessions. It is instead the honest caring for, the desire for the best for, and the feeling of comradery with other human beings, which should ultimately lead to action (See the story of the good Samaritan in Luke 10:25-37). Jesus summarized God's fifth through tenth commandments in the statement that people should love one another, and that must also even include love of ones enemies. Paul epitomized love in First Corinthians chapter 13. He spoke of love as the only permanent thing in time and space, and that it is more important than even hope or faith. He then described the characteristics of Christian love as patience, kindness, not envious, nor boastful, nor arrogant, rude, nor insistent on its own way, nor resentful. He also said that love opposes wrong-doing and rejoices in truth (See First Corinthians 13:6).

In the apostle John's first letter, he also spoke extensively of love and its inherent importance in the Christian existence (See First john 3:11 through 4:21).

Recognize of God's love for humans

Jesus had said in conversation with the Pharisee Nicodemus in the gospel of John "that God so loved the world that he sent his only begotten son". Also, the letters of the New Testament are full of references of God's love for us, not just for Christians but for all of humanity (For example, see Romans 5:5, Ephesians 5:2, First John 2:5, 4:8-9, and 4:16, etc.).

Love God

In the Old Testament, the first four of the Ten Commandments dealt with love and respect for God. In the New Testament, Jesus summarized those into a statement that we are to love the Lord with all our heart, soul, strength, and mind (See Luke 10:25-27). **And he said that this was the first and greatest commandment.** Because without God there would be no creation, guidance, nor purpose. And without God we would not exist.

Practice Christian love within one's Christian family

In both Ephesians 5:22-26 and Colossians 3:18-19 Paul said that wives must respect and submit to their husbands, and accept the idea that the husband is the head of the wife. But also husbands must love their wives as they do their own bodies. Also, the husband must hold his wife as more important than his parents, and hold fast to her so that they become one in the flesh. In addition, children must honor and obey their parents. However, fathers must not provoke their children to anger, but instead be a teacher to bring them up in the discipline and instruction of the Lord (See Ephesians 5:22 through 6:4). Also, Peter said similar things about husbands and wives, that wives be subject to their husbands and not adorn themselves in gaudy fashion on the outside, but instead be adorned with inner beauty. And also, Paul devotes two whole sections of his first letter to the Corinthians to the issues of husband/wife relationships, and of marriage and children (See First Corinthians 7:1-16 and 11:2-15) However, he also suggested that the unmarried remain so unless sexual passion forces it, because he was concerned that in marriage, concerns for a spouse could dilute one's relationship with God (See First Corinthians 7:17-38).

Paul also said that women should not speak in church services (See First Corinthians 14:34-35). This instruction of Paul's however, is often ignored in current-day churches, where in some evangelical denominations, women are ordained as ministers and serve as preachers and pastors. Also, women often serve as Bible teachers in Christian churches. *I, unfortunately, must leave decisions on this issue up to individual and denominational interpretation. I sometimes wonder if Paul was influenced on this issue by the cultural standards of his time, rather than God's guidance. Blasphemy? I hope not.*

Apply Christian principles in master/slave relationships

Interestingly, the Bible does not condemn slavery as such, but rather gives important instructions as to the treatment of slaves. Paul said in Galatians 3:28 "under Christ, there is no distinction between slave and free". Paul also said in Ephesians 6:5-9 that slaves should obey their earthly masters, not just as people pleasers or with eye service, but rather from the heart, as servants of Christ. And, masters must do the same and stop their threatening behavior toward slaves, knowing that both are equal under Christ". And again in Colossians 3:22 and 4:1 are expressed what slave/master relations should be like. Also, the whole thrust of Paul's letter to Philemon, a slave owner, was to take back Onesimus, a run-away slave, without reprisal, but as a fellow Christian.

In more recent times, slavery has become an abhorrent practice not so much as over-under master to slave relationship but because of the assumptions among owners that slaves were lower forms of life, and were most often being considered property, just like farm animals or land, rather than as human beings, and were also manhandled and punished in very ungodly ways.

Unfortunately, it took a very bloody war in the U.S. to abolish this practice. But the associated attitudes have taken longer to resolve (skin color discrimination and overt attention to skin color in education, employment, and promotions, property ownership, etc.)

And other forms of slavery still exist in what is called "white slavery" (an abhorrent practice related to sex trade), and servitude bound by contract (such as professional athletes and military service).

Biblical teachings about slavery might also, in modern times, be related to and applied to employer-employee relationships as well.

It should also be noted that there is no mention of skin color in the Bible in connection with slavery.

Have no discrimination between Jewish and Gentile Christians

In his letters, Paul repeatedly denied that there was a difference between Jewish and Gentile Christians. In fact he often found that Gentiles were more receptive to his teaching than were Jews, and were endowed with the same Holy Spirit once they had accepted Christ as their saviour. Throughout Romans, Paul warned Jews not to depend on their heritage for salvation, but to be aware that salvation comes through faith and the gracious gift of God, and not through any other means. Also in Galatians 3:7-9 Paul preached that Gentiles who accepted Christ would be saved as well. And again in Galatians 5:6 he said that circumcision (a Jewish practice) counts for nothing in Christ's kingdom, only faith. And also, that the Gentiles have equal access to salvation, even if they had not been following the laws on Moses (See Romans 3:9 and 3:23). In addition, Paul praised the Gentiles for their acceptance and sincerity of their faith (See Romans 15:8-18).

This situation can be applied to many situations today, for instance animosity between Jews and Christians, Catholics and Evangelicals, congregations that mostly made up of black skinned people and white skinned people, and between the various evangelical denominations (liberal vs fundamental vs Pentecostal), (and also between mainstream Christian churches and Mormons, Jehovah's Witnesses, or Christian Scientists). All of these varieties contain many elements or concepts of Christianity, and thus are not enemies. They are only the products of often earnest believers in Christ who may have taken divergent tracks due to human limitations and misunderstandings. One should always remember that Jesus taught that we should love even our enemies.

Follow Biblical guidance in dealing with homosexuality

Like slavery, the Bible does not condemn homosexuality as a sin, but rather the sexual practices relating to it. In his letter to the church in Rome, Paul roundly condemns such practices by both men and women, but also liking thiese practices to a whole list of other unrighteous acts, saying those who practice these things deserve to die *(as do all sinners)*. And this condemnation includes not only those who practice them but also those who give approval of these acts (See Romans 1:24-32). *So it looks to me like those who consider homosexual acts not a sin or support the legitimacy of gay marriage, are as guilty of sinning as much as those who practice same sex intercourse.*

169

However, we are taught by Christ that if we acknowledge our sins, and sincerely feel and accept the guilt, and confess them, we will be given the power through belief in Christ to try to avoid sinning, and our sins will be forgiven. Thus, we all, even those with homosexual tendencies, can become citizens of God's kingdom and have eternal life, if we recognize our sins and ask forgiveness of those sins, and accept of the lordship of Christ as our guide and saviour (See John 8:10-11 and Romans 6:3-11).

Do not judge others

In Matthew, chapter 7 Jesus condemned judging others because in doing so, we open ourselves to being judged. And he gave an example of not recognizing our own sins when we pass judgement on others. He said that we must clear out own sins first. In Paul's letter to the Romans, he said that we have no excuse for passing judgement on others, because in doing so we only store up wrath within ourselves instead of love and caring, and will ourselves be judged by God for finding fault in others while we ourselves are sinners (See Romans 2:1-5).

However, I believe this admonition to not judge others does not apply to courts of law, since those courts are intended to protect society from the dangers of the unjust, and where judgement is intended to be based on evidence, not on a person's personal opinion. And there are also laws that permit review in case personal biases might be found to have entered into a court's decision.

Speak in tongues only if this practice is beneficial to others

Speaking in tongues was first noted in the book of Acts at Pentecost (See Acts 2:4-12), where believers were given the gift of speaking in "other languages" as a method of reaching people who spoke the various languages of the time, to tell them of Jesus/Christ. It soon however, became a general sign of proof that the tongue speaker was a child of God, whether or not the members of the speakers' audience could understand what they were saying. The Pentecostal faith embraces speaking in tongues as an inherent and basic part of worship. Paul had a lot to say in his first letter to the Corinthians about speaking in tongues. First, he told the Corinthians to, most importantly, pursue love and prophesy in one's worship practice. Then he downplayed speaking in tongues because one did so might not be understood by another person, and would less effective than if he were prophesying, and that a tongue speaker does not uplift anyone unless there is an interpreter. Then Paul, using himself as an example, admitted that he was fluent in several languages, but that this was a useless talent if what he said could not be understood by his listeners (See First Corinthians 14:1-25). Then Paul went on to say that when believers assemble to worship, there should be only two or three who speak in tongues and each in turn, and there must be someone present to interpret what they are saying (See First Corinthians 14:26-28).

Respect governmental authority

Both Paul in his letter to the Romans and Peter in his first letter told the readers of their correspondence to respect and be subject to governing authorities. Paul went so far as to say that this authority was from God. He also insisted that rulers were not a terror to good conduct

(See Romans 13:1-5). Also Peter said that one must be subject for the Lord's sake to every human institution whether that was the Roman emperor or to governors sent by him. And that this was the duty of the servants of God (See First Peter 2:13-17). The irony of this was that some were eventually executed by the very authorities they told others to respect. Also, the book of Acts records several interactions between Paul and local authorities (some good and some bad) both before and after his conversion, as well as various Roman and royal authorities just prior to and during his trip to Rome. And however though they may have seemed demeaning, they appear to have benefitted his ability to travel to Rome and to witness there (See various references above).

Recognize and practice Fruits of the Spirit

In most of Paul's letters he compared lives that are controlled by sin to those guided by the holy spirit. As an example, in Galatians he said that the works of the flesh are evident; sexual immorality, idolatry, sorcery, enmity, strife, jealousy, fits of anger (*rages*), rivalries, dissensions, envy, divisions, drunkenness, orgies, conceit, provocational attitudes, etc. (*We can see a lot of these in our public lives today: political attacks, worship of entertainment stars and athletes, college partying, work rivalries, demeaning others, alcoholism and drug addiction, road rage, etc.*) But the fruits of the spirit are (*such things as*); love, joy, peace (*of mind*), patience, kindness, goodness, faithfulness, gentleness, and self-control (See Galatians 5:19-26 and also Colossians 3:12-14). (*Fortunately, there is a lot of these approaches to life today. However, we just don't see it on the news.*) Also, in his book, James said the faith should produce good works. This was confirmed by Jesus himself in both his curse on the fig tree that did not bear fruit (*negative*) (See Mark 11:12-14 and 20-21) and his parable of the good Samaritan (*positive*).

Seek and find the proper path to Salvation

First of all, Paul stated that one is justified by faith alone and not by works. He also gave a path to salvation and eternal life that seems simple. In Paul's letter to the Romans, he declared that "if you confess with your mouth that Jesus is Lord and believe in your heart that God raised him from the dead you will be saved" (*into God's kingdom and eternal life*) (See Romans 6:23 and Romans 10:9-10 and also First John 5:13). However, true confession is really difficult, because it requires an undying faith and sincere belief. In Paul's letter to the Ephesians, Paul stated that it is by God's grace that we are saved by faith (in God through the blood of Jesus Christ). And it is not of our own doing, (but) it is a gift of God (See Ephesians 2:5-8). Thus, salvation does not come from the laws of Moses or other Old Testament prophets, or from being of Hebrew heritage, nor even from good works, but from God's grace only, through faith in Jesus Christ (See Romans 3:23-25).

Be confident in the promise of eternal life

In First Corinthians, Paul confirmed that believers will have eternal life when he pronounced that Christ rose from the dead as the first-fruits of those who believe in him, saying "For as by a man came death, by a man (Jesus) has come also the resurrection of the dead. For as in Adam all die, so also in Christ shall also be made alive" (See First Corinthians 15:19-22)..

Look forward and not fear Life after (Physical) Death

Jesus told some of what life after death would be like in Matthew 22:30-32, where he said that the saved would be like angels and that there would be no marriages. In Ephesians 2:6, Paul said that we will be seated with Christ. In Philippians 3:20-21 Paul said that Christ will "transform our lowly bodies to be like his glorious body". And Paul in First Corinthians chapter 15 gave a more thorough explanation of life after death. He explained that there are two states of being, earthly and heavenly (See First Corinthians 15:35-38, 40, and 42-49). Thus, it appears that all earthly limitations and infirmities will be wiped away and one's heavenly body will be perfect and eternal. Also, while full of allegory and symbolism, the book of Revelation gives an interesting view of paradise and our destination there (Especially see Rev. 22:1-5). And even though life after death might sound strange, we are repeatedly told that it will be wonderful beyond all understanding.

Part III Section 6 - Special and unique books of the New Testament, Hebrews and The Revelation of Christ

I have grouped these New Testament books separately because of the uniqueness of their content. One is a letter (Hebrews) which reiterates the past, and one (Revelation) contains seven letters to selected churches in what is now the country of Turkey, but also gives a unique look into the future..

Hebrews

This book was written as a general letter to the children of Israel wherever they might be living. It appears to me and some others that it is generally in the style of Paul's letters. But it is different in that it has no introductory greeting. It does have a final statement referring to "our brother Timothy", indicating that it might have been written by Paul. However, numerous Bible scholars seem to believe he was not the author due what they consider that it was not done in Paul's general writing style. However, I don't believe this is, in any way, a major issue. So I will lay this aside to be considered by someone else.

The letter as a whole indicates that the author had a profound belief in the kingship and inherency of Jesus Christ. It strongly supports the concept that Jesus was the Son of God, reiterating several statements to that effect in the gospels. It warns against rejecting salvation offered by Jesus, but instead to continue to honor him as the one "who, for a little while, was made lower than the angels", so that he might face physical death for our sins. The author also strongly stated that Jesus was greater than Moses (who died), and that Jesus was both God's direct son and "...a priest forever after the order of Melchizedek". The author further stated that Moses brought a covenant with God that included not only repeated blood sacrifices but also an intervening earthly priesthood and a physical earthly place for worship. But Jesus bought a new covenant that abolished the need for repeated blood sacrifices, and for an earthly central place to worship (the Jerusalem temple), and for an intervening priesthood. That new covenant instead provided the blood of Christ as a <u>once-for-all blood sacrifice</u>, and the implantation of the law in the hearts of believers, as a substitute for an earthly place of worship, and by the example of the torn Temple veil, believers given direct access to God. And then after Christ offered his body as the once-for-all sacrifice he was given a seat at the right hand of the throne of God.

This to me however, does not mean that there is not a benefit for places where Christians can gather to help support each other's faiths, nor where there should be places where those who are especially blessed with prophetic, preaching, or teaching skills to speak out. Just as in Jesus' time, the local synagogues provided places where believers could teach each other and strengthen their individual beliefs, local churches provide critical places to assist in spiritual growth among existing believers, and for additional people to be introduced to faith in Jesus/ Christ .

Then the author led the people through their whole heritage from the sacrifice of Able (in Genesis), to the faith of Abraham and the stories of many important people of the Old Testament, to Jesus "the founder a perfecter of our faith". He followed that by admonishing the Hebrews to hold fast to their faith and continue to follow the teachings of Jesus with respect to love and caring for all. Thus, the book of Hebrews brought the people of God from the beginning to the advent of Jesus Christ.

And now we shall, in the book of "The Revelation of Christ", see the future of the world and of those who believe.

Part III Section 6 - The Revelation of Christ

Note: The following is <u>my interpretation</u> of the book of Revelation in the New Testament of the Judeo/Christian Bible, as it appears in the English Standard Version (ESV) translation. I have used no other intermediate source material. All of the below are my own observations, views, musings, and discernment based on that document (except in one place as noted).

The Revelation of Jesus Christ (Revelation for short) is the last book of the Judeo/Christian Bible. And it is unique in that it is a forecast of the future of world and of Christianity. It was written during the later part of the first century after the crucifiction of Jesus. Although it is the words of Jesus/Christ, it was ghost-written by John the Elder. John the Elder is assumed to also be the John who was one of the original twelve disciples of Jesus. At the time of his writing of this document he was a house-arrest prisoner of Rome on the island of Patmos, just off the southwest coast of Turkey.

Revelation is also quite unique in that it uses a plethora of innuendo, allegory, symbolism, sacred numerology, and what often appears to be fantasy, to depict what will happen in God's kingdom in the future. It starts off in chapter one with a meeting between John and, by then, a mature Jesus/Christ, with whom John fell at his feet and worshiped. In this meeting, Christ expressed his intent to write letters to seven individual Christian churches which were located in what is now the country of Turkey. And the contents of those letters are recorded in chapters two and three of the book of Revelation. And then in the rest of the book, Christ lead John through a series of prophesies about God, Christianity, and the world

Christ's letters to his churches

John documented those letters in the book of Revelation. In them, Christ told each church what was right and what was wrong in their individual promulgation of the faith. He praised five of the churches (the churches in Ephesus, Smyrna, Pergamum, Thyatira, and Philadelphia) for their success and fortitude, even though warning them of dangers of earthly compromises.

But for two churches he had only concerns. In his letter to the church in Sardis he told them that even though their works were good, their faith was actually dead. He also told them to wake up before it was too late. (I believe this is a lesson for many non-faith-related charities today. The lesson, I believe, is that charities should grow from faith, not stand alone, because they are often in danger of being victimized by profiteers or can easily fall victim to political issues.) The other church Christ condemned was in Laodicea. He told them that they were only "luke warm", and that because of that, he would "spew them out of my mouth". He based this on the fact the they were a well-off, self satisfied church with no strong drive for their faith (See Rev. Chapters 2 and 3). (This condemnation unfortunately could apply to many large churches in America today.)

After Revelation Chapter Three - Prophecies of the future

Then in chapter four begins a series of allegorical and symbolic visions that Christ used to lead the Apostle John into the future, many with overtones of sacred numbers, seven and twelve. Since this part of Revelation is prophetic, I will use the future tense in my comments from here on where-ever appropriate (except for chapter ten)..

The Sacred Numbers

The numbers "seven" and "twelve" are used in many contexts in the Judeo/Christian Bible, along with multiples of those numbers. The number twelve was often used to indicate completeness. For instance, both Ishmael and Jacob/Israel had twelve sons. There were twelve tribes of Hebrews led out of Egypt by Moses, who maintained their separate identities throughout the Old Testament. In the New Testament Jesus chose twelve men to be his inner circle of disciples. And when Judas Iscariot betrayed Jesus, the remaining eleven were quick to choose a replacement to make the number again twelve.

In Biblical terms, the number twelve indicates totality or completeness. In Revelation the number twelve and multiples thereof (twenty four, one hundred forty four, twelve thousand, and one hundred forty four thousand) are used to signify wholeness, all, full, and completeness, assuring that praise, respect, and love for God is compete among all believers (a horizontal or breadth dimension).

On the other hand, the number seven and multiples thereof were used to indicate the ultimate, best, or finest (a height dimension), thus the identification of God as the Great "**I Am Who I Am**" as He informed Moses in Exodus 3:13 as being the all-in-all of existence, of understanding, and of creation. And also in the New Testament, when Jesus was asked if one should forgive seven times for a wrong done by someone else, Jesus said "no, seventy times seven".

These sacred numbers (seven and twelve) and their meanings are used extensively throughout Revelation from chapter four onward, as the reader will see.

A look at Heaven

Chapter four opens the door to heaven. In its center is God, sitting on his great throne. And surrounding that throne are twenty four other thrones occupied by twenty four elders of the faith. Also, standing by are "Four Living Creatures" often identified as the four gospels. of the New Testament, (Matthew, Mark, Luke, and John), who, without pause, continue to praise and worship God (See Rev. 4:1-11).

The words of God, the first six of the seven seals, and impending dangers

In God's right hand John saw a sealed scroll. And he recognized that Christ (the lamb that was slain) would be designated as the only one worthy to open the scroll (The word of God). But this time, Christ has a different appearance. This time he appears, not as a lamb, but as a mature Ram, and endowed by God with seven spirits which are represented by special physical characteristics; seven horns *(indicating ultimate power)* and seven eyes *(indicating ultimate vision and understanding)*. And the four living creatures are seen to fall down before him and confirm Christ's worthiness to open the seven seals that protect the scroll. Then they will continue in worship of both God and Christ (See Rev. 5:1-14).

Christ then will open the first four seals to release onto earth what is known as the "four horsemen of the apocalypse", (1) capability and propensity to make war, (2) war itself, (3) human suffering during war, and (4) and genocide and chaos resulting from war. He then will open the fifth seal to reveal the myriads of people who have died for their worship of God and their witnessing for Christ. Then Christ's opening of the sixth seal will bring terrible natural disasters on the earth; earthquakes, floods, wind storms, and droughts (See Rev. 6:1-17).

These forecasts of calamities are similar to the forecasts of the catastrophic events in Matthew that will happen before the return of Christ (See Mat. 24:1-8), but in significantly more detail.

The protection of the believers

But during these calamities, the chosen, will be represented by a multiple of the number twelve (144,000), and that number will be broken up into twelve parts represented by the twelve tribes of Israel (12,000 each) and will be protected from harm. Thus, those protected will all be equal, no matter how relatively powerful or numerous the people of the twelve tribes had become. Again being the sacred number representing the fullness and totality of Christ's followers. This is reminiscent of what Jesus taught in his parable about the land owner who hired crop reapers, some in the morning, some at midday, and some in the evening, but who he paid all the same wages. (Where Jesus, in essence, taught that all are equal in the kingdom of God.) (See Mat. 20:1-16).

Then John saw an un-countable number of people from all the earth standing before God and Christ, crying out "Salvation belongs to our God and to Christ who was crucified". These were identified as those who had suffered through the calamities listed above. These will also be protected and will be in continuing service to and in worship of God (See Rev. 7:1-17).

The Seventh seal and further disasters

Then Christ will open the seventh seal, to reveal seven angels with trumpets and also an eighth angel who will light a censer to spread the pleasant odor of heaven. But then he will throw the censer to earth to cause further earthquakes, lightning, and thunder.

Then the seven angels will blow their trumpets to cause further disasters on and to the earth, which will be brought particularly against those who had not been previously chosen and protected. The result of the trumpet blast of the first angel will be fire and volcanic eruptions. Then the second angle will cause the earth to be struck by an asteroid. The third angel will cause darkness over the earth. Then, after a warning by an eagle, the fourth angel will cause the earth to be struck by another asteroid, which will cause a swarm of stinging locusts to be unleashed on the people who were not among the chosen. Then the horn of the sixth angel will release a huge army of soldiers from the east who will kill many more people. But even after all these disasters, John was told that the remaining unchosen people will not repent of their sinning.

A little scroll

Then in Revelation Chapter Ten, John saw a new angel who presented him with a quite small scroll, and ordered him to take and eat it. *This to me is another way of presenting the communion bread of the Last Supper when Jesus told the disciples that the bread represented his body (his life force, his teachings, and his miracles as a human being on earth).* John ate the scroll (the acceptance of Christ as the son of God) and it tasted good, but resulted in digestive problems. Thus, just as Jesus' words and actions were pleasant to hear and see, but they would result in physical dangers and difficulties for those who take him into their hearts. *And this will be a small scroll, representing only Christ's earthly presence, as opposed to the timelessness and infinite power of Christ as the Son of God, seated at his right hand for all time and eternity* (See John 1:1-3, Colossians 3:1, and Revelation 1:17-18). Then, John was told to continue with his effort to document the Revelation of Christ (See Revelation 10:1-11).

John Continued His Prophesies

Apparently renewed by his ingestion of the Little Scroll, John continued to prophesy. In Revelation chapter eleven John was first asked to measure the temple in Jerusalem apparently in order to preserve knowledge of it, because the whole of Jerusalem will be destroyed. This did occur in AD 70, when the Roman army attacked the city. But John also predicted the rise of two strong witnesses for Christ. *(I assume that he was referring to Peter and Paul)*. And he also predicted that they would eventually be killed by Satan, and the followers of Satan will celebrate their deaths. But, however, they will enter heaven at God's personal request. And when this happens, a significant part of the remains of Jerusalem will be destroyed by an earthquake, and many people will be killed by it. And the seventh angel will blow his trumpet and the leaders of the faith will again worship God. And then another significant event will occur. **God's temple will open up in heaven** (See Rev. chapter 11).

John then prophesied about Satan and the early church

John said that there will be a woman honored by God. But she will be pregnant. And there will be Satan, in the form of a red dragon, who will be waiting to devour the child as soon as he is born. *To my thinking, the woman was the early church, and her child would be the worldwide spread of the gospel of Christ.* But Satan will be defeated by the angels of God and will be cast down to earth. And Satan's plans to devour the child will be thwarted, *(This child has been suspected of possibly being someone who would be responsible for great advances in Christianity, possibly Roman emperor Constantine, who in the fifth century AD turned Christianity from a mistrusted, demeaned, and persecuted body of believers, to the primary religion of the Roman Empire, an area that covered much of Europe, North Africa, and the Middle East.)*

When Satan fails to devour the child, he will go after the mother, and try to drown her. When this fails, he will go after the individual disciples, to try to corrupt them individually, *(something that is still going on today)* (See Rev. chapter12).

After this, John prophesied about two powerful beasts

*This prophesy appears to me to be different from others, because John seems to possibly identify these two beasts as specific individuals who he said ay have been known to the readers of his book. I think it could be referring to two Roman emperors of the time, one beast who was thought declared himself to be god, and also one who required the people to worship the first beast, and to be slaves to his own whims. John ends this prophesy with a identification of the second beast with the number **666**, and notes that discerning people should be able to figure out why. Unlike the rest of this prophesy, some of the source material I have used and some of the assumptions I have made are based on data from Wikipedia.*

A first beast will rise out of the sea, and will be ugly, powerful, and aggressive, and will speak with numerous obscenities. It will be severely injured *(poisoned)*, but will recover. And it will be highly popular and will be worshiped as immortal by those on earth who's names had not previously been identified as followers of Christ. And it will make war against Christ's followers who must have endurance against this beast's attacks (See Rev. 13:1-10). *It is possible that this beast is a caricature of emperor Nero, who in the later part of the first century had many Christians tortured and killed (including Peter and Paul). He was considered divine by many who were expecting him to return from the dead.*

Then a second beast (or identified later as a "false prophet") will rise out of the land. It will look acceptable and innocent, but will speak like a dragon, and will encourage worship of the first beast <u>and make an image of it.</u> This second beast will be able to perform seaming miracles that will impress people, and will also attempt to control commerce by requiring business people to be branded and licensed in order to conduct their businesses. He also was a sworn enemy of Christianity and Christians. And this beast will have a number associated with it, **666** (See Rev. 13:11-18). *It is assumed by some that this was the caricature of Emperor Diocletian who ruled the Roman empire in the third century AD, not from Rome, but from the land across the Adriatic Sea, in what is in area that is now part of modern-day Croatia. Diocletian appears identified with the number 666 because his name is quite similar in Latin vernacular to the letters in the Roman numbering system for six hundred sixty six.*

John saw the crucified Christ standing among a large special group of believers

John then had a vision of the slain lamb (Christ) standing at the center of worship among a huge group of men who had not married nor had sexual intercourse with a woman. And he identified these as having been protected and taken out of the world before the tragedies that were to befall mankind. And John heard God speak from heaven, and also heard singing in praise of him (See Rev. 14:1-5).

John then saw angels proclaiming that the end (of all things) had come

Then he foresaw an angel flying over the earth, proclaiming that all should worship God, for the <u>end</u> has come. (This is the first time in Revelation that John predicted the end of time and that the judgement had come.)

Then he saw a second angel that will proclaim the fall of what appears to be the corrupt and sinful world order (Babylon), (and apparently in the process of the fall, the first beast will be conquered and and its image will be destroyed).

And a third angel will follow, who will declare that anyone who has been worshiping the first beast (mentioned above) will be thrown into the fires of hell. But there will remain believers on earth who must endure and hold fast to their faith in Jesus Christ. And some of them will die, but they will be blessed.

John prophesied that Christ will come again, this time with dire purpose

At this point and beyond, John's dire prophetic writing becomes almost lyrical, with the prediction that Christ will come to earth again, but this time he will come as a harvester with a sharp sickle to harvest the earth. And those not of the faith will be crushed like grapes in a wine press, and their blood will flood over the land (See Rev. 14:14-26). This prophesy is similar to the statements of Jesus about his purpose and actions at his second coming as documented in the twenty fourth chapter of the gospel of Matthew. But John's prophesy of Christ's second coming adds a note that angels will come from the new temple in heaven who will encourage and assist him in this action.

And again John prophesied, this time about seven more angels and seven bowls of plagues

Special note: It appears to me that John's prophesies are not ordered by time, but are independent of each other. This prophesy and others following appear thus not in sequential order. This particular prophesy appears to be about events that will precede the ones described in the prophesy above. And it also may be of a one-time occurrence or several similar events recurring over and over again over time. Also, although some might consider this prophesy a harbinger of the last days, I suspect it might simply be a forecast of future dire events that will occur over a period of time. Together, the events below seem to be an ominous grouping of catastrophes. However, one must remember that this book is the "Revelation of Christ", and he had told his disciples that even he did not know the time of his second coming nor the timing of the end of all things.

This time, John prophesied that these seven angels will carry bowls containing seven plagues of God's wrath that will infect the earth until the end of time. But first, John again saw the throne room of God and its sea of glass. And standing beside it will be those who had conquered the beast. And they will be singing a song of praise to both Moses and Christ. After this, the seven angels will appear, and be given seven bowls containing the seven plagues. And God himself will tell the angels to pour the contents of the bowls onto the earth.

The contents of the first bowl will cause painful sores to appear on the bodies of those who had followed the beast. *(Could this be resurgence of smallpox?)* The contents of the second bowl will cause the sea to be poisoned and the sea life to be killed *(Red tide?)*. The contents of the third bowl will poison the rivers and streams *(Blue green algae?)*. The fourth bowl will make the sun hotter to scorch the people *(Global warming?)*. The fifth bowl will increase the pain and anguish of the beast worshipers *(Arthritis, sciatica, gout, etal?)*. The sixth bowl will cause a drought over the earth *(Brought on by global warming?)*. And the seventh bowl will bring about increases in earthquakes and weather disasters on the earth *(Happening now)*, the destruction of powerful nations *(Prospects of societal breakdowns and another even more destructive global war)*, and disappearance of islands and mountains *(Sea level rise, also happening now)* (See Rev. Chapters 15 and 16). *Wow, frightening.*

179

John next prophesied about a "Great Prostitute" and the end of Rome

This time John was carried away to a wilderness, where he saw a great prostitute sitting on the back of the beast. He described the beast as red. But otherwise his description appears to be the same one as identified as the "first beast" in Rev. 13. *I believe that in this case John fairly clearly identified the first east as the rule and power of The Roman empire. And also he appeared to identify the great prostitute as the immoral and debouched culture of the people of the city of Rome and the influence of this culture on the whole Roman empire .* He prophesied that there already have been and will continue to be a series of corrupt rulers. And he also prophesied that many kings of the earth will continue to pay homage to the beast, and will continue for a while to share the benefits and profits of cooperating with the beast and to enjoy the sumptuous living and the misguided pride of the great prostitute. And also the beast will make war on the chosen of Christ. John also, in the prophesy, further called the beast and its culture by the additional name "Babylon".

However, John prophesied that Christianity will eventually win, and that plagues will come and destroy "the beast/the great prostitute/Babylon" in one day, and fire will consume it. But he also predicted that the whole business and trade culture that prospered as part of this entity will also collapse, bringing death, mourning, and famine (See Rev. 17 and 18). (This is an amplification of John's previous statements about the fall of Babylon, the rescue of the chosen, and the torture of the beast's followers in Rev.14:8-11.)

In the fourth century AD Rome was actually invaded and destroyed by a barbarian hoard, and all aspects of John's prophesy occurred. The city of Rome has never again become a world power, and for a time, due to destitution and disease, its population was reduced from millions to only a few thousand people. However, a century later the empire was resurrected as a <u>*Christian*</u> *nation in Constantinople, under the leadership the Christian emperor Constantine.*

Also, in this prophecy is special reference to the disasters that will happen even to the good parts of the culture and the economy. I think no one really recognizes the fragility of manufacturing, trade, exchange, and transportation of goods that are dependant on stability of governments and the currencies of those governments and their economies when a world order collapses if or when the political governing bodies are destroyed, as to the examples cited in John's prophesies about the destruction of the beast/Babylon (See Rev.18:11-19 and 22).

Another special note: The economic stability of the world today appears far more fragile than many assume. A breakdown of law and order in a major country or a major war today can do far more damage to world standards of living and can bring on mass starvation and famine on a vast scale, far greater than anything previously experienced in the history of the world. A world apocalypse is a real risk and would be an awful catastrophe. And it could easily happen in our time, and only God can save us if it does.

Heaven will rejoice at the fall of the great prostitute

John's next prophesy was that there will be great rejoicing in heaven, praising God's judgement against the great prostitute (and the beast/Babylon). And that the previously mentioned twenty four elders and four living creatures will fall down again and worship God, saying "Amen, Hallelujah". And that this will signal a marriage between the slain saints and the churches they represent to the resurrected lamb (Christ). And the symbolic bride *(who is the body of believers in him)*, who will be clothed for the wedding ceremony in **"the righteous deeds of the saints"** (See Rev. 19:1-10).

The second coming of Christ, this time as a judge and righteous conqueror

Then John prophesied a second time about the Christ's return. (For the first time see John *Rev. 14:14-26 above*.) And he described the event this time as follows: The heavens will be opened and another white horse will appear (not the white horse of the apocalypse). And this time the rider will be "called faithful and true, and in righteousness he will judge and make war" (this time against the forces of evil). And he will be crowned with many crowns and will be clothed in a robe dipped in blood *(which I believe is both Christ's blood and the blood of the saints who will be killed for their belief and witness). A*nd he will be confirmed again as "the Word of God". And he will lead an angel army. And there will be great disasters, death, and destruction of the followers of the beast. And the beast and a "false prophet" *(which I believe is a revised definition of the second beast mentioned previously in Rev. 13:11-18)* will be captured and thrown into a lake of fire. And the flesh of their followers will be eaten by birds (See Rev. 19:11-21).

Then John prophesied about the capture of Satan himself and the salvation of the martyrs

In John's next prophesy he told that Satan himself (as a red dragon) will be captured and thrown into a bottomless pit and locked away for a thousand years. And the people who were not followers of the beast who had died or who had become martyrs, will come back to life and will reign with Christ for that thousand years.(See Rev.20:1-6)

And following this, John prophesied about the temporary release and recapture of Satan.

John next prophesied that after a thousand years Satan will be temporarily released from the bottomless pit, and will build an army to make war against the saints. But Satan's new armies will be consumed by fire, and Satan himself will be thrown into the same lake of fire as were the beasts. And this will be followed by a judgement event by God, that will result in the also casting into the lake of fire of those who's names do not appear in the "Book of Life" See Rev. 20:7-15). *I assume that the names in the Book of Life are of those who have accepted Christ into their hearts.*

Special note: During the period of about one thousand AD several very unsettling events occurred. One was the rise of the political and military power of Islamic faith, and its eventual destruction of the eastern Roman empire, along with the strongholds of the Christian faith and the early Christian churches in Turkey and the middle east. The second was the several mostly unsuccessful attempts by basically uneducated Christian warriors to drive the Muslim faith and its armies out of southern and eastern Europe, and to take back the holy land for Christianity during the Crusades. The third was the return of and often satanic earthly political power of the Christian faith in central Europe during what is called the Renaissance. A fourth was the beginning of the rise of antisemitism throughout Europe, especially in Spain and the slavic nations. All of these appear to me to be signs of the temporary return of Satan.

Since that time, despite the fact of two recent world wars and numerous territorial conflicts, Satan's influence seems to me to have settled down somewhat. However, there still remains a threat of a new horrific global conflict, the potential impact on Truth threatened by AI, and dangerous effects of uncontrolled drug use. So there are many signs that even though Satan has been assigned to the lake of fire, he seems to still remain alive in the hearts of many people.

And the final judgement will take place

Then John saw the great throne of God, with God seated on it. The books of life will then be opened and the righteous who's names appear in the books will be identified. Then death and hades will be cast into the lake of fire, followed by those who's names are not in the books of life.

Then John saw that all things will be made anew

Note: Then starting in Revelation Chapter 21, there is a change from the predictions of dire, dangerous, and deadly circumstances, to new, more positive visions of God, Heaven, Christ, and the human race. See following.

Then John predicted that all the old will pass away and that a new Jerusalem will come, adorned for her husband (Christ). And John then heard a loud voice from God's throne saying **"Behold the dwelling place of God is with man. He will dwell with them, and they will be his people, and God will be with them as their God. He will wipe away every tear from their eyes, and death shall be no more. Neither shall there be mourning or crying nor pain any more, for the former things have passed away."** (See Rev. 21:3-4). Then God also will assure John by saying **"Write this down for these words are trustworthy and true. It is done! I am the alpha and the omega, the beginning and the end. To the thirsty I will give the water of life. And to the one who conquers** *(over death and Satan)* **will have this heritage, and I will be his God and he will be my Son."** Then God went on to condemn the faithless and other (non-believing) sinners who would be cast "into the lake of fire".

Following this, there is a change in the tenor of the predictions in Revelation, to the celebration of the eventual victory of God over the earth, as a whole new radiantly beautiful Jerusalem will be presented as coming down from Heaven. And John will be asked to measure it. And all its dimensions will be multiples of twelve, indicating total completeness.

However, there will be no physical temple in this new city, because God and Christ themselves will be the temple. And there will be no need for the sun or the moon because the radiancy of God will light the city. And it will be populated only by those who's names appear in the book of life.

Then an angel will show John the river of the water of life, flowing from the throne of God and also of Christ, and also the tree of life who's leaves will heal the nations of the earth. And the thrones of God and Christ will be in the city, and there will be no darkness. And God and Christ will rule forever.

Then Christ himself appeared to John again

Then Christ himself appeared to John and blessed him by saying **"And behold, I am coming soon. Blessed is the one who keeps the prophesy of this book."** And John fell down and worshiped him. Then Christ repeated the words of God by saying **"I am the alpha and the omega, the first and the last, the beginning and the end".** *For God and Christ are one (see the gospel of John chapter 1 verses one and two).*

The end of all things

<u>This is the end of Revelation and the end of the New Testament, and also the end of the whole Judeo/Christian Bible. But it is the beginning and the core of the religion that is now the light for at least 40% of the world's population, and a hope and a forecast that it will some day be the whole, the 100% of all humanity, and that this exhistance will last forever</u>.

AND BLESSED ARE THOSE WHO BELIEVE IN GOD'S WORD.

Part III - CODA of The Story of Christ

Apparently the world in the first century AD was hungry for something of value to believe in. This was a troubling time of the decline of the moral and ethical standards of the so-called civilized world, where unbridled sex and sometimes bloody mass entertainment was the order of the day. Subliminally, people were beginning to realize that, despite seeming prosperity, there needed to be a higher purpose in life; something that was outside of one's self that would bring meaning, order, and purpose. Thus, the appeal of the idea that there was one with great ethereal power, who taught with a higher standard, and who died for the sins of others, was very appealing. So at first small Christian communities, and then larger ones, began to spring up in both the middle east and Europe with a common bond that brought together these communities in common belief and worship.

Wayne Sherman

And of course wherever there was rapid growth, there were accompanying growing pains. Fortunately, there were several highly motivated and spiritually infused individuals who had the knowledge and persuasive power, at least in part, to provide stimulus, direction, and control of this growth. They also provided the dedication that made it possible for this new faith to survive, despite strong and sometimes lethal opposition of the powerful and ruling individuals. **This to the point that three centuries later, it became accepted and validated by those same individuals, who went so far as to declare Christianity as the official religion of the Roman empire, and to collect the existing documents about Christ and his coming and his life, into the Judeo/ Christian Bible as we know it today.**

However, per the prophesies of the last book in this story, many trials and tribulations still lie ahead for the world and for humanity before completion of God's plan.

A CODA TO THE BOOK OF CHRIST

So ends this story of Christ, but not of his eternal existence

"The story of Christ", as depicted in this document, is of course only an excerpt from the story of the voice of the creator and sustainer of the universe, time, space, and all of existence. But this excerpt is the narrative of the time on earth of that voice as a human being, in the person of Jesus of Nazareth, who offered a path to freedom from the condemnation of sin and to a reward of eternal life. And it is the story of how he changed the world.

This story began with the predictions about him in the Old Testament of the Judea/Christian Bible. It then documents his birth and becoming a human adult. It continues with his ministry, the miracles he performed to prove his divinity, his death and sacrifice for our sins, his resurrection from the dead, and commission to believers to carry his message to all humanity.

It is also the story of the beginning of his continuing influence on society and humanity, and in addition, a prediction that he will someday return at the end of all things and validate his rightful place in eternity.

Blessings on all who read this document. And is my fervent hope that those who read this book might find their own path to belief in Jesus and take him into their hearts. Or otherwise, that those who are more eloquent than I, will use this writing as a resource to further offer belief in Jesus Christ, the Messiah to human beings around the world to gain believers in him as their saviour and to eternal life.

In the beauty of the lilies Christ was born across the sea, with the glory in his bosom that transfigures you and me. As he died to make men holy, let us live to make men free. While God is marching on. Glory, Glory, Hallelulia.

Printed in the United States
by Baker & Taylor Publisher Services